Eliza Ruhamah Scidmore

Java, the Garden of the East

Eliza Ruhamah Scidmore

Java, the Garden of the East

ISBN/EAN: 9783743322394

Manufactured in Europe, USA, Canada, Australia, Japa

Cover: Foto ©ninafisch / pixelio.de

Manufactured and distributed by brebook publishing software (www.brebook.com)

Eliza Ruhamah Scidmore

Java, the Garden of the East

CONTENTS

		PAGE
I.	SINGAPORE AND THE EQUATOR	1
II.	IN "JAVA MAJOR"	17
III.	BATAVIA, QUEEN OF THE EAST	25
IV.	THE KAMPONGS	37
V.	TO THE HILLS	49
VI.	A DUTCH SANS SOUCI	62
VII.	IN A TROPICAL GARDEN	79
VIII.	THE "CULTURE SYSTEM"	94
IX.	THE "CULTURE SYSTEM" (Continued)	109
X.	SINAGAR	126
XI.	PLANTATION LIFE	136
XII.	ACROSS THE PREANGER REGENCIES	147
XIII.	"TO TISSAK MALAYA!"	156
XIV.	PRISONERS OF STATE AT BORO BOEDOR	167
XV.	BORO BOEDOR	182
XVI.	BORO BOEDOR AND MENDOET	203
XVII.	BRAMBANAM	216
XVIII.	SOLO: THE CITY OF THE SUSUNHAN	240
XIX.	THE LAND OF KRIS AND SARONG	253
XX.	DJOKJAKARTA	265
XXI.	PAKOE ALAM: THE "AXIS OF THE UNIVERSE"	283
XXII.	"TJILATJAP," "CHALACHAP," "CHELACHAP"	301
XXIII.	GAROET AND PAPANDAYANG	312
XXIV.	"SALAMAT!"	324

LIST OF ILLUSTRATIONS

Malays Diving for Money	*Frontispiece*
	PAGE
A Street in Singapore	5
Map of Java	16
A Javanese Young Woman	27
Painting Sarongs	43
Rice-fields	53
Mount Salak, from the Resident's Garden, Buitenzorg	63
Frangipani and Sausage-tree	73
Tropical Fruits	81
Tropical Fruits	89
A Market in Buitenzorg	99
Scenes around the Market	105
A View in Buitenzorg	111
Javanese Coolies Gambling	123
Javanese Dancing-girl	139
A Mohammedan Mosque	159
Wayside Pavilion on Post-road	177
Boro Boedor, from the Passagrahan	183
Ground-plan of Boro Boedor	187
Four Bas-reliefs from Boro Boedor	191
On the Second Terrace	195
The Latticed Dagobas on the Circular Terraces	199

The Right-hand Image at Mendoet	207
Temple of Loro Jonggran at Brambanam	217
Clearing Away Rubbish and Vegetation at Brambanam Temples	221
Krishna and the Three Graces	225
Loro Jonggran and her Attendants	229
Plan of Chandi Sewou ("Thousand Temples")	233
Fragment from Loro Jonggran Temple	235
Ganesha, the Elephant-headed God	238
The Susunhan	243
The Dodok	249
Java, Bali, and Madura Krises	255
The Brambanam Baby	267
Tying the Turban	279
Wayang-wayang	285
Topeng Troupe with Masks	291
Transplanting Rice	315

JAVA
THE GARDEN OF THE EAST

I

SINGAPORE AND THE EQUATOR

SINGAPORE (or S'pore, as the languid, perspiring, exhausted residents near the line most often write and pronounce the name of Sir Stamford Raffles's colony in the Straits of Malacca) is a geographical and commercial center and cross-roads of the eastern hemisphere, like to no other port in the world. Singapore is an ethnological center, too, and that small island swinging off the tip of the Malay Peninsula holds a whole congress of nations, an exhibit of all the races and peoples and types of men in the world, compared to which the Midway Plaisance was a mere skeleton of a suggestion. The traveler, despite the overpowering, all-subduing influence of the heat, has some thrills of excitement at the tropical pictures of the shore, and the congregation of varicolored humanity grouped on the Singapore wharf; and there and in Java, where one least and last expects to find such modern conveniences, his ship swings up to solid wharves, and he walks down a gang-plank in civilized fashion—something to be appreciated after the excitements and discomforts of landing in small boats among the screaming heathen of all other Asiatic ports.

On the Singapore wharf is a market of models and a life-class for a hundred painters; and sculptors, too, may study there all the tones of living bronze and the beauties of human patina, and more of repose than of muscular action, perhaps. Japanese, Chinese, Siamese, Malays, Javanese, Burmese, Cingalese, Tamils, Sikhs, Parsees, Lascars, Malabars, Malagasy, and sailor folk of all coasts, Hindus and heathens of every caste and persuasion, are grouped in a brilliant confusion of red, white, brown, and patterned drapery, of black, brown, and yellow skins; and behind them, in ghostly clothes, stand the pallid Europeans, who have brought the law, order, and system, the customs, habits, comforts, and luxuries of civilization to the tropics and the jungle. All these alien heathens and picturesque unbelievers, these pagans and idolaters, Buddhists, Brahmans, Jews, Turks, sun- and fire-worshipers, devil-dancers, and what not, have come with the white man to toil for him under the equatorial sun, since the Malays are the great leisure class of the world, and will not work. The Malays will hardly live on the land, much less cultivate it or pay taxes, while they can float about in strange little hen-coops of houseboats that fill the river and shores by thousands. Hence the Tamils have come from India to work, and the Chinese to do the small trading; and the Malay rests, or at most goes a-fishing, or sits by the canoeloads of coral and sponges, balloon-fish and strange sea treasures that are sold at the wharf.

A tribe of young Malays in dugout canoes meet every steamer and paddle in beside it, shrieking and gesticulating for the passengers to toss coins into the water. Their mops of black hair are bleached auburn by the action of sun and salt water, and the canoe and paddle fit as naturally to these amphibians as a turtle's shell and flipper. They bail with an automatic sweep of the hollowed foot in regular time with the dip of the paddle; and when a coin drops, the Malay lets go the paddle and sheds his canoe without concern. There is a flash of brown heels, bubbles and commotion below, and the diver comes up, and chooses and rights his wooden shell and flipper as easily and naturally as a man picks out and assumes his coat and cane at a hall door. And in their hearts, the civilized folk on deck, hampered with their multiple garments and conventions, envy these happy-go-lucky, care-free amphibians in the land of the breadfruit, banana, and scant raiment, with dives into the cool, green water, teeming with fish and glittering with falling coins, as the only exertion required to earn a living. Cold and hunger are unknown; flannels and soup are no part of charity; and even that word, and the many organizations in its name, are hardly known in the lands low on the line.

S'pore is the great junction where travelers from the East or the West change ship for Java; a commercial cross-roads where all who travel must stop and see what a marvel of a place British energy has raised from the jungle in less than half a century. The Straits Settlements date from the time when Sir Stamford

Raffles, after Great Britain's five years' temporary occupancy of Java, returned that possession to the Dutch in 1816, the fall of Napoleon removing the fear that this possession of Holland would become a French colony and menace to British interests in Asia. It had been intended to establish such a British commercial entrepôt at Achin Head, the north end of Sumatra; but Sir Stamford Raffles's better idea prevailed, and the free port of Singapore in the Straits of Malacca has won the commercial supremacy of the East from Batavia, and has prospered beyond its founder's dreams. It is a well-built and a beautifully ordered city, and the municipal housekeeping is an example to many cities of the temperate zone. Even the untidy Malay and the dirt-loving Chinese, who swarm to this profitable trading-center, and have absorbed all the small business and retail trade of the place, are held to outer cleanliness and strict sanitary laws in their allotted quarters. The stately business houses, the marble palace of a bank, the long iron pavilions shading the daily markets, the splendid Raffles Museum and Library, are all regular and satisfactory sights; but the street life is the fascination and distraction of the traveler before everything else. The array of turbans and sarongs gives color to every thoroughfare; but the striking and most unique pictures in Singapore streets are the Tamil bullock-drivers, who, sooty and statuesque, stand in splendid contrast between their humped white oxen and the mounds of white flour-bags they draw in primitive carts. Tiny Tamil children, shades blacker, if that could really be, than their ebon- and charcoal-skinned parents, are seen on suburban roads, clothed only in silver chains,

A STREET IN SINGAPORE.
After photograph by E. S. Platt.

bracelets, and medals; and these lithe, lean people from the south end of India are first in the picturesque elements of the great city of the Straits. The Botanical Garden, although so recently established, promises to become famous; and one arriving from the farther East meets there for the first time the beautiful red-stemmed Banka palm, and the symmetrical traveler's palm of Madagascar, the latter all conventionalized ready for sculptors' use. Scores of other splendid palms, giant creepers, gorgeous blossoms and fantastic orchids, known to us only by puny examples in great conservatories at home, equally delight one—all the wealth of jungle and swamp growing beside the smooth, hard roads of an English park, over which one may drive for hours in the suburbs of Singapore.

The Dutch mail-steamers to and from Batavia connect with the English mail-steamers at Singapore; a French line connects with the Messagerie's ships running between Marseilles and Japan; an Australian line of steamers gives regular communication; and independent steamers, offering as much comfort, leave Singapore almost daily for Batavia. The five hundred miles' distance is covered in forty-eight or sixty hours, for a uniform fare of fifty Mexican dollars or ninety Dutch gulden—an excessive and unusual charge for a voyage of such length in that or any other region. The traveler is usually warned long beforehand that living and travel in the Netherlands Indies is the most expensive in the world; and the change from the depreciated Mexican silver-dollar standard and the profitable exchange of the far East to the gold standard of Holland dismays one at the start. The completion of railways across and to all parts of the island of Java, however, has greatly reduced tourist expenses, so that they are not now two or three times the average of similar expenses in India, China, and Japan.

At Singapore, only two degrees above the equator, the sun pursues a monotony of rising and setting that ranges only from six minutes before to six minutes after six o'clock, morning and evening, the year round. Breakfasting by candle-light and leaving the hotel in darkness, there was all the beauty of the gray-and-rose dawn and the pale-yellow rays of the early sun to be seen from the wet deck when our ship let go from the wharf and sailed out over a sea of gold. For the two days and two nights of the voyage, with but six passengers on the large blue-funnel steamer, we had the deck and the cabins, and indeed the equator and the Java Sea, to ourselves. The deck was furnished with the long chairs and hammocks of tropical life, but more tropical yet were the bunches of bananas hanging from the awning-rail, that all might pick and eat at will; for this is the true region of plenty, where selected bananas cost one Mexican cent the dozen, and a whole bunch but five cents, and where actual living is far too cheap and simple to be called a science.

The ship slipped out from the harbor through the glassy river of the Straits of Malacca, and on past points and shores that to me had never been anything but geographic names. There was some little thrill of excitement in being "on the line" in the heart of the tropics, the half-way house of all the world, and one expected strange aspects and effects. There was a magic stillness of air and sea; the calm was as of enchantment, and one felt as if in some hypnotic trance, with all nature chained in the same spell. The pale, pearly sky was reflected in smooth stretches of liquid, pearly sea, with vaporous hills, soft green visions of land beyond. Everywhere in these regions the shallow water shows pale green above the sandy bottom, and the anchor can be dropped at will. All through the breathless day the ship coursed over this shimmering yellow and gray-green sea, with faint pictures of land, the very landscapes of mirage, drawn in vaporous tints on every side. We were threading a way through the thousand islands, the archipelago lying below the point of the Malay Peninsula, a region of unnamed, uncounted "summer isles of Eden," chiefly known to history as the home of pirates.

The high mountain-ridges of Sumatra barred the west for all the first equatorial day, the land of this "Java Minor" sloping down and spreading out in great green plains and swamps on the fertile but unhealthy eastern coast. The large settlements and most attractive districts are on the west coast, where the hills rise steeply from the ocean, and coffee-trees thrive luxuriantly. Benkoelen, the old English town, and Padang, the great coffee-mart, are on that coast, and from the latter a railway leads to high mountain districts of great picturesqueness. There are few government plantations on Sumatra, where land-tenures and leases are the same as in Java. Immense areas have been devoted to tobacco-culture near Deli, on the north or Straits coast, planters employing there and on lower east-coast estates more than forty-three thousand Chinese coolies—the Chinese, the one Asiatic who toils with ardor and regularity, whom the tropics cannot debilitate, and to whom malaria and all germs, microbes, and bacilli seem but tonic agents.

When the British returned Java, after the Napoleon scare was over, they retained Ceylon and the Cape of Good Hope, and sovereign rights over Sumatra, relinquishing this latter suzerainty in 1872, in exchange for Holland's imaginary rights in Ashantee and the Gold Coast of Africa. The Dutch then attempted to reduce the native population of Sumatra to the same estate as the more pliant people of Java; but the wild mountaineers and bucaneers, of the north, or Achin, end of the island in particular, warned by the sad fate of the Javanese, had no intention of being conquered and enslaved, of giving their labor and the fruit of their lands to the strangers from Europe's cold swamps. The Achin war has continued since 1872, with little result save a general loss of Dutch prestige in the East, an immense expenditure of Dutch gulden, causing a deficit in the colonial budget every year, a fearful mortality among Dutch troops, and the final abandonment, in this decade of trade depression, of the aggressive policy. Dutch commanders are well satisfied to hold their chain of forts along the western hills, and to punish the Achinese in a small way by blockading them from their supplies of opium, tobacco, and spirits. In one four years of active campaigning the Achin war cost seventy million gulden, and seventy out of every hundred Dutch soldiers succumbed to the climate before going into an encounter. The Achinese merely retired to their swamps and jungles and waited, and the climate did the rest, their confidence in themselves only shaken during the command of General Van der Heyden, who for a time actually crushed the rebellion. This picturesque fighter, a half-brother of Baron de Stuers, inherited Malay instincts from a native mother, and carried on such a warfare as the Achinese understood. He lost an eye in one encounter, and the natives, then remembering an old tradition that their country would be conquered by a one-eyed man, practically gave up the struggle—to resume it, however, as soon as General Van der Heyden retired and sailed for Holland, and military vigilance was relaxed in consequence of Dutch economy. The Achinese leader, Toekoe Oemar, has several times apparently yielded to the Dutch, only to perpetrate some greater injury; and his treachery and crimes have given him repute as the very prince of evil ones.

One's sympathy goes naturally with the brave, liberty-loving Achinese; and in view of their indomitable spirit, Great Britain did not lose so much when she let go unconquerable Sumatra. British tourists are saddened, however, when they see what their ministers let slip with Java, for with that island and Sumatra, all Asia's southern shore-line, and virtually the far East, would have been England's own.

Geologically this whole Malay Archipelago was one with the Malay Peninsula, and although so recently made, is still subject to earthquake change, as shown in the terrible eruption of the island of Krakatau in the narrow Sunda Strait, west of Java, in August, 1883. Native traditions tell that anciently Sumatra, Java, Bali, and Sumbawa were one island, and " when three thousand rainy seasons shall have passed away they will be reunited"; but Alfred Russel Wallace denies it, and proves that Java was the first to drop away from the Asiatic mainland and become an island.

While the sun rode high in the cloudless white zenith above our ship the whole world seemed aswoon. Hills and islands swam and wavered in the heat and mists, and the glare and silence were terrible and oppressive. One could not shake off the sensation of mystery and unreality, of sailing into some unknown, eerie, other world. Every voice was subdued, the beat of the engines was scarcely felt in that glassy calm, and the stillness of the ship gave a strange sensation, as of a magic spell. It was not so very hot,—only 86° by the thermometer,—but the least exertion, to cross the deck, to lift a book, to pull a banana, left one limp and exhausted, with cheeks burning and the breath coming faster, that insidious, deceptive heat of the tropics declaring itself—that steaming, wilting quality in the sun of Asia that so soon makes jelly of the white man's brain, and that in no way compares with the scorching, dry 96° in the shade of a North American, hot-wave summer day.

At five o'clock, while afternoon tea and bananas were being served on deck, we crossed the line—that imaginary parting of the world, the invisible thread of the universe, the beginning and the end of all latitude —latitude 0°, longitude 103° east, the sextant told. The position was geographically exciting. We were literally "down South," and might now speak disrespectfully of the equator if we wished. A breeze sprang up as soon as we crossed the line, and all that evening and through the night the air of the southern hemisphere was appreciably cooler. The ship went slowly, and loitered along in order to enter the Banka Straits by daylight; and at sunrise we were in a smooth river of pearl, with the green Sumatra shores close on one hand, and the heights of Banka's island of tin on the other. A ship in full sail swept out to meet us, and four more barks under swelling canvas passed by in that narrow strait, whose rocks and reefs are fully attested by the line of wrecks and sunken masts down its length. The harbor of Muntuk, whence there is a direct railway to the tin-mines, was busy with shipping, and the white walls and red roofs of the town showed prettily against the green.

The open Java Sea was as still and glassy as the straits had been, and for another breathless, cloudless day the ship's engines beat almost inaudibly as we went southward through an enchanted silence. When the heat and glare of light from the midday sun so directly overhead drove us to the cabin, where swinging punkas gave air, we had additional suggestion of the tropics; for a passenger for Macassar, just down from Penang and Malacca, showed us fifty freshly cured specimens of birds, whose gorgeous plumage repeated the most brilliant and dazzling tints of the rainbow, the flower-garden, and the jewel-case, and left us bereft of adjectives and exclamations. Here we found another passenger, who spoke Dutch and looked the Hollander by every sign, but quickly claimed citizenship with us as a naturalized voter of the great republic. He asked if we lived in Java, and when we had answered that we were going to Java *en touriste*, "merely travelers," he established comradeship by saying, "I am a traveling man myself—New York Life." This naturalized American citizen said quite naturally, "We Dutchmen" and "our queen"—Americanisms with a loyal Holland ring.

After the gold, rose, gray, and purple sunset had shown us such a sky of splendor and sea of glory as we had but dreamed of above the equator, banks of dark vapor defined themselves in the south. A thin young moon hung among the huge yellow stars, that glowed steadily, with no cold twinkling, in that intense night sky; but before the Southern Cross could rise, dense clouds rolled up, and flashes, chains, and forks of angry lightning made a double spectacular play against the inky-black sky and the mirror-black sea. The captain promised us a tropical thunder-storm from those black clouds in the south, and went forward to give ship's orders, advising us to make all haste below when the first drop should fall, as in an instant a sheet of blinding rain would surround the decks, against which the double awnings would be no more protection than so much gauze, and through which one could not see the ship's length. The clouds remained stationary, however, and we missed the promised sensation, although we waited for hours on deck, the ship moving quietly through the soft, velvety air of the tropic's blackest midnight, and the lightning-flashes becoming fainter and fainter.

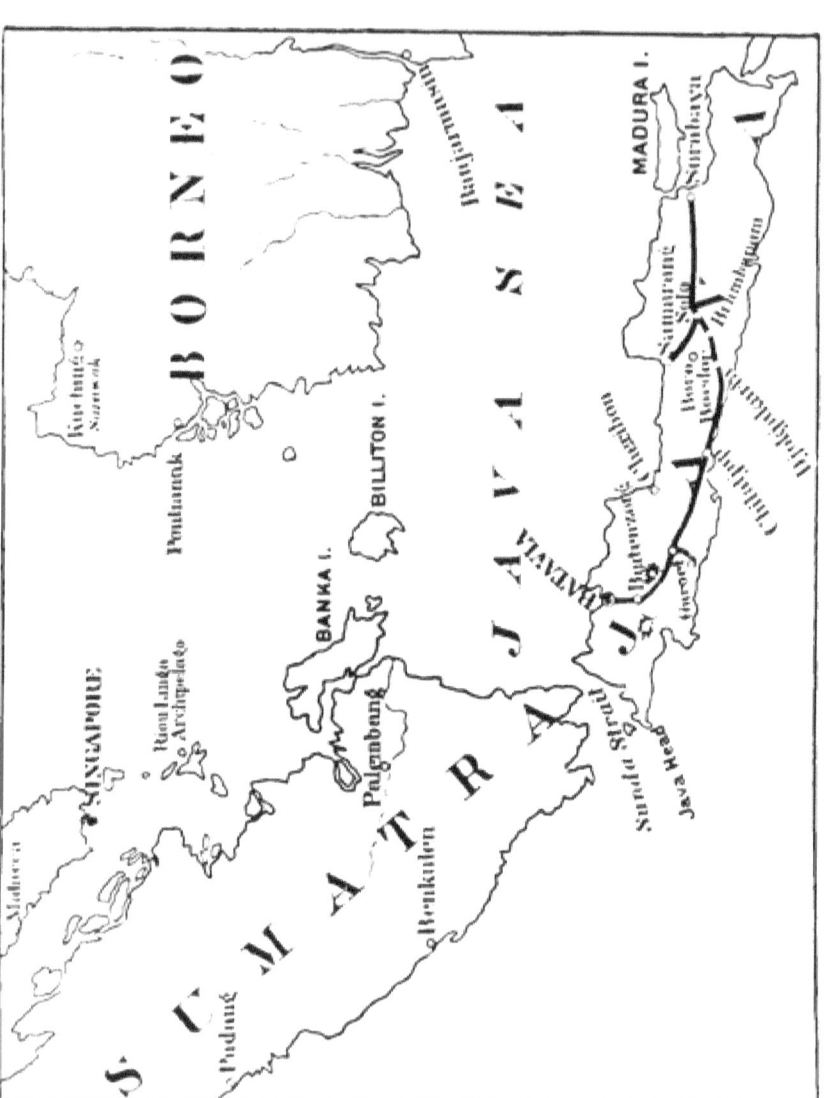

MAP OF JAVA

II

IN "JAVA MAJOR"

IN the earliest morning a clean white lighthouse on an islet was seen ahead, and as the sun rose, bluish mountains came up from the sea, grew in height, outlined themselves, and then stood out, detached volcanic peaks of most lovely lines, against the purest, pale-blue sky; soft clouds floated up and clung to the summits; the blue and green at the water's edge resolved itself into groves and lines of palms; and over sea and sky and the wonderland before us was all the dewy freshness of dawn in Eden. It looked very truly the "gem" and the "pearl of the East," this "Java Major" of the ancients, and the Djawa of the native people, which has called forth more extravagant praise and had more adjectives expended on it than any other one island in the world. Yet this little continent is only 666 miles long and from 56 to 135 miles wide, and on an area of 49,197 square miles (nearly the same as that of the State of New York) supports a population of 24,000,000, greater than that of all the other islands of the Indian Ocean put together. With 1600 miles of coast-line, it has few harbors, the north shore being swampy and flat, with shallows extending far out, while the southern coast is steep and bold, and the one harbor of Tjilatjap breaks the long line of surf where the Indian Ocean beats against the southern cliffs. Fortunately, hurricanes and typhoons are unknown in the waters around this "summer land of the world," and the seasons have but an even, regular change from wet to dry in Java. From April to October the dry monsoon blows from the southeast, and brings the best weather of the year—dry, hot days and the coolest nights. From October to April the southwest or wet monsoon blows. Then every day has its afternoon shower, the air is heavy and stifling, all the tropic world is asteam and astew and afloat, vegetation is magnificent, insect life triumphant, and the mountains are hidden in nearly perpetual mist. There are heavy thunder-storms at the turn of the monsoon, and the one we had watched from the sea the Hallowe'en night before our arrival had washed earth and air until the foliage glistened, the air fairly sparkled, nature wore her most radiant smiles, and the tropics were ideal.

It was more workaday and prosaic when the ship, steaming in between long breakwaters, made fast to the stone quays of Taudjon Priok, facing a long line of corrugated-iron warehouses, behind which was the railway connecting the port with the city of Batavia. The gradual silting up of Batavia harbor after an eruption of Mount Salak in 1699, which first dammed and then sent torrents of mud and sand down the Tjiliwong River, finally obliged commerce to remove to this deep bay six miles farther east, where the colonials have made a model modern harbor, at a cost of twenty-six and a half million gulden, all paid from current revenues, without the island's ceasing to pay its regular tribute to the crown of Holland. The customs officers at Tandjon Priok were courteous and lenient, passing our tourist luggage with the briefest formality, and kindly explaining how our steamer-chairs could be stored in the railway rooms until our return to port. It is but nine miles from the Tandjon Priok wharf to the main station in the heart of the original city of Batavia—a stretch of swampy ground dotted and lined with palm-groves and banana-patches, with tiny woven baskets of houses perched on stilts clustered at the foot of tall cocoa-trees that are the staff and source of life and of every economical blessing of native existence. We leaped excitedly from one side of the little car to the other, to see each more and more tropical picture; groups of bare brown children frolicking in the road, and mothers with babies astride of their hips, or swinging comfortably in a scarf knotted across one shoulder, and every-day life going on under the palms most naturally, although to our eyes it was so strange and theatrical.

At the railway-station we met the *sadoe* (dos-à-dos), a two-wheeled cart, which is the common vehicle of hire of the country, and is drawn by a tiny Timor or Sandalwood pony, with sometimes a second pony attached outside of the shafts. The broad cushioned seat over the axles will accommodate four persons, two sitting each way. The driver faces front comfortably; but the passenger, with no back to lean against but the driver's, must hold to the canopy-frame while he is switched about town backward in the footman's place, for one gulden or forty cents the hour.

Whether one comes to Java from India or China, there is hasty change from the depreciated silver currency of all Asia to the unaltered gold standard of Holland, and the sudden expensiveness of the world is a sad surprise. The Netherlands unit of value, the gulden (value, forty cents United States gold), is as often called a florin, a rupee, or a dollar—the "Mexican dollar" or the equivalent "British dollar" of the Straits Settlements, a coin which trade necessities drove British conservatism to minting, which act robs the Briton of the privilege of making further remarks upon "the almighty dollar" of the United States, with its unchanging value of one hundred cents gold. This confusion of coins, with prices quoted indifferently in guldens, florins, rupees, and dollars, is further increased by dividing the gulden into one hundred cents, like the Ceylon rupee, so that, between these Dutch fractions, the true cents of the United States dollar that one instinctively thinks of, and the depreciated cents of the British or the battered Mexican dollar, one's brain begins to whirl when prices are quoted, or any evil day of reckoning comes.

No Europeans live at Tandjon Priok, nor in the old city of Batavia, which from the frightful mortality during two centuries was known as "the graveyard of Europeans." The banks and business houses, the Chinese and Arab towns, are in the "old town"; but Europeans desert that quarter before sundown, and betake themselves to the "new town" suburbs, where every house is in a park of its own, and the avenues are broad and straight, and all the distances are magnificent. The city of Batavia, literally "fair meadows," grandiloquently "the queen of the East," and without exaggeration "the gridiron of the East," dates from 1621, when the Dutch removed from Bantam, where quarrels between Portuguese, Javanese, and the East India Company had been disturbing trade for fifteen years, and built Fort Jacatra at the mouth of a river off which a cluster of islands sheltered a fine harbor. Its position in the midst of swamps was unhealthy, and the mortality was so appalling as to seem incredible. Dutch records tell of 87,000 soldiers and sailors dying in the government hospital between 1714 and 1776, and of 1,119,375 dying at Batavia between 1730 and August, 1752—a period of twenty-two years and eight months.[1] The deadly Java fever occasioning this seemingly incredible mortality was worst between the years 1733 and 1738, during which time 2000 of the Dutch East India Company's servants and free Christians died annually. Staunton, who visited Batavia with Lord Macartney's embassy in 1793, called it the "most unwholesome place in the universe," and "the pestilential climate" was considered a sufficient defense against attack from any European power.

The people were long in learning that those who went to the higher suburbs to sleep, and built houses of the most open construction to admit of the fullest sweep of air, were free from the fever of the walled town, surrounded by swamps, cut by stagnant canals, and facing a harbor whose mud-banks were exposed at

[1] See Sir Stamford Raffles's "History of Java," Appendix A.

low tide. The city walls were destroyed at the beginning of this century by the energetic Marshal Daendels, who began building the new town. The quaint old air-tight Dutch buildings were torn down, and streets were widened; and there is now a great outspread town of red-roofed, whitewashed houses, with no special features or picturesqueness to make its street-scenes either distinctively Dutch or tropical. Modern Batavia had 111,763 inhabitants on December 31, 1894, less than a tenth of whom are Europeans, with 26,776 Chinese and 72,934 natives. While the eighteenth-century Stadhuis might have been brought from Holland entire, a steam tramway starts from its door and thence shrieks its way to the farthest suburb, the telephone "hellos" from center to suburb, and modern inventions make tropical living possible.

The Dutch do not welcome tourists, nor encourage one to visit their paradise of the Indies. Too many travelers have come, seen, and gone away to tell disagreeable truths about Dutch methods and rule; to expose the source and means of the profitable returns of twenty million dollars and more for each of so many years of the last and the preceding century—all from islands whose whole area only equals that of the State of New York. Although the tyrannic rule and the "culture system," or forced labor, are things of the dark past, the Dutch brain is slow and suspicious, and the idea being fixed fast that no stranger comes to Java on kindly or hospitable errands, the colonial authorities must know within twenty-four hours why one visits the Indies. They demand one's name, age, religion, nationality, place of nativity, and occupation, the name of the ship that brought the suspect to Java, and the name of its captain—a dim threat lurking in this latter query of holding the unlucky mariner responsible should his importation prove an expense or embarrassment to the island. Still another permit—a *toelatings-kaart*, or "admission ticket"—must be obtained if one wishes to travel farther than Buitenzorg, the cooler capital, forty miles away in the hills. The tourist pure and simple, the sight-seer and pleasure traveler, is not yet quite comprehended, and his passports usually accredit him as traveling in the interior for "scientific purposes." Guides or efficient couriers in the real sense do not exist yet. The English-speaking servant is rare and delusive, yet a necessity unless one speaks Dutch or Low Malay. Of all the countries one may ever travel in, none equals Java in the difficulty of being understood; and it is a question, too, whether the Malays who do not know any English are harder to get along with than the Dutch who know a little.

Thirty years ago Alfred Russel Wallace inveighed against the unnecessary discomforts, annoyances, and expense of travel in Java, and every tourist since has repeated his plaint. The philippics of returned travelers furnish steady amusement for Singapore residents; and no one brings back the same enthusiasm that embarked with him. It is not the Java of the Javanese that these returned ones berate so vehemently, but the Netherlands India, and the state created and brought about by the merciless, cold-blooded, rapacious Hollanders who came half-way round the world and down to the equator, nine thousand miles away from their homes, to acquire an empire and enslave a race, and who impose their hampering customs and restrictions upon even alien visitors. Java undoubtedly is "the very finest and most interesting tropical island in the world," and the Javanese the most gentle, attractive, and innately refined people of the East, after the Japanese; but the Dutch in Java "beat the Dutch" in Europe ten points to one, and there is nothing so surprising and amazing, in all man's proper study of mankind, as this equatorial Hollander transplanted from the cold fens of Europe; nor is anything so strange as the effect of a high temperature on Low-Country temperament. The most rigid, conventional, narrow, thrifty, prudish, and Protestant people in Europe bloom out in the forcing-house of the tropics into strange laxity, and one does not know the Hollanders until one sees them in this "summer land of the world," whither they threatened to emigrate in a body during the time of the Spanish Inquisition.

III

BATAVIA, QUEEN OF THE EAST

WHEN one has driven through the old town of Batavia and seen its crowded bazaars and streets, and has followed the lines of bricked canals, where small natives splash and swim, women beat the family linen, and men go to and fro in tiny boats, all in strange travesty of the solemn canals of the old country, he comes to the broader avenues of the new town, lined with tall tamarind- and waringen-trees, with plumes of palms, and pyramids of blazing Madagascar flame-trees in blossom. He is driven into the long garden court of the Hotel Nederlanden, and there beholds a spectacle of social life and customs that nothing in all travel can equal for distinct shock and sensation. We had seen some queer things in the streets,—women lolling barefooted and in startling dishabille in splendid equipages,—but concluded them to be servants or half-castes; but there in the hotel was an undress parade that beggars description, and was as astounding on the last as on the first day in the country. Woman's vanity and man's conventional ideas evidently wilt at the line, and no formalities pass the equator, when distinguished citizens and officials can roam and lounge about hotel courts in pajamas and bath slippers, and bare-ankled women, clad only in the native sarong, or skirt, and a white dressing-jacket, go unconcernedly about their affairs in streets and public places until afternoon. It is a dishabille beyond all burlesque pantomime, and only shipwreck on a desert island would seem sufficient excuse for women being seen in such an ungraceful, unbecoming attire—an undress that reveals every defect while concealing beauty, that no loveliness can overcome, and that has neither color nor grace nor picturesqueness to recommend it.

The hotel is a series of one-storied buildings surrounding the four sides of a garden court, the projecting eaves giving a continuous covered gallery that is the general corridor. The bedrooms open directly upon this broad gallery, and the space in front of each room, furnished with lounging-chairs, table, and reading-lamp, is the sitting-room of each occupant by day. There is never any jealous hiding behind curtains or screens. The whole hotel register is in evidence, sitting or spread in reclining-chairs. Men in pajamas thrust their bare feet out bravely, puffing clouds of rank Sumatra tobacco smoke as they stared at the new arrivals; women rocked and stared as if we were the unusual spectacle, and not they; and children sprawled on the cement flooring, in only the most intimate undergarments of civilized children. One turned his eyes from one undressed family group only to encounter some more surprising dishabille; and meanwhile servants were hanging whole mildewed wardrobes on

A JAVANESE YOUNG WOMAN.

clothes-lines along this open hotel corridor, while others were ironing their employers' garments on this communal porch.

We were sure we had gone to the wrong hotel; but the Nederlanden was vouched for as the best, and when the bell sounded, over one hundred guests came into the vaulted dining-room and were seated at the one long table. The men wore proper coats and clothes at this midday *riz tavel* (rice table), but the women and children came as they were—*sans gêne*.

The Batavian day begins with coffee and toast, eggs and fruit, at any time between six and nine o'clock; and the affairs of the day are despatched before noon, when that sacred, solemn, solid feeding function, the riz tavel, assembles all in shady, spacious dining-rooms, free from the creaking and flapping of the punka, so prominent everywhere else in the East. Rice is the staple of the midday meal, and one is expected to fill the soup-plate before him with boiled rice, and on that heap as much as he may select from eight or ten dishes, a tray of curry condiments being also passed with this great first course. Bits of fish, duck, chicken, beef, bird, omelet, and onions rose upon my neighbors' plates, and spoonfuls of a thin curried mixture were poured over the rice, before the conventional chutneys, spices, cocoanut, peppers, and almond went to the conglomerate mountain resting upon the "rice table" below. Beefsteak, a salad, and then fruit and coffee brought the midday meal to a close. Squeamish folk, unseasoned tourists, and well-starched Britons with small sense of humor complain of loss of appetite at these hotel riz tavels; and those Britons further criticize the way in which the Dutch fork, or most often the Dutch knife-blade, is loaded, aimed, and shoveled with a long, straight stroke to the Dutch interior; and they also criticize the way in which portions of bird or chicken are managed, necessitating and explaining the presence of the finger-bowl from the beginning of each meal. But we forgot all that had gone before when the feast was closed with the mangosteen—nature's final and most perfect effort in fruit creation.

After the riz tavel every one slumbers—as one naturally must after such a very "square" meal—until four o'clock, when a bath and tea refresh the tropic soul, the world dresses in the full costume of civilization, and the slatternly women of the earlier hours go forth in the latest finery of good fortune, twenty-six days from Amsterdam, for the afternoon driving and visiting, that continue to the nine-o'clock dinner-hour. Batavian fashion does not take its airing in the jerky sadoe, but in roomy "vis-à-vis" or barouches, comfortable "milords" or giant victorias, that, being built to Dutch measures, would comfortably accommodate three ordinary people to each seat, and are drawn by gigantic Australian horses, or "Walers" (horses from New South Wales), to match these turnouts of Brobdingnag.

Society is naturally narrow, provincial, colonial, conservative, and insular, even to a degree beyond that known in Holland. The governor-general, whose salary is twice that of the President of the United States, lives in a palace at Buitenzorg, forty miles away in the hills, with a second palace still higher up in the mountains, and comes to the Batavia palace only on state occasions. This ruler of twenty-four million souls, who rules as a viceroy instructed from The Hague, with the aid of a secretary-general and a Council of the Indies, has, in addition to his salary of a hundred thousand dollars, an allowance of sixty thousand dollars a year for entertaining, and it is expected that he will maintain a considerable state and splendor. He has a standing army of thirty thousand, one third Europeans, of various nationalities, raised by volunteer enlistment in Holland, who are well paid, carefully looked after, and recruited by long stays at Buitenzorg after short terms of service at the seaports. After the Indian mutiny the Dutch were in great fear of an uprising of the natives of Java, and placed less confidence in native troops. Only Europeans can hold officers' commissions; and while the native soldiers are all Mohammedans, and great consideration is paid their religious scruples, care is taken not to let the natives of any one province or district compose a majority in any one regiment, and these regiments frequently change posts. The colonial navy has done great service to the world in suppressing piracy in the Java Sea and around the archipelago, although steam navigation inevitably brought an end to piracy and picturesque adventure. The little navy helps maintain an admirable lighthouse service, and with such convulsions as that of Krakatau always possible, and changes often occurring in the bed of the shallow seas, its surveyors are continually busied with making new charts.

The islands of Amboyna, Borneo, Celebes, and Sumatra are also ruled by this one governor-general of the Netherlands Indies, through residents; and the island of Java is divided into twenty-two residencies or provinces, a resident, or local governor, ruling—or, as "elder brother," effectually advising—in the few provinces ostensibly ruled by native princes. A resident receives ten thousand dollars a year, with house provided and a liberal allowance made for the extra incidental expenses of the position—for traveling, entertaining, and acknowledging in degree the gifts of native princes. University graduates are chosen for this colonial service, and take a further course in the colonial institute at Haarlem, which includes, besides the study of the Malay language, the economic botany of the Indies, Dutch law, and Mohammedan justice, since, in their capacity as local magistrates, they must make their decisions conform with the tenets of the Koran, which is the general moral law, together with the unwritten Javanese code. They are entitled to retire upon a pension after twenty years of service—half the time demanded of those in the civil service in Holland. All these residents are answerable to the secretary of the colony, appointed by the crown, and much of executive detail has to be submitted to the home government's approval. Naturally there is much friction between all these functionaries, and etiquette is punctilious to a degree. A formal court surrounds the governor-general, and is repeated in miniature at every residency. The pensioned native sovereigns, princes, and regents maintain all the forms, etiquette, and barbaric splendor of their old court life, elaborated by European customs. The three hundred Dutch officials condescend equally to the rich planters and to the native princes; the planters hate and deride the officials; the natives hate the Dutch of either class, and despise their own princes who are subservient to the Dutch; and the wars and jealousies of rank and race and caste, of white and brown, of native and imported folk, flourish with tropical luxuriance.

Batavian life differs considerably from life in British India and all the rest of Asia, where the British-built and conventionally ordered places support the same formal social order of England unchanged, save for a few luxuries and concessions incident to the climate. The Dutchman does not waste his perspiration on tennis or golf or cricket, or on any outdoor pastime more exciting than horse-racing. He does not make well-ordered and expensive dinners his one chosen form of hospitality. He dines late and dines elaborately, but the more usual form of entertainment in Batavia is in evening receptions or musicales, for which the spacious houses, with their great white porticos, are well adapted. Batavian residents have each a paradise park around their dwellings, and the white houses of classic architecture, bowered in magnificent trees and palms, shrubs and vines and blooming plants, are most attractive by day. At night, when the great portico, which is drawing-room and living-room and as often dining-room, is illuminated by many lamps, each lovely villa glows like a fairyland in its dark setting. If the portico lamps are not lighted, it is a sign of "not at home," and mynheer and his family may sit in undress at their ease. There are weekly concerts at the Harmonie and Concordia clubs, where the groups around iron tables might have been summoned by a magician from some continental garden. There are such clubs in every town on the island, the government subsidizing the opera and supporting military bands of the first order; and they furnish society its center and common meeting-place. One sees fine gowns and magnificent jewels; ladies wear the heavy silks and velvets of an Amsterdam winter in these tropical gardens, and men dance in black coats and broadcloth uniforms. Society is brilliant, formal, and by lamplight impressive; but when by daylight one meets the same fair beauties and bejeweled matrons sockless, in sarongs and flapping slippers, the disillusionment is complete.

The show-places of Batavia are easily seen in a day: the old town hall, the Stadkirche, the lighthouse, the old warehouse, and the walled gate of Peter Elberfeld's house, with the spiked skull of that half-caste rebel against Dutch rule pointing a more awful reminder than the inscription in several languages to his "horrid memory." The pride of the city, and the most creditable thing on the island, is the Museum of the Batavian Society of Arts and Sciences ("Bataviaasch Genootschap von Kunsten en Wepenschappen"), known sufficiently to the world of science and letters as "the Batavian Society," of which Sir Stamford Raffles was the first great inspirer and exploiter, after it had dreamed along quietly in colonial isolation for a few years of the last century. In his time were begun the excavations of the Hindu temples and the archæological work which the Dutch government and the Batavian

Society have since carried on, and which have helped place that association among the foremost learned societies of the world. The museum is housed in a beautiful Greek temple of a building whose white walls are shaded by magnificent trees, and faces the broad Koenig's Plein, the largest parade-ground in the world, the Batavians say. The halls, surrounding a central court, shelter a complete and wonderful exhibit of Javanese antiquities and art works, of arms, weapons, implements, ornaments, costumes, masks, basketry, textiles, musical instruments, models of boats and houses, examples of fine old metal-work, and of all the industries of these gifted people. It is a place of absorbing interest; but with no labels and no key except the native janitor's pantomime, one's visit is often filled with exasperation.

There is a treasure-chamber heaped with gold shields, helmets, thrones, state umbrellas, boxes, salvers, betel and tobacco sets of gold, with jeweled daggers and krises of finest blades, patterned with curious veinings. Tributes and gifts from native sultans and princes display the precious metals in other curious forms, and a fine large *coco-de-mer*, the fabled twin nut of the Seychelles palm, that was long supposed to grow in some unknown, mysterious isle of the sea-gods, is throned on a golden base with all the honors due such a talisman. The ruined temples and sites of abandoned cities in Middle Java have yielded rich ornaments, necklaces, ear-rings, head-dresses, seals, plates, and statuettes of gold and silver. A room is filled with bronze weapons, bells, tripods, censers, images, and all the appurtenances of Buddhist worship, characteristic examples of the Greco-Buddhist art of India, which even more surprisingly confronts one in these treasures from the jungles of the far-away tropical island. A central hall is filled with bas-reliefs and statues from these ruins of Buddhist and Brahmanic temples, in which the Greek influence is quite as marked, and Egyptian and Assyrian suggestions in the sculptures give one other ideas to puzzle over.

The society's library is rich in exchanges, scientific and art publications of all countries; and the row of reports of the Smithsonian Institution, the Geological Survey and Bureau of Ethnology, are as much a matter of pride to the American visitor as the framed diplomas of institutes and international expositions are to the Batavian curator. The council-room contains the state chairs of native sovereigns, and portraits and souvenirs of the great explorers and navigators who passed this way in the last century and in the early years of this cycle. Captain Cook left stores of South Sea curios on his way to and fro, and during this century the museum has been the pet and pride of Dutch residents and officials, and the subject of praise by all visitors.

The palace of the governor-general on this vast Koenig's Plein is a beautiful modern structure, but more interest attaches to the old palace of the Waterloo Plein, the *palys* built by the great Marshal Daendels, who, supplanted by the British after but three years' energetic rule, withdrew to Europe.

IV

THE KAMPONGS

THE *Tjina*, or China, and the Arab *kampongs*, are show-places to the stranger in the curious features of life and civic government they present. Each of these foreign kampongs, or villages, is under the charge of a captain or commander, whom the Dutch authorities hold responsible for the order and peace of their compatriots, since they do not allow to these yellow colonials so-called "European freedom"—an expression which constitutes a sufficient admission of the existence of "Asiatic restraint." Great wealth abides in both these alien quarters, whose leading families have been there for generations, and have absorbed all retail trade, and as commission merchants, money-lenders, and middlemen have garnered great profits and earned the hatred of Dutch and Javanese alike. The lean and hooked-nosed followers of the prophet conquered the island in the fifteenth century, and have built their *messigits*, or mosques, in every province. The Batavian messigit is a cool little blue-

and-white-tiled building, with a row of inlaid wooden clogs and loose leather shoes at the door; and turbaned heads within bow before the mihrab that points northwestward to Mecca. Since the Mohammedan conquest of 1475, the Javanese are Mohammedan if anything; but they take their religion easily, and are so lukewarm in the faith of the fire and sword that they would easily relapse to their former mild Brahmanism if Islam's power were released. The Dutch have always prohibited the pilgrimages to Mecca, since those returning with the green turban were viewed with reverence and accredited with supernatural powers that made their influence a menace to Dutch rule. Arab priests have always been enemies of the government and foremost in inciting the people to rebellion against Dutch and native rulers; but little active evangelical work seems to have been done by Christian missionaries to counteract Mohammedanism, save at the town of Depok, near Batavia.

In all the banks and business houses is found the lean-fingered Chinese comprador, or accountant, and the rattling buttons of his abacus, or counting-board, play the inevitable accompaniment to financial transactions, as everywhere else east of Colombo. The 251,-325 Chinese in Netherlands India present a curious study in the possibilities of their race. Under the strong, tyrannical rule of the Dutch they thrive, show ambition to adopt Western ways, and approach more nearly to European standards than one could believe possible. Chinese conservatism yields first in costume and social manners; the pigtail shrinks to a mere symbolic wisp, and the well-to-do Batavian Chinese dresses faultlessly after the London model, wears spotless duck coat and trousers, patent-leather shoes, and, in top or derby hat, sits complacent in a handsome victoria drawn by imported horses, with liveried Javanese on the box. One meets correctly gotten-up Celestial equestrians trotting around Waterloo Plein or the alleys of Buitenzorg, each followed by an obsequious groom, the thin remnant of the Manchu queue slipped inside the coat being the only thing to suggest Chinese origin. The rich Chinese live in beautiful villas, in gorgeously decorated houses built on ideal tropical lines; and although having no political or social recognition in the land, entertain no intention of returning to China. They load their Malay wives with diamonds and jewels, and spend liberally for the education of their children. The Dutch tax, judge, punish, and hold them in the same regard as the natives, with whom they have intermarried for three centuries, until there is a large mixed class of these Paranaks in every part of the island. The native hatred of the Chinese is an inheritance of those past centuries when the Dutch farmed out the revenue to Chinese, who, being assigned so many thousand acres of rice-land, and the forced labor of the people on them, gradually extended their boundaries, and by increasing exactions and secret levies oppressed the people with a tyranny and rapacity the Dutch could not approach. In time the Chinese fomented insurrection against the Dutch, and in 1740, joining with disaffected natives, entrenched themselves in a suburban fort. The Dutch in alarm gave the order, and over 20,000 Chinese then within the walls were put to death, not an infant, a woman, nor an aged person being spared. In fear of the wrath of the Emperor of China, elaborate excuses were framed and sent to Peking. Sage old Keen-Lung responded only by saying that the Dutch had served them right, that any death was too good for Chinese who would desert the graves of their ancestors.

After that incident they were restrained from all monopolies and revenue farming, and restricted to their present humble political state. An absolute exclusion act was passed in 1837, but was soon revoked, and the Chinese hold financial supremacy over both Dutch and natives, trade and commerce being hopelessly in the hands of the skilful Chinese comprador. The Dutch vent their dislike by an unmerciful taxation. They formerly assessed them according to the length of their queues and for each long finger-nail. The Chinese are mulcted on landing and leaving, for birth and death, for every business venture and privilege; yet they prosper and remain, and these Paranaks in a few more generations may attain the social and political equality they seek. It all proves that under a strong, tyrannical government the Chinese make good citizens, and can easily put away the notions and superstitions that in China itself hold countless millions in the bondage of a long-dead past. The recent exposure of Chinese forgeries of Java bank-notes to the value of three million pounds sterling has put the captains of Batavia and Samarang kampongs in prison, and has led to wholesale arrests of rich Chinese throughout the island.

Native life swarms in this land of the betel and

banana, where there seems to be more of inherent dream and calm than in other lands of the lotus. The Javanese are the finer flowers of the Malay race—a people possessed of a civilization, arts, and literature in that golden period before the Mohammedan and European conquests. They have gentle voices, gentle manners, fine and expressive features, and are the one people of Asia besides the Japanese who have real charm and attraction for the alien. They are more winning, too, by contrast, after one has met the harsh, unlovely, and unwashed people of China, or the equally unwashed, cringing Hindu. They are a little people, and one feels the same indulgent, protective sense as toward the Japanese. Their language is soft and musical—"the Italian of the tropics"; their ideas are poetic; and their love of flowers and perfumes, of music and the dance, of heroic plays and of every emotional form of art, proves them as innately esthetic as their distant cousins, the Japanese, in whom there is so large an admixture of Malay stock. Their reverence for rank and age, and their elaborate etiquette and punctilious courtesy to one another, are as marked even in the common people as among the Japanese; but their abject, crouching humility before their Dutch employers, and the brutality of the latter to them, are a theme for sadder thinking, and calculated to make the blood boil. When one actually sees the quiet, inoffensive peddlers, who chiefly beseech with their eyes, furiously kicked out of the hotel courtyard when mynheer does not choose to buy, and native children actually lifted by an ear and hurled away from the vantage-point on the curbstone which a pajamaed Dutchman wishes for himself while some troops march by, one is content not to see or know any more.

These friendly little barefoot people are of endless interest, and their daily markets, or *passers*, are panoramas of life and color that one longs to transplant entire. Life is so simple and primitive, too, in the sunshine and warmth of the tropics. A bunch of bananas, a basket of steamed rice, and a leaf full of betel preparations comprise the necessaries and luxuries of daily living. With the rice may go many peppers and curried messes of ground cocoanut, which one sees made and offered for sale in small dabs laid on bits of banana-leaf, the wrapping-paper of the tropics. Pinned with a cactus-thorn, a bit of leaf makes a primitive bag, bowl, or cup, and a slip of it serves as a sylvan spoon. All classes chew the betel- or areca-nut, bits of which, wrapped in betel-leaf with lime, furnish cheer and stimulant, dye the mouth, and keep the lips streaming with crimson juice. In Canton and in all Cochin China, across the peninsula, and throughout island and continental India, men and women have equal delight in this peppery stimulant. The Javanese lays his quid of betel tobacco between the lower lip and teeth, and so great seem to be the solace and comfort of it that dozing venders and peddlers will barely turn an eye and grunt responses to one's eager "*Brapa?*" ("How much?")

Peddlers bring to one's doorway fine Bantam basketry and bales of the native cotton cloth, or *battek*, patterned in curious designs that have been in use from time out of mind. These native art fabrics are sold at the passers also, and one soon recognizes the con-

PAINTING SARONGS

ventional designs, and distinguishes the qualities and
merits of these hand-patterned cottons that constitute
the native dress. The sarong, or skirt, worn by men
and women alike, is a strip of cotton two yards long
and one yard deep, which is drawn tightly around the
hips, the fullness gathered in front, and by an adroit
twist made so firm that a belt is not necessary to native wearers. The sarong has always one formal panel
design, which is worn at the front or side, and the
rest of the surface is covered with the intricate ornaments in which native fancy runs riot. There are
geometrical and line combinations, in which appear the
swastika and the curious latticings of central Asia;
others are as bold and natural as anything Japanese;
and in others still, the palm-leaves and quaint
animal forms of India and Persia attest the rival art
influences that have swept over these refined, adaptive,
assimilative people. One favorite serpentine pattern
running in diagonal lines does not need explanation
in this land of gigantic worms and writhing crawlers;
nor that other pattern where centipedes and insect
forms cover the ground; nor that where the fronds of
cocoa-palm wave, and the strange shapes of mangos,
jacks, and breadfruit are interwoven. The deer and
tapir, and the "hunting-scene" patterns are reserved
for native royalty's exclusive wear. In village and
wayside cottages up-country we afterward watched
men and women painting these cloths, tracing a first
outline in a rich brown waxy dye, which is the foundation and dominant color in all these batteks. The
parts which are to be left white are covered with wax,
and the cloth is dipped in or brushed over with the

dye. This resist, or mordant, must be applied for each color, and the wax afterwards steamed out in hot water, so that a sarong goes through many processes and handlings, and is often the work of weeks. The dyes are applied hot through a little tin funnel of an implement tapering down to a thin point, which is used like a painter's brush, but will give the fine line- and dot-work of a pen-and-ink drawing. The sarong's value depends upon the fineness of the drawing, the elaborateness of the design, and the number of colors employed; and beginning as low as one dollar, these brilliant cottons, or hand-painted calico sarongs, increase in price to even twenty or thirty dollars. The Dutch ladies vie with one another in their sarongs as much as native women, and their dishabille dress of the early hours has not always economy to recommend it. The battek also appears in the *slandang*, or long shoulder-scarf, which used to match the sarong and complete the native costume when passed under the arms and crossed at the back, thus covering the body from the armpits to the waist. It is still worn knotted over the mother's shoulder as a sling or hammock for a child; but Dutch fashion has imposed the same narrow, tight-sleeved *kabaia*, the *baju*, or jacket, that Dutch women wear with the sarong. The *kam kapala*, a square handkerchief tied around men's heads as a variant of the turban, is of the same figured battek, and, with the slandang, often exhibits charming color combinations and intricate Persian designs. When one conquers his prejudices and associated ideas enough to pay seemingly fancy prices for these examples of free-hand calico printing, the taste grows, and he soon shares the native longing for a sarong of every standard and novel design.

The native silversmiths hammer out good designs in silver relief for betel- and tobacco-boxes, and exhibit great taste and invention in belt- and jacket-clasps, and in heavy knobs of hairpins and ear-rings, that are often made of gold and incrusted over with gems for richer folk.

There are no historic spots nor show-places of native creation in Batavia; no *kratons*, or *aloon-aloons*, as their palaces and courtyards are called; and only a sentimental interest for a virtual exile pining in his own country is attached to the villa of Raden Saleh. This son of the regent of Samarang was educated in Europe, and lived there for twenty-three years, developing decided talents as an artist, and enjoying the friendship of many men of rank and genius on the Continent, among the latter being Eugène Sue, who is said to have taken Raden Saleh as model for the Eastern Prince in "The Wandering Jew." In Java he found himself sadly isolated from his own people by his European tastes and habits; and he had little in common with the coarse, rapacious mynheers whose sole thoughts were of crops and gulden. "Coffee and sugar, sugar and coffee, are all that is talked here. It is a dreary atmosphere for an artist," said Raden Saleh to D'Almeida, who visited him at Batavia sixty odd years ago. He has left a monument of his taste in this charming villa, in a park whose land is now a vegetable-patch, its shady pleasance a beer-garden and exposition-ground, and the sign "*Te Huur*" ("To Hire") hung from the royal entrance. The exposition of arts and industries in these grounds in 1893 was a great event in Java, the governor-general Van der Wyk opening and closing the fair by electric signal, and the natives making a particularly interesting display of their products and crafts.

V

TO THE HILLS

ONE'S most earnest desire, in the scorch of Batavian noondays and stifling Batavian nights, is to seek refuge in "the hills" — in the dark-green groves and forests of the Blue Mountains, that are ranged with such admirable effect as background when one steams in from the Java Sea. At Buitenzorg, only forty miles away and seven hundred and fifty feet above the sea, heat-worn people find refuge in an entirely different climate, an atmosphere of bracing clearness tempered to moderate summer's warmth. Buitenzorg ("without care"), the Dutch Sans Souci, has been a general refuge and sanitarium for Europeans, the real seat of government, and the home of the governor-general for more than a century. It is the pride and show-place of Java, the great center of its social life, leisure interests, and attractions. The higher officials and many Batavian merchants and bankers have homes at Buitenzorg, and residents from other parts of the island make it their place of recreation and goal of holiday trips.

Undressed Batavia was just rousing from its afternoon nap, and the hotel court was surrounded with barefoot guests in battek pajamas and scant sarongs, a sockless, collarless, unblushing company, that yawned and stared as we drove away, rejoicing to leave this Sans Gêne for Sans Souci. The Weltevreden Station, on the vast Koenig's Plein, a spacious, stone-floored building, whose airy halls and waiting- and refreshment-rooms are repeated on almost as splendid scale at all the large towns of the island, was enlivened with groups of military officers, whose heavy broadcloth uniforms, trailing sabers, and clanking spurs transported us back from the tropics to some chilly European railway-station, and presented the extreme contrast of colonial life. The train that came panting from Tandjon Priok was made up of first-, second-, and third-class cars, all built on the American plan, in that they were long cars and not carriages, and we entered through doors at the end platforms. The first-class cars swung on easy springs; there were modern car-windows in tight frames, also window-frames of wire netting; while thick wooden venetians outside of all, and a double roof, protected as much as possible from the sun's heat. The deep arm-chair seats were upholstered with thick leather cushions, the walls were set with blue-and-white tiles repeating Mauve's and Mesdag's pictures, and adjustable tables, overhead racks, and a dressing-room furnished all the railroad comforts possible. The railway service of Netherlands India is a vast improvement on, and its cars are in striking contrast to, the loose-windowed, springless, dusty, hard-benched carriages in which first-class passengers are jolted across British

India. The second-class cars in Java rest on springs also, but more passengers are put in a compartment, and the fittings are simpler; while the open third-class cars, where native passengers are crowded together, have a continuous window along each side, and the benches are often without backs. The fares average 2.2 United States cents a kilometer (about five eighths of a mile) for first class, 1.6 cents second class, and 6 mills third class. The first-class fare from Batavia to Sourabaya, at the east end of the island, is but 50 gulden ($20) for the 940-kilometer journey, accomplished in two days' train-travel of twelve and fourteen hours each, so that the former heavy expense (over a dollar a mile for post-horses, after one had bought or rented a traveling-carriage) and the delays of travel in Java are done away with.

The railways have been built by both the government and private corporations, connecting and working together, the first line dating from 1875. The continuous railway line across the island was completed and opened with official ceremonies in November, 1894. The gap of one hundred miles or more across the "*terra ingrata*," the low-lying swamp and fever regions either side of Tjilatjap, had existed for years after the track was completed to the east and west of it. Dutch engineers built and manage the road, but the staff, the working force of the line, are natives, or Chinese of the more or less mixed but educated class filling the middle ground between Europeans and natives, between the upper and lower ranks. Wonderful skill was shown in leading the road over the mountains, and in building a firm track and bridges through the reeking swamps, where no white man could labor, even if he could live. The trains do not run at night, which would be a great advantage in a hot country, for the reason that the train crews are composed entirely of natives (since such work is considered beneath the grade of any European), and the cautious Dutch will not trust native engineers after dark. Through trains start from either end of the line and from the half-way stations at five and six o'clock each morning, and run until the short twilight and pitch-darkness that so quickly succeed the unchanging six-o'clock tropical sunset. These early morning starts, and the eight- and nine-o'clock dinner of the Java hotels, make travel most wearisome. One may buy fruit at every station platform, and always tea, coffee, chocolate, wine and schnapps, bread and biscuits at the station buffets. At the larger stations there are dining-rooms, or a service of lunch-baskets, in which the Gargantuan riz tavel, or luncheon, is served hot in one's compartment as the train moves on.

The hour-and-a-half's ride from Batavia to Buitenzorg gave us an epitome of tropical landscapes as the train ran between a double panorama of beauty. The soil was a deep, intense red, as if the heat of the sun and the internal fires of this volcanic belt had warmed the fruitful earth to this glowing color, which contrasted so strongly with the complemental green of grain and the groves of palms and cacao-trees. The level rice-fields were being plowed, worked, flooded, planted, weeded, and harvested side by side, the several crops of the year going on continuously, with seemingly no regard to seasons. Nude little boys, astride

RICE-FIELDS.

of smooth gray water-buffaloes, posed statuesquely while those leisurely animals browsed afield; and no pastoral pictures of Java remain clearer in memory than those of patient little brown children sitting half days and whole days on buffalo-back, to brush flies and guide the stupid-looking creatures to greener and more luscious bits of herbage. Many stories are told of the affection the water-ox often manifests for his boy keeper, killing tigers and snakes in his defense, and performing prodigies of valor and intelligence; but one doubts the tales the more he sees of this hideous beast of Asia. Men and women were wading knee-deep in paddy-field muck, transplanting the green rice-shoots from the seed-beds, and picturesque harvest groups posed in tableaux, as the train shrieked by. Children rolled at play before the gabled baskets of houses clustered in toy villages beneath the inevitable cocoa-palms and bananas, the combination of those two useful trees being the certain sign of a kampong, or village, when the braided-bamboo houses are invisible.

At Depok there was a halt to pass the down-train, and the natives of this one Christian village and mission-station, the headquarters of evangelical work in Java, flocked to the platform with a prize horticultural display of all the fruits of the season for sale. The record of mission work in Java is a short one, as, after casting out the Portuguese Jesuit missionaries, the Dutch forbade any others to enter, and Spanish rule in Holland had perhaps taught them not to try to impose a strange religion on a people. During Sir Stamford Raffles's rule, English evangelists began work among the natives, but were summarily interrupted and obliged to withdraw when Java was returned to Holland. All missionaries were strictly excluded until the humanitarian agitation in Europe, which resulted in the formal abolition of slavery and the gradual abandonment of the culture system, led the government to do a little for the Christianization and education of the people. The government supports twenty-nine Protestant pastors and ten Roman Catholic priests, primarily for the spiritual benefit of the European residents, and their spheres are exactly defined— proselytizing and mutual rivalries being forbidden. Missionaries from other countries are not allowed to settle and work among the people, and whatever may be said against this on higher moral grounds, the colonial government has escaped endless friction with the consuls and governments of other countries. The authorities have been quite willing to let the natives enjoy their mild Mohammedanism, and our Moslem servant spoke indifferently of mission efforts at Depok, with no scorn, no contempt, and apparently no hostility to the European faith.

Until recently, no steps were taken to educate the Javanese, and previous to 1864 they were not allowed to study the Dutch language. All colonial officers are obliged to learn Low Malay, that being the recognized language of administration and justice, instead of the many Javanese and Sundanese dialects, with their two forms of polite and common speech. These officials receive promotion and preferment as they make progress in the spoken and written language. Low Malay is the most readily acquired of all languages, as there are no harsh gutturals or difficult consonants, and the construction is very simple. Children who learn the soft, musical Malay first have difficulty with the harsh Dutch sounds, while the Dutch who learn Malay after their youth never pronounce it as well or as easily as they pronounce French. The few Javanese, even those of highest rank, who acquired the Dutch language and attempted to use it in conversation with officials, used to be bruskly answered in Malay, an implication that the superior language was reserved for Europeans only. This helped the conquerors to keep the distinctions sharply drawn between them and their subject people, and while they could always understand what the natives were saying, the Dutch were free to talk together without reserve in the presence of servants or princes. Dutch is now taught in the schools for natives maintained by the colonial government, 201 primary schools having been opened in 1887, with an attendance of 39,707 pupils. The higher schools at Batavia have been opened to the sons of native officials and such rich Javanese as can afford them, and conservatives lament the "spoiling" of the natives with all that the government now does for them. They complain that the Javanese are becoming too "independent" since schoolmasters, independent planters, and tourists came, just as the old-style foreign residents of India, the Straits, China, and Japan bemoan the progressive tendencies and upheavals of this era of Asiatic awakening and enlightenment; and tourist travel is always harped upon as the most offending and corrupting cause of the changes in the native spirit.

Once above the general level of low-lying rice-lands, cacao-plantations succeeded one another for miles beyond Depok; the small trees hung full of fat pods just ripening into reddish brown and crimson. The air was noticeably cooler in the hills, and as the shadows lengthened the near green mountains began to tower in shapes of lazuli mist, and a sky of soft, surpassing splendor made ready for its sunset pageant. When we left the train we were whirled through the twilight of great avenues of trees to the hotel, and given rooms whose veranda overhung a strangely rustling, shadowy abyss, where we could just discern a dark silver line of river leading to the pale-yellow west, with the mountain mass of Salak cut in gigantic purple silhouette.

The ordinary bedroom of a Java hotel, with latticed doors and windows, contains one or two beds, each seven feet square, hung with starched muslin curtains that effectually exclude the air, as well as lizards or winged things. The bedding, as at Singapore, consists of a hard mattress with a sheet drawn over it, a pair of hard pillows, and a long bolster laid down the middle as a cooling or dividing line. Blankets or other coverings are unneeded and unknown, but it takes one a little time to become acclimated to that order in the penetrating dampness of the dewy and reeking hours before dawn. If one makes protest enough, a thin blanket will be brought, but so camphorated and mildew-scented as to be insupportable. Pillows are not stuffed with feathers, but with the cooler, dry, elastic down of the straight-armed cotton-tree, which one sees growing everywhere along the highways, its rigid, right-angled branches inviting their use as the regulation telegraph-pole. The floors are made of a smooth, hard cement, which harbors no insects, and can be kept clean and cool. Pieces of coarse ratan matting are the only floor-coverings used, and give an agreeable contrast to the dirty felts, dhurries, and carpets, the patches of wool and cotton and matting, spread over the earth or wooden floors of the unspeakable hotels of British India. And yet the Javanese hotels are disappointing to those who know the solid comforts and immaculate order of certain favorite hostelries of The Hague and Amsterdam. Everything is done to secure a free circulation of air, as a room that is closed for a day gets a steamy, mildewed atmosphere, and if closed for three days blooms with green mold over every inch of its walls and floors. The section of portico outside each room at Buitenzorg was decently screened off to serve as a private sitting-room for each guest or family in the hours of startling dishabille; and as soon as the sun went down a big hanging-lamp assembled an entomological congress. Every hotel provides as a night-lamp for the bedroom a tumbler with an inch of cocoanut-oil, and a tiny tin and cork arrangement for floating a wick on its surface. For the twelve hours of pitch-darkness this little lightning-bug contrivance burns steadily, emitting a delicious nutty fragrance, and allowing one to watch the unpleasant shadows of the lizards running over the walls and bed-curtains, and to look for the larger, poisonous brown gecko, whose unpleasant voice calling "*Becky! Becky! Becky!*" in measured gasps, six times, over and over again, is the actual, material nightmare of the tropics.

British tourists, unmindful of the offending of their own India in more vital matters, berate and scorn the tiny water-pitcher and basin of the Java hotels, brought from the continent of Europe unchanged; and rage at the custom of guests in Java hotels emptying their basins out of doors or windows on tropical shrubbery or courtyard pavings at will. There are swimming-pools at some hotels and in many private houses, but the usual bath-room of the land offers the traveler a barrel and a dipper. One is expected to ladle the water out and dash it over him in broken doses, and as the swimming-pool is a rinsing-tub for the many, the individual is besought not to use soap. Naturally the British tourist's invectives are deep and loud and long, and he will not believe that the dipper-bath is more cooling than to soak and soap and scour in a comfortable tub of his own. He will not be silenced or comforted in this tubless tropical land, which, if it had only remained under British rule, might be— would be—etc. All suffering tourists agree with him, however, that the worst laundering in the world befalls one's linen in Java, the cloth-destroying, button-exterminating *dhobie* man of Ceylon and India being a careful and conscientious artist beside the clothes-pounder of Java. In making the great circle of the earth westward one leaves the last of laundry luxury at Singapore, and continues to suffer until, in the substratum of French civilization in Egypt, he finds the *blanchisseuse*.

The order of living is the same at the up-country hotels as at Batavia, and the charges are the same everywhere in Java, averaging about three dollars gold each day, everything save wine included; and at Buitenzorg corkage was charged on the bottle of filtered water which a dyspeptic tourist manufactured with a patent apparatus he carried with him. Landlords do not recognize nor deal with fractions of days, if they can help it, in charging one for board on this "American plan"; but when that reckless royal tourist, the King of Siam, makes battle over his Java hotel bills, lesser travelers may well take courage and follow his example. The King of Siam has erected commemorative columns crowned with white marble elephants, as souvenirs of his visits to Singapore and Batavia, and after the king's financial victory over Buitenzorg and Garoet hotels, the tourist sees the white elephant as a symbol of victory more personally and immediately significant than the lion on the Waterloo column. It has been said that "no invalid nor dyspeptic should enter the portals of a Java hotel," and this cannot be insisted upon too strongly, to deter any such sufferers from braving the sunrise breakfasts and bad coffee, the heavy riz tavel, and the long-delayed dinner-hour, solely for the sake of tropical scenery and vegetation, and a study of Dutch colonial life.

VI

A DUTCH SANS SOUCI

AT daylight we saw that our portico looked full upon the front of Mount Salak, green to the very summit with plantations and primeval forests. Deep down below us lay a valley of Eden, where thousands of palm-trees were in constant motion, their branches bending, swaying, and fluttering as softly as ostrich-plumes to the eye, but with a strange, harsh, metallic rustle and clash, different from the whispers and sighs and cooing sounds of temperate foliage. As stronger winds threshed the heavy leaves, the level of the valley rippled and tossed in green billows like a barley-field. There was a basket village on the river-bank, where tropic life went on in as plain pantomime as in any stage presentation. At sunrise the people came out of their fragile toy houses, stretched their arms to the sky and yawned, took a swim in the river, and then gathered in the dewy shade to eat their morning curry and rice from their plantain-leaf plates. Then the baskets and cooking-utensils were held in the swift-flowing stream,—such a fastidious, ideal,

MONT SALAK, FROM THE RESIDENT'S GARDEN, BUITENZORG.

adorable sort of dish-washing!—and the little community turned to its daily vocations. The men went away to work, or sat hammering and hewing with implements strangely Japanese, and held in each instance in the Japanese way. The women pounded and switched clothing to and fro in the stream, and spread it out in white and brilliant-colored mosaics on the bank to dry. They plaited baskets and painted sarongs, and the happy brown children, in nature's dress, rolled at play under the cocoanut-trees, or splashed like young frogs in and out of the stream.

While this went on below, and we watched the dark indigo mass of Salak turning from purple and azure to sunlit greens in the light of early day, the breakfast of the country was brought to our porch: cold toast, cold meats, eggs, fruit, tea or the very worst coffee in all the world—something that even the American railway restaurant and frontier hotel would spurn with scorn. Java coffee, in Java, comes to one in a stoppered glass bottle or cruet, a dark-brown fluid that might as well be walnut catsup, old port, or New Orleans molasses. This double extract of coffee, made by cold filtration, is diluted with hot water and hot milk to a muddy, gray-brown, lukewarm drink, that is uniformly bad in every hotel and public place of refreshment that a tourist encounters on the island. In private houses, where the fine Arabian berry is toasted and powdered, and the extract made fresh each day, the morning draught is quite another fluid, and worthy the cachet the name of Java gives to coffee in far countries.

Buitenzorg, the Bogor of the natives, who will not

call it by its newer name, is one of the enchanted spots where days can slip by in dateless delight; one forgets the calendar and the flight of time, and hardly remembers the heavy, sickening heat of Batavia stewing away on the plains below. It is the Versailles of the island, the seat of the governor-general's court, and the social life of the colony, a resort for officials and the leisure class, and for invalids and the delicate, who find strength in the clear, fresh air of the hills, the cool nights, and the serenely tempered days, each with its reviving shower the year round. Buitenzorg is the Simla of Netherlands India, but it awaits its Kipling to record its social life in clear-cut, instantaneous pictures. There are strange pictures for the Kipling to sketch, too, since the sarong and the native jacket are as much the regular morning dress for ladies at the cool, breezy hill-station as in sweltering Batavia, a fact rather disproving the lowland argument that the heat demands such extraordinary concessions in costume. But as that "Bengal Civilian" who wrote "*De Zieke Reiziger;* or, Rambles in Java in 1852," and commented so freely upon Dutch costume, cuisine, and Sabbath-keeping, succeeded, Mr. Money said, in shutting every door to the English traveler for years afterward, and added extra annoyances to the toelatings-kaart system, budding and alien Kiplings may take warning.

The famous Botanical Garden at Buitenzorg is the great show-place, the paradise and pride of the island. The Dutch are acknowledgedly the best horticulturists of Europe, and with the heat of a tropical sun, a daily shower, and nearly a century's well-directed efforts, they have made Buitenzorg's garden first of its kind in the world, despite the rival efforts of the French at Saigon, and of the British at Singapore, Ceylon, Calcutta, and Jamaica. The governor-general's palace, greatly enlarged from the first villa of 1744, is in the midst of the ninety-acre inclosure reached from the main gate, near the hotel and the passer, by what is undoubtedly the finest avenue of trees in the world. These graceful kanari-trees, arching one hundred feet overhead in a great green cathedral aisle, have tall, straight trunks covered with stag-horn ferns, bird's-nest ferns, ratans, creeping palms, blooming orchids, and every kind of parasite and air-plant the climate allows; and there is a fairy lake of lotus and *Victoria regia* beside it, with pandanus and red-stemmed Banka palms crowded in a great sheaf or bouquet on a tiny islet. When one rides through this green avenue in the dewy freshness of the early morning, it seems as though nature and the tropics could do no more, until he has penetrated the tunnels of waringen-trees, the open avenues of royal palms, the great plantation of a thousand palms, the grove of tree-fern, and the frangipani thicket, and has reached the knoll commanding a view of the double summit of Gedeh and Pangerango, vaporous blue volcanic heights, from one peak of which a faint streamer of smoke perpetually floats. There is a broad lawn at the front of the palace, shaded with great waringen-, sausage-, and candle-trees, and trees whose branches are hidden in a mantle of vivid-leafed bougainvillea vines, with deer wandering and grouping themselves in as correct park pictures as if under branches of elm or oak, or beside the conventional ivied trunks of the North.

It is a tropical experience to reverse an umbrella and in a few minutes fill it with golden-hearted white frangipani blossoms, or to find nutmegs lying as thick as acorns on the ground, and break their green outer shell and see the fine coral branches of mace enveloping the dark kernel. It is a delight, too, to see mangosteens and rambutans growing, to find bread, sausages, and candles hanging in plenty from benevolent trees, and other fruits and strange flowers springing from a tree's trunk instead of from its branches. There are thick groves and regular avenues of the waringen, a species of *Ficus*, and related to the banian- and the rubber-tree, a whole family whose roots crawl above the ground, drop from the branches and generally comport themselves in unconventional ways. Bamboos grow in clumps and thickets, ranging from the fine, feathery-leafed canes, that are really only large grasses, up to the noble giants from Burma, whose stems are more nearly trunks easily soaring to a hundred feet in air, and spreading there a solid canopy of graceful foliage.

The creepers run from tree to tree, and writhe over the ground like gray serpents; ratans and climbing palms one hundred feet in length are common, while uncommon ones stretch to five hundred feet. There is one creeper with a blossom like a magnified white violet, and with all a wood-violet's fragrance; but with only Dutch and botanical names on the labels, one wanders ignorantly and protestingly in this paradise of strange things. The rarer orchids are grown in matted sheds in the shade of tall trees; and although we saw them at the end of the dry season, and few plants were in bloom, there was still an attractive orchid-show.

But the strangest, most conspicuous bloom in that choice corner was a great butterfly flower of a pitcher-plant (a *nepenthes*), whose pale-green petals were veined with velvety maroon, and half concealed the pelican pouch of a pitcher filled with water. It was an evil-looking, ill-smelling, sticky thing, and its unusual size and striking colors made it haunt one longest of all vegetable marvels. There were other more attractive butterflies fluttering on pliant stems, strange little woolly white orchids, like edelweiss transplanted, and scores of delicate Java and Borneo orchids, not so well known as the Venezuelan and Central American orchids commonly grown in American hothouses, and so impossible to acclimate in Java.

Lady Raffles died while Sir Stamford was governor of Java, and was buried in the section of the palace park that was afterward (in 1817) set apart as a botanical garden, and the care of the little Greek temple over her grave near the kanari avenue was provided for in a special clause in the treaty of cession. The bust of Theismann, who founded the garden and added so much to botanical knowledge by his studies in Java and Borneo, stands in an oval pleasance called the rose-garden; and there one may take heart and boast of the temperate zone, since that rare exotic, the rose, is but a spindling bush, and its blossoming less than scanty at Buitenzorg, when one remembers California's, and more especially Tacoma's, perennial prodigalities in showers of roses. In 1895 Professor Lotsy of Johns Hopkins University, Baltimore, was called to assist the learned curator, Dr. Treub, in the management of this famous *Hortus Bogoriensis*, which provides laboratory and working-space for, and invites foreign botanists freely to avail themselves of, this unique opportunity of study. Over one hundred native gardeners tend and care for this great botanic museum of more than nine thousand living specimens, all working under the direction of a white head-gardener. The Tjiliwong River separates the botanic garden from a culture-garden of forty acres, where seventy more gardeners look to the economic plants—the various cinchonas, sugar-canes, rubber, tea, coffee, gums, spices, hemp, and other growths whose introduction to the colony has so benefited the planters. Experiments in acclimatization are carried on in the culture-garden, and at the experimental garden at Tjibodas, high up on the slopes of Salak, where the governor-general has a third palace, and there is a government hospital and sanatorium.

Theismann's famous museum of living twig- and leaf-insects was abandoned some years ago, the curator deciding to keep his garden strictly to botanical lines. One no longer has the pleasure of seeing there those curious and most extraordinary freaks of nature —the fresh green or dry and dead-looking twigs that suddenly turn their heads or bend their long angular legs and move away; or leaves, as delusive in their way, that detach themselves from a tree-branch and fly away. These insects bearing so astonishing a resemblance to their environment may be purchased now and then from Chinese gardeners; but otherwise, if one asks where they can be found or seen, there comes the usual answer, "In Borneo or Celebes,"—always on the farther, remoter islands,—tropic wonders taking wing like the leaf-insects when one reaches their reputed haunts.

All Java is in a way as finished as little Holland itself, the whole island cultivated from edge to edge like a tulip-garden, and connected throughout its length with post-roads smooth and perfect as park drives, all arched with waringen-, kanari-, tamarind-, or teak-trees. The rank and tangled jungle is invisible, save by long journeys; and great snakes, wild tigers, and rhinoceroses are almost unknown now. One must go to Borneo and the farther islands to see them, too. All the valleys, plains, and hillsides are planted in formal rows, hedged, terraced, banked, drained, and carefully weeded as a flower-bed. The drives are of endless beauty, whichever way one turns from Buitenzorg, and we made triumphal progresses through the kanari- and waringen-lined streets in an enormous "milord." The equipage measured all of twenty feet from the tip of the pole to the footman's perch behind, and with a cracking whip and at a rattling gait we dashed through shady roads, past Dutch barracks and hospitals, over picturesque bridges, and through villages where the native children jumped and clapped their hands with glee as the great Juggernaut vehicle rolled by. We visited the grave of Raden Saleh, a lonely little pavilion or temple in a tangle of shrubbery that was once a lovely garden shaded by tall cocoa-palms; and we drove to Batoe Toelis, "the place of the written stone," and in the little thatched basket of a temple saw the sacred stone inscribed in ancient Kawi characters, the original classic language of the Javanese. In another basket shrine were shown the veritable footprints of Buddha, with no explanation as to how and when he rested on the island, nor yet how he happened to have such long, distinctively Malay toes. Near these temples is the villa where the poor African prince of Ashantee was so long detained in exile—an African chief whose European education had turned his mind to geology and natural sciences, and who led the life of a quiet student here until, by the exchange from Dutch to British ownership of Ashantee, a way was opened for him to return and die in his own country. There is a magnificent view from the Ashantee villa out over a great green plain and a valley of palms to the peaks of Gedeh and Pangerango, and to their volcanic neighbor, Salak, silent for two hundred years. Peasants, trooping along the valley roads far below, made use of a picturesque bamboo bridge that is accounted one of the famous sights of the neighborhood, and seemed but processions of ants crossing a spider's web. All the suburban roads are so many botanical exhibitions approaching that in the great garden, and one's interest is claimed at every yard and turn.

It takes a little time for the temperate mind to accept the palm-tree as a common, natural, and inevitable object in every outlook and landscape; to realize that the joyous, living thing with restless, perpetually threshing foliage is the same correct, symmetrical, motionless feather-duster on end that one knows in the still life of hothouses and drawing-rooms at home; to realize that it grows in the ground, and not in

FRANGIPANI AND SAUSAGE-TREE

a pot or tub to be brought indoors for the winter season. The arches of gigantic kanari-trees growing over by-lanes and village paths, although intended for triumphal avenues and palace driveways, overpower one with the mad extravagance, the reckless waste, and the splendid luxury of nature. One cannot accept these things at first as utilities, just as it shocks one to have a servant black his shoes with bruised hibiscus flowers or mangosteen rind, or remove rust from kris- or knife-blades with pineapple-juice, thrusting a blade through and through the body of the pine. The poorest may have his hedge of lantana, which, brought from the Mauritius by Lady Raffles, now borders roads, gardens, and the railway-tracks from end to end of the island. The humblest dooryard may be gay with tall poinsettia-trees, and bougainvilleas may pour a torrent of magenta leaves from every tree, wall, or roof. The houses of the great planters around Buitenzorg are ideal homes in the tropics, and the Tjomson and other large tea and coffee estates are like parks. The drives through their grounds show one the most perfect lawns and flower-beds and ornamental trees, vines, and palms, and such ranks on ranks of thriving tea-bushes and coffee-bushes, every leaf perfect and without flaw, every plant in even line, and the warm red earth lying loosely on their roots, that one feels as if in some ornamental *jardin d'acclimatation* rather than among the most staple and serious crops of commerce. Yet from end to end of the island the cultivation is as intense and careful, entitling Java to its distinction as "the finest tropical island in the world." It is the gem of the Indies, the one splendid jewel in the Netherlands crown, and a possession to which poor Cuba, although corresponding exactly to it geographically and politically, has been vainly compared.

There were often interesting *table d'hôte* companies gathered at noon and at night in the long dining-room of the Buitenzorg hotel. While many of the Dutch officials and planters, and their wives, maintained the wooden reserve and supercilious air of those uncertain folk of the half-way strata in society everywhere, there were others whose intelligence and courtesy and friendly interest remain as green spots in the land. There was one most amiable man, who, we thought, in his love of country, was anxious to hear us praise it. We extolled the cool breezes and the charming day, and said: "You have a beautiful country here."

"This is not my country," he answered.

"But are you not Dutch?"

"Oh, yes."

"Then Java is yours. It is the Netherlands even if it is India."

"Yes; but I am from East Java, near Malang"—a section all of three hundred miles away, off at the other end of the island; but a strong distinction—an extreme aloofness or estrangement—exists between residents of East, West, and Middle Java, and between those of this island and of the near-by Sumatra, Celebes, and Molucca, all Indonesians as they are, under the rule of the one governor-general of Netherlands India, representing the little queen at The Hague.

Often when we spoke of "India" or "southern

India," or referred to Delhi and Bombay as "cities of India," the Hollanders looked puzzled.

"Ah, when you say 'India,' you mean Hindustan or British India?"

"Certainly; that is India, the continent—the greater India."

"But what, then, do you call this island and all the possessions of the Netherlands out here?"

"Why, we speak of this island as Java. Every one knows of it, and of Sumatra and Borneo, by their own names."

The defender of Netherlands India said nothing; but soon a reference was made to a guest who had been in official residence at Amboyna.

"Where?" we inquired with keen interest in the unknown.

"Amboyna. Do you in America not know of Amboyna?"

Average Americans must confess if, since early geography days, they have not remembered carefully that one tiny island in the group of Moluccas off the east end of Java—an island so tiny that even on the school atlases used in Buitenzorg it is figured the size of a pea, and on the maps for the rest of the world is but a nameless dot in the clustered dots of the group that would better be named the Nutmeg Isles, since the bulk of the world's supply of that spicy fruit comes from their shores.

Then, away down there, out of the world, I was taken to task for that chief sin and offending of my country against other countries—the McKinley Bill of so long ago.

"Why, *we* could n't make any money out of tobacco while such a law was in existence," said one Sumatra planter.

"But we are concerned with the prosperity of our own American tobacco-growers. It is for the Dutch government to make laws to benefit the tobacco-planters of Sumatra."

"Ah! but you have new and better laws now since that last revolution in the States, and we are all planting all the tobacco we can. We shall be very prosperous now."

VII

IN A TROPICAL GARDEN

THE Buitenzorg passer proper is housed in a long, tiled pavilion facing an open common, on which the country folk gather with their produce twice a week, and, overflowing, stretch in a scattering encampment down the broad street leading from the gate of the Botanical Garden. The permanent passer, or regular bazaar in the covered building, is stocked with the staples and substantials of life, and is open every day. The town tailors have their abode under that cover, and squat in rows before their little American hand-sewing machines, and sew the single seam of a sarong skirt, or reel off a native jacket, while the customer waits. It is the semi-weekly, early morning, outdoor market of chattering country folk that most delights and diverts a stranger, however. The lines of venders, strung along the shady street and grouped under palm-patched umbrellas in the open, provide horticultural and floral exhibits of the greatest interest, and afford the most picturesque scenes of native life. The long street of the Tjina kampong beyond is dull and monotonous by comparison, for when Dutch rules force the Chinese to be clean and orderly all picturesqueness and character are gone from their quarter. All the tasseled lanterns and strips of vermilion paper will not "tell" artistically without their concomitant grease and dirt.

As a very new broom, a clever child pleased with the toy of a new employer, Amat, our mild-mannered Moslem servant, was a treasure and delight during those first days at Buitenzorg. He entered gleefully into the spirit of our reckless purchase from the heaps of splendid fruits poured from the great horn of plenty into the open passer. He gave us the name of each particular strange fruit, taught us the odd tricks and sleight-of-hand methods of opening these novelties of the market-place; and it was quite like kindergarten play when he unbraided and wove together again the ribbed palm-leaf reticules in which *dukus* and such small fruits are sold. We carried baskets of strange fruits back to the hotel, and Amat added every vegetable curio and market's marvel he could find to the heaps of fruits and flowers. Our veranda was a testing- and proving-ground, and there seemed to be no end to the delights and surprises the tropics provided.

Tons of bananas were heaped high in the passer each day, the great golden bunches making most decorative and attractive masses of color, and their absurd cheapness tempting one to buy and to buy. The Java *pisang*, or banana, however, is but a coarse plantain with a pinkish-yellow, dry pulp, of a pumpkiny flavor that sadly disappoints the palate. Yet it

TROPICAL FRUITS.

is nature's greatest and most generously bestowed gift in the tropics, and it was pleasant to eat it picked ripe in its native home, instead of receiving it steam-ripened from Northern fruiterers' warehouses. Every tiny village and almost every little native hut in Java has its banana-patch or its banana-tree, which requires nothing of labor in cultivation, save the weeding away of the old stalks. It was intended as a humane concentration of benefits when nature gave man this food-plant, four thousand pounds of whose fruit will grow with so little human aid in the same space of ground required to raise ninety-nine pounds of potatoes or thirty-three pounds of wheat; both those Northern crops acquired, too, only by incessant sweat of the brow and muscular exertion. The pisang is the tropical staff of life for whites as well as natives, as wholesome and necessary as bread, and an equivalent for the latter as a starchy food. It comes to one with the earliest breakfast cup, appears at every meal, arrives with the afternoon tea-tray, and always ends the late dinner as the inevitable accompaniment of cheese, the happiest substitute for bread or biscuits, tropical gourmets insist.

The lovely red rambutans (*Nephelium lappaceum*) we would have bought for their beauty alone—those clusters of seemingly green chestnut-burs, with spines tinted to the deepest rose, affording the most exquisite color-study of all the fruits in the passer. The spiny shell pulls apart easily, and discloses a juicy, half-transparent mass of white pulp around a central core of smooth stones. The duku, looking like a big green grape, a fresh almond, or an olive, contains just such another ball of pulp within its leathery rind, and both fruits much resemble the fresh *lychees* of China in flavor. The *salak*, or "forbidden fruit," is a hard, scaly, pear-shaped thing, which very appropriately grows on a prickly bush, and whose strange brown rind reminds one of a pine-cone or a rattlesnake's skin. This scaly, snaky shell prejudices one against it; but the salak is as solid as an apple, with a nutty flavor and texture. It is not unpleasant, nor is it distinctively anything in flavor—nothing unique or delicious enough to make one seek hard or long for a second taste of it. The *jamboa*, the eugenia or rose-apple (*Eugenia malaccensis*), is a fruit of the same size and shape as the salak, and in spite of its exquisite coloring it impresses one as being an albino, a skinless or some other monstrous and unnatural product of nature. Its outer integument, thinner than any nectarine's rind, shades from snow-white at the stem to the deepest rose-pink at the blossom end, and it looks as if it were the most fragrant, delicious, and juicy fruit. One bites into the fine, crisp, succulent pulp, and tastes exactly nothing, and never forgives the beautiful, rose-tinted, watery blank for its deluding. The *carambola* (*Averrhoa*), the five-ribbed yellow "star-fruit," popularly known in real Cathay as the "Chinese gooseberry," is a favorite, fragrant study in spherical geometry, and the cutting apart of its triangular sections is the nicest sort of after-dinner amusement and demonstration; but its fine, deliciously acid pulp is usually known to one before he reaches Java. Its relative, the *bilimbi*, is the sharpest of acid fruits, and lends an edge to chutneys and curried conglomerates.

The breadfruit and its gigantic relative, the *nanko* (*Artocarpus integrifolia*), or jackfruit, which often weighs thirty and even forty pounds, and is sufficient load for a man to bring to market on his back, are the vegetable mainstays of native life; but as both must be cooked to a tasteless mush to be relished, one is satisfied only to look at them in the passer. That swollen monstrosity, the nanko, grows goiter-like on the trunk of a tree, and is supported in ratan slings while the great excrescence ripens. One must speak of the breadfruit with respect, though, after all that scientists have said, philosophers and political economists have argued, concerning it. Since ten breadfruit-trees will support a large family the year round, and a man may plant that many within an hour and need give them no further care, Captain Cook observed that such a man has then "as completely fulfilled his duty to his own and future generations as the native of our less genial climate by plowing in the cold of winter and reaping in the summer heat as often as the seasons return."

The prickly durian (*Durio Zibethinus*), which is almost as large as the nanko, has a pulp a little like that of a cantaloup melon, only smoother and more solid—a thick, creamy, "almondy-buttery" custard, which is agreeable to the palate, but offends the nose with an odor of onion and stale egg. It is spoken of with bitterness and contempt by most Europeans, is extolled as "the king and emperor of fruits" by Wallace and a few other intrepid ones, and the little English children in Java, who all are fond of it, call it "darling durian." In 1599 Linschott declared it to surpass in flavor "all the other fruits of the world." Crawfurd said that it tasted like "fresh cream and filberts," a description which conjures up the cloying modern fantasia of English-walnut kernels in a mayonnaise. Another great one has said that "to eat durians is a new sensation worth a voyage to the East to experience"; and Dr. Ward, in his "Medical Topography of the Straits," says: "Those who overcome the prejudice excited by the disagreeable, fetid odor of the external shell reckon it delicious. From experience I can pronounce it the most luscious and the most fascinating fruit in the universe; the pulp covering the seeds, the only part eaten, excels the finest custards which could be prepared by either Ude or Kitchener." One sees the monster retailed in segments in every passer; the natives are always munching it inconveniently to windward of one, and they not only praise it, but write poems to it, and respectfully salute the tree they see it growing on. This fruit of discordant opinions hangs high upon a tall tree, and is never picked, but allowed to fall to the ground when it becomes perfectly ripe. A falling durian is justly dreaded and guarded against by the natives, who tell of men whose shoulders have been lacerated and heads half crushed by the sudden descent of one of these great green cannon-balls. Its unpleasant odor is said to come with age, and they tell one that a freshly fallen durian is free from such objection; but the watched durian never falls, I found, after maintaining the attitude of the fox toward the grapes for a reasonable time before a durian-tree.

The papaya, a smaller custard-fruit, with unpleasant

little curly gray seeds in the mess, is like a coarse, flavorless melon, but is highly extolled as a febrifuge and tonic. The much-heralded and disappointing cherimoyer is grown too, and mangos ripen in every yard; but the Java mangos are coarse and turpentiny, of a deep pumpkiny hue. Pineapples, the *nanas*, or Portuguese *ananassa*, grow to perfection all over the low, hot country; but one is warned to be careful in eating them, and they are called the most dangerous, the most choleraic and fever-causing of tropical fruits. The native orange on this south side of the equator is not orange at all, even when ripe, but its peel is a deep, dark, beautiful green, and its flavor unequaled. The big *Citrus decumana*, the pomelo of China, the *pumplemoos* of Java, the Batavian lime in British India, the shaddock of the West Indies, and the grape-fruit of Florida, appears in the passers, but is coarse, dry, and tasteless, save for the turpentine flavor, which does not lurk within, but stalks abroad.

The fruit of fruits, the prize of the Indies and of all the Malay equatorial regions, where the tree is indigenous, is the mangosteen (*Garcinia mangosteen*), and the tourist should avail himself of November and December as the months for a tour in Java, if only to know the mangosteen in its perfection. The dark-purple apples hang from the tall trees by woody stems, and the natives bring the *manggis* to market tied together in bunches of twenties like clusters of gigantic grapes. It is delight enough to the eye alone to cut the thick, fibrous rind, bisect the perfect sphere at the equator line, and see the round ball of "perfumed snow" resting intact in its rose-lined cup. The five white segments separate easily, and may be lifted whole with a fork, and they melt on the tongue with a touch of tart and a touch of sweet; one moment a memory of the juiciest, most fragrant apple, at another a remembrance of the smoothest cream ice, the most exquisite and delicately flavored fruit-acid known—all the delights of nature's laboratory condensed in that ball of *neige parfumée*. It is fortunate that the mangosteen is a harmless and wholesome fruit, and that one may eat with impunity, laying store for a lifetime in his one opportunity. I often wondered how it would be if the mangosteen were a dangerous or a forbidden fruit; if it were wicked or a little of a sin to eat it; if mangosteens could be obtained singly, at great risk or expense; or if they should be prescribed for one as a tonic, something antimalarial, a substitute for quinine, to be taken in doses of one, two, or ten before or after each meal. The mangosteen cannot be transported to the temperate zone of Europe,—not even with the aid of modern ships' refrigerating-machines and when coated with wax,—as in less than a week after leaving the trees the pulp melts away to a brown mass. By the alternation of seasons the mangosteen is always in market at Singapore, as it ripens north of the equator during the summer six months of the northern hemisphere's year, and during this rainy season of Cochin China is carried from Saigon successfully as far north as Shanghai and Yokohama. The offer by the leading British steamship company of thirty pounds sterling to the ship-captain who will get a basket of mangosteens to the Queen is still open. The tree grows throughout the Malay Peninsula and

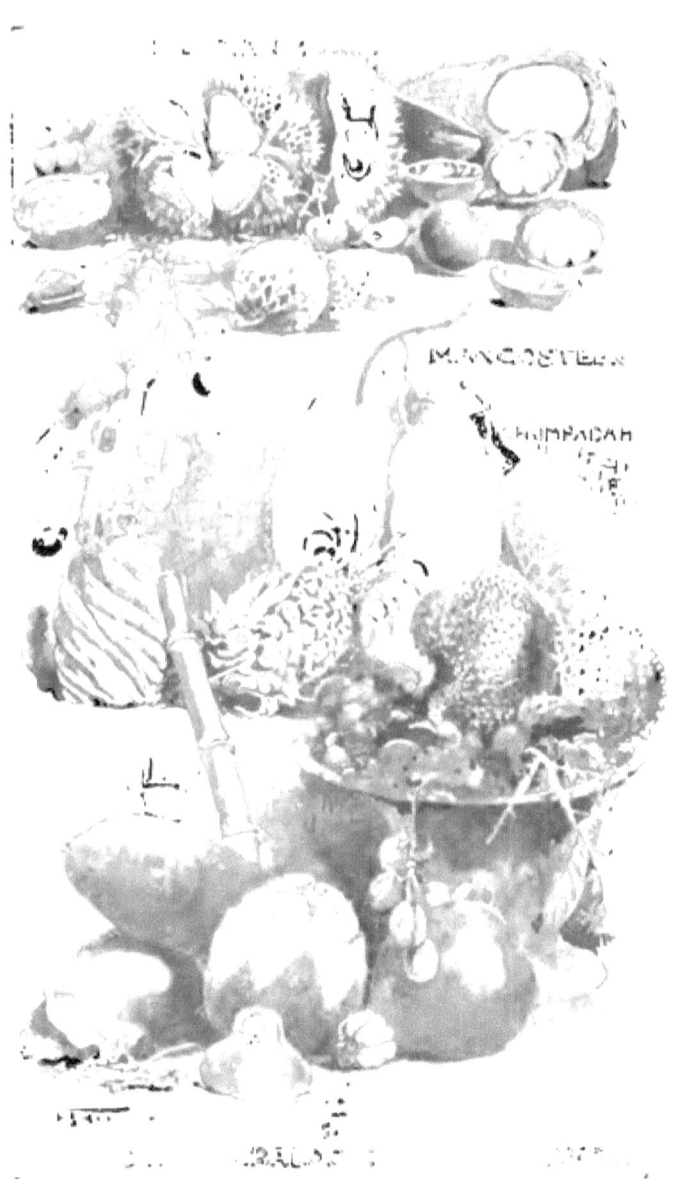

TROPICAL FRUITS.

Archipelago, and groves have been successfully planted in Ceylon, so that there is hope that this incomparable fruit may finally be acclimated in the West Indies, and fast steamers make it known in New York and London. The mangosteen is tinned for export at Singapore; but the faded segments floating in tasteless syrup give one little idea of this peerless fruit in its natural state.

It had been my particular haunting dream of the tropics to have a small black boy climb a tree and throw cocoanuts down to me; and while we sat admiring the rank beauty of the deserted garden around Raden Saleh's tomb, one afternoon, the expression of the wish caused a full-grown Malay to saunter across the grass, and, cigarette in mouth, walk up the straight palm-stem as easily as a fly. The Malay toes are as distinct members as the fingers, and almost as long; and clasping the trunk with the sole of the foot at each leaf-scar, that Malay climber gripped the rough palm-stem as firmly with his toes as with claws or extra fingers. It was so easily and commonly done that palm-tree climbing soon ceased to be any more of a feat to watch than berry-picking; but the first native who walked up a palm-tree for my benefit held me rapt, attentive, while he picked the big nuts and sent twenty-pounders crashing down through the shrubbery. We paid him well, and carried two of the nuts home with us; and from them the servant brought us tall glasses, or schooners, filled with the clear, colorless, tasteless milk, and a plate full of a white, leathery stuff—tough, tasteless too, and wilted, like cold omelet without eggs—the saddest sort of a feast of fresh cocoanuts.

We found all the countless common fragrant flowers that are so necessary to these esthetic, perfume-loving people heaped for sale in the flower-market of the passer, along with the oils and the gums and spices that give out, and burn with, such delicious odors. Short-stemmed roses and heaps of loose rose-petals were laid on beds of green moss or in bits of palm-leaf in a way to delight one's color-sense, and, with the mounds of pale-green petals of the *kananga*, or ylang-ylang-tree's blossoms, filled the whole air with fragrance. We dried quantities of kananga flowers for sachets, as they will crisp even in the damp air of Java, and retain their spicy fragrance for years; but the exquisite white-and-gold "Bo-flowers," the sacred *sumboja* or frangipani (the *Plumeria acutifolia* of the botanists), would not dry, but turned dark and mildewed wherever one petal fell upon another. This lovely blossom of Buddha is sticky and unpleasant to the touch when pulled from the tree, and the stem exudes a thick milk. After they have fallen to the ground they may be handled more easily, and fallen flowers retain the spotless, waxen perfection of their thick, fleshy petals for even two days. One wonders that the people do not more often wear these flowers of the golden heart in their black hair; but the sumboja is a religious flower in Java, as in India, and in Buddhist times was almost as much an attribute and symbol of that great faith as the lotus. This Bo-flower is still the favorite offering, together with the *champaka*, or Arabian jasmine, in the Buddhist temples of Burma and Ceylon, and is often laid before the few images of that old religion now remaining in Java.

All through the Malay world, however, it is especially the flower of the dead, associated everywhere with funeral rites and graves, as conventional an expression or accompaniment of grief, death, and burial as the cypress and the weeping willow. For this reason one rarely sees it used as an ornamental tree or hedge, even in a European's garden or pleasure-grounds, and its presence in hedges or copses indicates that there are graves, or one of Islam's little open-timbered temples of the dead, within reach of its entrancing fragrance. Our Malay servant would never accept our name of "frangipani" when told to spread out or stir the petals we tried to dry in the sun. He stoically repeated the native "sumboja" after me each time, very rightly resenting the baptism in honor of an Italian marquis, who only compounded an essence imitating the perfume of the West Indian red jasmine, which breathes a little of the cloying sweetness of the peerless sumboja. After but a few trials of its syllables, "sumboja" soon expressed to me more of the fragrance, the sentiment and spirit, of the lovely death-flower than ever could the word "frangipani." Chinese Buddhists seem not to have any traditions or associations with the Bo-flower, as in South China, where the tree is grown in gardens, it is only the *kai tan fa*, or "egg-flower," those hideously matter-of-fact people noting only the resemblance of the lovely petals to the contrasting yolk and albumen of a hard-boiled egg.

VIII

THE "CULTURE SYSTEM"

WHILE the Dutch East India Company held the monopoly of trade and production in Java, farmed out the revenues, and exacted forced labor and forced delivery of produce, this tropical possession yielded an enormous revenue. With the company's monopoly of trade with Japan, and only Portugal as Holland's great rival in the ports of China, the company made Amsterdam the tea- and spice-market and the center of Oriental trade in Europe. The early Dutch traders not only cut down all the spice-trees on the Molucca Islands, and forbade the planting of clove-, cinnamon-, and nutmeg-trees, save on certain Dutch islands, but they burned tons of spices in the streets of Amsterdam, in order to maintain prices in Europe and realize their usual profit of three hundred per cent.

The Dutch East India Company acquired control of Java through pioneer preëmption, purchase, conquest, strategy, and crooked diplomacy, and, finally, as residuary legatee by the will of the Mohammedan emperor at Solo. The company then claimed the same sovereign rights over the people as the native rulers, who had exacted one fifth of the peasant's labor and one fifth of his crops as ground-rent, the land being all the inalienable property of the princes. When the colony passed from the company to the crown of Holland, Marshal Daendels at once turned such feudal rights to profitable account and instituted public works on a great scale. With such forced labor he built the great double post-road over the island from Anjer Head to Banjoewangi,—that road upon whose building twenty thousand miserable lives were expended,—so that difficulty of communication no longer interfered with the delivery of products at government warehouses on the seashore. He further established government teak- and coffee-plantations, but the natives who were forced to cultivate them were no more tyrannized over nor oppressed than they had been under their own princes, the change of masters making small difference in their condition. Previous to Daendels's time all the coffee came from the Preangers, whose princes, having yielded their territories by treaty in the middle of the last century, retained sovereignty and their old land-revenues on condition of paying the Dutch East India Company an annual tribute in coffee, and after that selling the balance of the crop to the company at the fixed rate of three and a half florins the picul ($133\frac{1}{3}$ pounds).

Although the East India Company practically ended its rule in 1798, the States-General canceled the lease in 1800, and the colony passed to the crown of Holland, the same trade monopoly continued until the happy interval of British rule (1811–16), and there was a continual movement of natives from the Dutch to the native states up to 1811. Under Sir Stamford Raffles's enlightened control the Java ports were made free to the ships of all nations, the peasants were given individual ownership of lands, great estates were bestowed upon native chiefs, and a bewildering doctrine of liberty and equality before the law was preached to the people. Free trade, free culture, and free labor were decreed at once. The same treaty of London (August, 1814) which restored Java to the Dutch (August, 1816), at the close of the Napoleonic wars, secured the freedom of the ports; but the Dutch quickly resumed the old system of land-tenure by village communities paying ground-rent in produce and labor through their *wedana*, or head man, who answered to a district chief, who in turn reported to the native prince acting as regent for the Dutch government. Dutch residents "advised" these native regents, who ruled wholly under their orders and were mere middlemen between the Dutch and the natives. These regents were always chosen from the greatest family of the province, and the Dutch *contrôleurs* directed the chiefs and wedanas. The Dutch retained the excellent British police and judicial system in the main, while having more regard for the native aristocracy, their prejudices and their laws of caste. British philanthropy had introduced the British India ryot system of separate property in the soil and a separate land-tax, along with equality of rights, duties, and imposts, while abolishing all monopolies, forced labor and productions. The natives, like true Orientals, preferred their own old communal land system, with yearly allotments of village lands and the just rotation of the best lands, to any modern system of individual property, and to what was most dreaded by the native, individual liability. The Dutch resumed the old land system, exacted the old one fifth of produce as landrent, and obliged the peasants to plant one fifth of the village land in crops, to be sold to the government at fixed prices; but they only demanded one day's labor in seven, instead of one day in five. The lands which Sir Stamford Raffles had given to the chiefs and petty princes soon passed into the hands of Europeans or Chinese; and except for this one tenth of the land held by private owners, and two tenths held by the Preanger regents, the rest of the island became crown land, subject to lease, but never to be sold. The Preanger princes resumed their payment of a revenue in coffee and the sale of the surplus crop to the government at a fixed price. Marshal Daendels's plantations, so long neglected, were put in order again and cultivated by seventh-day labor. Each family was required to keep one thousand coffee-trees in bearing on village lands, to give two fifths of the crop to the government, and deliver it cleaned and sorted at government warehouses established all through the coffee districts.

But with the open ports, the abolition of the government's spice monopoly in 1824, and the expenses of a protracted war with the native ruler of Middle Java (1817–30), the revenues still only met the expenses; and there was great concern in Holland at the decrease of the golden stream of Indian revenue, and consequent satisfaction in England that its statesmen had handed back the island, that might have proved only an embarrassment and intolerable expense instead of a profit to the British crown. The King of Holland had established and guaranteed the Netherlands Trading Company, which acted as the commission agent of the government in Europe, importing in its own ships exclusively, selling all the produce in Europe, and conducting a general business in the colony. The partial failure of this company, which obliged the king to meet the guaranteed interest, brought about a new order of things destined to increase the colonial trade and crown revenues.

As private enterprise could not make the Java trade what it had been, Governor Van den Bosch, who originated the "culture system" as a means of relieving the distressed finances, was sent out from Holland in 1830, with power to grant cash credits and make ten-year contracts with private individuals who would assist in developing the sugar industry. Sufficient advances were made to these colonists to enable them to erect sugar-mills and to maintain themselves until, by the sales of their products, they were able to repay the capital and own their mills. The government agreed that the natives of each community or district should grow sufficient sugar-cane on their lands to supply the mills' capacity, and deliver it at the mills at fixed rates. The natives were obliged to plant one fifth of the village lands in sugar-cane, and each man to give one day's labor in seven to tending the crop. The village head man was paid for the community three and a half florins for each picul of

A MARKET IN BUTENZORG.

sugar made from their cane, and the natives who worked in the mills were paid regular wages. The mill-owner sold one third of the finished product of his mill to the government, at rates rising from eight to ten florins the picul; the mill-owner paid back each year one tenth of the government's cash advanced to him in sugar at the same rate, and was then free to ship, as his own venture, the balance of his sugar to the Netherlands Trading Company, which held the monopoly of transport and sale of government produce. Enormous profits resulted to the government and mill-owners from the sales of such sugar in Europe, and during one prosperous decade the crown of Holland enjoyed a revenue amounting to more than five million dollars United States gold each year from its Java sugar sales. The whole east end of the island and the low, hot lands along the coast were green at their season with the giant grass whose cultivation has forced or encouraged slavery everywhere throughout the earth's tropic belt. Slavery itself ceased in Java by royal edict in 1859, but sugar-culture went on under the admirable Van den Bosch system so profitably that mill-owners did not grumble at having to sell one third of their product to the government at a merely nominal price.

The great success in sugar led the government to extend the culture system's method to other crops. Would-be colonists competed for such profitable contracts, and all young Holland cherished the ambition to sail away to the East and make fortunes on Java plantations. A choice was exercised to secure the best class of young men as colonists; education, cultivation, and gentlemanly manners were made essentials, and it was known that no absenteeism would be tolerated, that the planters were expected to settle in Java in permanence, and that leaves of absence would be granted during the ten-year contracts only for actual illness. By providing military bands and subsidizing an opera, by establishing libraries and fostering the museum of the Batavian Society, and by encouraging a liberal social life among the higher officials, everything was done to secure all the advantages of civilization and to make life tolerable in the far-away tropics.

Early experiments had been made with the tea-plant in Java, and the government initiated tea-growing with great anticipations. Tea-plants and -seeds were brought by botanists from Japan as early as 1826, and later from China, together with skilled cultivators and workmen to instruct the natives. Crown lands were leased on long terms, and cash advances made during the first years of hill-clearing and planting. The government obliged the planters to produce equal quantities of green and black tea, and four grades or qualities of each kind; the planters were to repay the government's cash advances in tea, to sell the whole crop to the government at a fixed rate, and to pay the workmen fixed wages. Tea-growing was not profitable at first, as there was difficulty in securing a market in Europe for the bitter, weedy Java leaf, until, by a great reduction in the selling-price, its cheapness gained it a sale in Germany. The discovery of the wild Assam tea-plant in India, and the results obtained by grafting it on the Chinese plant, marked a new departure in tea-growing, and with better understanding of new methods and the aid of machinery in curing the leaf, tea-gardens became profitable ventures. After fostering the industry to success, the government refused further contracts after 1865, and the tea-planters were free to dispose of their crops as they wished. All through the hill-country of the Preangers tea-bushes stripe the rolling ground for miles, and new ground is being cleared and leased each season. Java teas have greatly improved in quality, and win medals and mention at every exposition; but they have India and Ceylon as formidable rivals, in addition to China and Japan, and their market remains in Holland and Germany, and in Persia and Arabia by way of Bombay—this Mohammedan trade an inheritance of those early times, when the Dutch drove the Moormen out of Ceylon and the far Eastern trade.

While the culture system was succeeding with sugar and tea, the government coffee-plantations were extended, and more and more hill-country cleared for such cultivation. Coffee-culture was carried on by the government without contractors' aid. Each native was obliged to plant six hundred Arabian or Mocha coffee-trees and keep them in bearing, and deliver the crop cleaned and sorted at the government warehouses at a fixed price—nine and twelve florins the picul previous to 1874, although forty and forty-five florins were paid in the open market of the ports. By careful supervision and by percentages paid to native officials for any superior quality in the berries produced in their district, the coffee from Java government stores was superior to anything else sold in Europe, and maintained its average steadily. Coffee was indeed "the pivot of the Netherlands colonial régime," a staple of greater economic value than spices had been. In 1879, the year of the greatest production of the government plantations in Java, some 79,400 tons of coffee were shipped to Europe. Blight and scale and insect pests were afterward to reduce the shipments to but 17,750 tons in 1887.

Indigo was at first cultivated on the same terms as sugar, but the government soon dispensed with such contracts, bought back the fabriks, and continued the industry without contract aid, obliging the natives to plant indigo on all village land not required for rice, and deliver the crop to the mills at fixed prices. Cinnamon, pepper, cinchona, and cochineal were grown by the natives in the same way, under merely official supervision, and delivered to the government for a trifling price.

In 1850 the government sent agents to Peru to obtain seeds of the cinchona-tree, and after fifteen years of effort and risk the indefatigable botanists and explorers secured the treasured seeds of the red-barked kina-tree. The records of those expeditions, the lives ventured and lost, are the romances of travel and exploration; and Sir Clements Markham's and Charles Ledger's narratives are most fascinating tales. The first little nursery of trees in the Buitenzorg Botanical Garden and in experimental gardens on higher ground near Bandong furnished the seeds and plants from which have sprung the great kina-plantations, or cinchona-groves, both government and private,

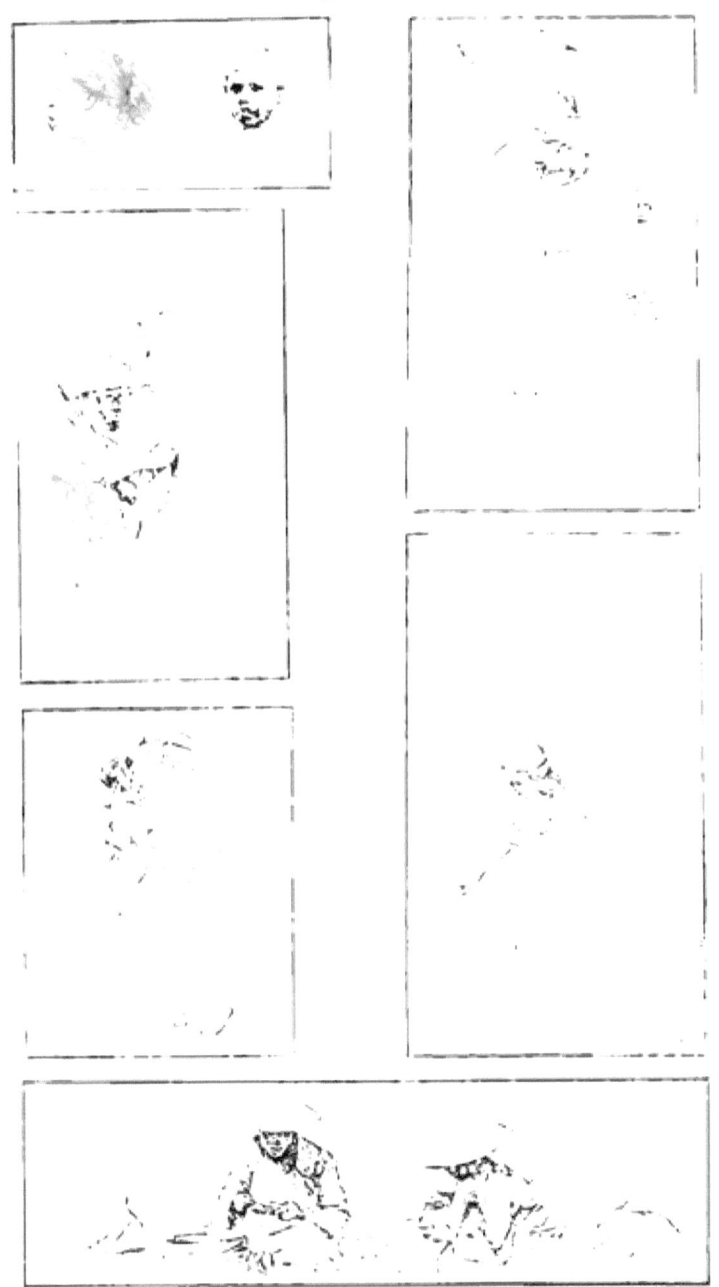

SCENES AROUND THE MARKET

whose red branches show in definite color-masses on every hillside of the Preangers, while the spindling young trees shade acres of tea-, coffee-, and cocoa-plants in their first growths. Java now produces, from government and private plantations together, one half of the world's supply of quinine, Ceylon and India furnishing the balance. Ship-loads of bark are sent to the laboratories or chemical factories of Europe, which produce the precious sulphate on which rest England's and Holland's conquest of the Indies and all European domination in the farther East, and laboratories are now building for manufacturing the sulphate from the bark in Java.

Poppy-culture has always been strictly prohibited, although the natives are greatly addicted to opium-smoking, especially in the middle or Hindu provinces. With all their zeal for revenue, the Dutch have resisted the example of the British in India and the Chinese in Szechuen and the western provinces of China, and have never let the land bloom with that seductive flower. The sale of opium is a closely guarded government monopoly, conducted at present under the *régie* system, the government itself importing all that is consumed in the colony and selling it from fixed offices throughout the island.

Salt-works and tin-mines were managed in as systematic and profitable a way as crops and cultures. No private individual was allowed to make or import salt into the colony. The government still holds the salt-supply as a monopoly, and there are large salt-works on Madura Island, where the natives are required to deliver fixed quantities of coarse salt at the government warehouses at the rate (in 1897) of ten gulden the *kojan* (1853 kilograms). The government manages the tin-mines on Banka Island in the Java Sea, while the mines of the neighboring Billeton Island are leased to private individuals.

IX

THE "CULTURE SYSTEM" (*Continued*)

THE culture system, as an experiment in colonial government and finance, was the greatest success and worked incalculable benefits to the islands and the native people, as well as to the assisted colonists and the crown of Holland. Great stretches of jungle were cleared and brought under cultivation, and more money was paid in wages directly to native cultivators and mill workmen each year than all the natives paid in taxes to the government. The Javanese acquired better homes, much personal wealth, and improved in all the conditions of living. The population increased tenfold during the half-century that the culture system was in operation—this alone an unanswerable reply to all critics and detractors, who declaimed against the oppression and outrage upon the Javanese. As the island became, under this system, a more profitable possession than it had been under the real tyranny exercised during the days of close-trade monopoly, the envy and attention of all the other colonizing nations of Europe were drawn to this new departure in colonial government. Spain copied the system in its tobacco-growing in the Philippine Islands, but could not follow further. Philanthropic and pharisaical neighbors, political economists, advanced political thinkers, humanitarians, and sentimentalists, all addressed themselves to the subject, and usually condemned the culture system in unmeasured terms. Holland's voluntary abolition of slavery in its East India possessions by no means stilled the storm of invective and abuse. Leaders, speeches, books, pamphlets, even novels,[1] showed up the horrors, the injustice and iniquities said to be perpetrated in Java. It was shown that almost nothing of the great revenues from the island was devoted to the education or benefit of the natives; that no mission or evangelical work was undertaken, or even allowed, by this foremost Protestant people of Europe; and that next to nothing in the way of public works or permanent improvements resulted to the advantage of those who toiled for the alien, absentee landlord, i. e., the crown of Holland,—the country being drained of its wealth for the benefit of a distant monarch. It was estimated that between 1831 and 1877 the natives were mulcted of one billion, seven hundred million francs by the forced labor exacted from them, and the sales of their produce to the government at the low market prices fixed by the purchaser. By continued philippics and exaggerated accusations, the names of Dutch government and Java planter became, to the average European, synonyms for all of rapacity, tyranny,

---

[1] "Max Havelaar," by Edouard Douwes Dekker (Multatuli); translation by Baron Nahuys (Edinburgh, 1868).

A VIEW IN BUITENZORG

extortion, and cruelty, and there was an impression that something worse than Spanish persecution in the Netherlands, in the name of religion, was being carried on by the Hollanders in Java in the name of the almighty florin. All the iniquities and horrors of the Dutch management of the cinnamon-gardens of Ceylon, and all the infamy of the Dutch East India Company's misrule in Java during the seventeenth and eighteenth centuries, were stupidly mixed up with and charged against the comparatively admirable, the orderly and excellently devised culture system of Governor Van den Bosch. Contractor planters vainly urged that the only tyranny and oppression of the people came from their own village chiefs; but philanthropists pointed steadily to the colonial government and the system which inspired and upheld the village tyrants.

In 1859 Mr. J. W. B. Money, a Calcutta barrister, visited Java, made exhaustive search and inquiry into every branch and detail of the culture system's working, and put the results in book form inwoven with a comparison with the less intelligent and successful management of the land and labor question in British India, where, with sixteen times the area and twelve times the population of Java, the revenue is only four times as great. His book, "Java: How to Manage a Colony" (London, Hurst & Blackett, 1861), is a most complete and reliable résumé of the subject, and his opinions throughout were an indorsement of the Van den Bosch culture system. He contrasted warmly the failure and inefficiency of the British India *ryot warree*, or land system, with the established communal system which the Oriental prefers and is fitted for, and showed how a similar culture system in Bengal and Madras would have worked to the advantage, benefit, and profit of Hindustan, the Hindus, and the British crown. Mr. Money especially noted how the Dutch refrained from interfering with native prejudices and established customs; how the prestige of the native aristocracy was as carefully maintained as that of the white race, with no modern, Western notions of equality, even before the law, the Dutch securing regentship to the leading noble of a district, and giving him more revenue and actual power than were possible under the native emperor. Mr. Money noted only the best of feeling apparently existing between natives and Europeans, a condition dating entirely from the establishment of the culture system, and the general prosperity that succeeded. "No country in the East can show so rich or so contented a peasantry as Java," he said.

Alfred Russel Wallace, who visited Java several times between 1854 and 1862, while the culture system was at the height of its successful working, spoke in approval and praise of what he saw of the actual system and its results, and commended it as the only means of forcing an indolent, tropical race to labor and develop the resources and industries of the island. His was one of the few clear, dispassionate, and intelligent statements given on that side, and he summed up his observations in the declaration that Java was "the very garden of the East, and perhaps, upon the whole, the richest, best-cultivated, and the *best-governed* island in the world."

The competition of French beet-sugar, fed by large government bounties of West Indian and Hawaiian sugars, so reduced the price of sugar in Europe that in 1871 the Dutch government began to withdraw from the sugar-trade, and by 1890 had no interest in nor connection with any of the many mills which colonists had built on the island. Java ranked second only to Cuba in the production of cane-sugar, and now (1897) ranks first in the world. Trade returns now show sugar exports to the value of six million pounds sterling from the private plantations of Java and Sumatra each year, and the distillation of arrack for the trade with Norway and Sweden is an important business.

At the time that sugar began to fall in price, owing to Western competition, Brazilian and Central American coffees began to command a place in the European market and to reduce prices; and then the blight, which reached Sumatra in 1876, attacked Java plantations in 1879, and spread slowly over the island, ruining one by one all the plantations of the choice Arabian or Mocha coffee-trees. As the area of thriving plantations decreased, and acres and acres of the white skeletons of blighted trees belted the hillsides, vain attempts were made at replanting. Only the tough, woody, coarse African or Liberian coffee-tree, with its large leaves and large, flat berries,—a plant which thrives equally in a damp or a dry climate, and luxuriates in the poorest, stoniest ground,—seems to be proof against the blight that devastated the Ceylon and Java coffee-plantations so thoroughly at the same time. Many of the old coffee-plantations in Java, as in Ceylon, were burned over and planted to tea; yet in many places in the Preangers one sees the bleached skeletons of Arabian trees still standing, and the abandoned plantations smothered in weeds and creepers, and fast relapsing to jungle. The virgin soil of Sumatra has so far escaped the severest attacks of the blight, and the center of coffee-production there is near Padang, on the west coast, whence the bulk of the crop goes directly to England or America in British ships.

The blight forced the Dutch government to begin its retirement from the coffee-trade, and but the smallest fraction of the coffee exported now goes from government plantations or warehouses. Nearly all the Sumatra plantations are owned or leased by private individuals, and the greater part of coffee lands in Java are cultivated by independent planters, who sell their crop freely in the open market. With the wholesale replanting of the Liberian tree in place of the Arabian, and the shipping only of the large, flat Liberian bean instead of the Mocha's small, round berry, it is questionable whether the little real "government Java" that goes to market is entitled to the name which won the esteem of coffee-drinking people for the century before the blight. The Dutch government still raises and sells coffee, but under strong protest and opposition in Holland, and as a temporary concession during these times of financial straits.

Public opinion was gradually aroused in Holland, and opponents of the culture system at last spoke out in the States-General; but not until the prices of sugar and coffee had fallen seriously, and the blight had ruined nearly all the government coffee-plantations, did the stirring of Holland's conscience bid the government retire from trade and agriculture, and leave the development of the island's resources, in natural and legitimate ways, to the enterprise of the many European settlers then established in permanence in Java, who had begun to see that the government was their most serious rival and competitor in the market.

The common sense and cooler vision of these days since its abandonment have shown that the culture system was an inspiration, a stroke of administrative genius of the first order, accomplishing in a few decades, for the material welfare of the island and its people, what the native race of a tropical country never could or would have done in centuries. The American mind naturally puzzles most over the idea that twenty odd millions of people of one race, language, and religion should ever have submitted to be ruled by a mere handful of over-sea usurpers and speculators. Considering the genius and characteristics of all Asiatic people, their superstitions, fatalism, self-abasement, and continuous submission to alien conquests and despotisms, which all their histories record and their religions almost seem to enjoin, and remembering the successive Buddhist, Brahmanic, and Mohammedan conquests and conversions of Java, and the domestic wars of three centuries since Islam's invasion, the half-century of the culture system's prosperous trial seems a most fortunate epoch and the cause of the admirable and surprising conditions existing to-day in that model garden and hothouse of the world.

It was much regretted later that some part of the

culture system's enormous profits was not devoted to railway construction and the making of the new harbor for Batavia at Tandjon Priok, as, immediately after the system's abandonment, railways and the new harbor became more urgent needs, and had to be provided for out of the current revenues, then taxed with the vigorous beginning of the Achinese struggle—Holland's thirty years' war in the Indies, which has so sadly crippled the exchequer. In order to provide a crown revenue in lieu of the sugar and coffee sales, a poll-tax was imposed on the natives in place of the seventh of their labor given to culture-system crops, and increased taxes were levied on lands and property; but through the extensive public works, the long-continued Achinese war in Sumatra, and the little war with the Sassaks in Lombok (1894), the deficits in the colonial budgets have become more ominous every year since 1876. The crown of Holland no longer receives a golden stream from the Indies, and is pushed to devise means to meet its obligations.

The culture system brought to Java a selected lot of refined, intelligent, capable, energetic colonists, who, settling there in permanence and increasing their holdings and wealth, have become the most numerous and important body of Europeans on the island. The great sugar and coffee barons, the patriarchal rulers of vast tea-gardens, the kina and tobacco kings, really rule Netherlands India. The planters and the native princes have much in common, and in the Preangers these horse-racing country gentlemen affiliate greatly and make common social cause against the small aristocracy of office-holders, who have been wont to regard the native nobles and the mercantile communities of the ports from on high.

The colonial government has never welcomed aliens to the isles, whether those bent on business or on pleasure. Dutch suspicion still throws as many difficulties as possible in the way of a tourist, and it took strong preventive measures against an influx of British or other *uitlander* planters when the abandonment of the culture system made private plantations desirable, and the opening of the Suez Canal brought Java so near to Europe. As a better climate, better physical conditions of every kind, and a more docile, industrious native race were to be found in Java than elsewhere in the Indies, there was a threatened invasion of coffee- and tea-planters, more particularly from India and Ceylon. The Boer of the tropics, like his kinsman in South Africa, found effectual means to so hamper as virtually to exclude the uitlander planters. Land-transfers and leases were weighted with inconceivable restrictions and impositions; heavy taxes, irksome police and passport regulations, and nearly as many restraints as were put upon Arabs and Chinese, urged the British planter to go elsewhere, since he could not have any voice in local or colonial government in a lifetime.[1] Six years' residence is required for naturalization, but the Briton is rarely willing to change his allegiance—it is his purpose rather to Anglicize, naturalize, annex, or protect all outlying countries as English.

The governor-general of the colony may revoke the toelatings-kaart of any one, Dutch as well as alien,

[1] See "A Visit to Java," W. Basil Worsfold, London, 1893.

and order him out of Netherlands India; and a resident is such an autocrat that he can order any planter or trader out of his domain if it is shown that he habitually maltreats or oppresses the natives, or does anything calculated to compromise the superior standing or prestige of the white people. The Dutch are severe upon this latter point, and the best of them uphold a certain noblesse oblige as imperative upon all who possess a white skin. The European military officer is sent to Holland for court martial and punishment, that the native soldiers may remain ignorant of his degradation, and the European who descends to drunkenness is hurried from native sight and warned. While the conquerors hold these people with an iron grasp, they aim to treat them with absolute justice. Many officials and planters have married native wives, and their children, educated in Europe, with all the advantages of wealth and cultured surroundings, do not encounter any race or color prejudice nor any social barriers in their life in Java. They are Europeans in the eye of the law and the community, and enjoy "European freedom." No native man is allowed to marry or to employ a European, not even as a tutor or governess, and no such subversion of social order as the employment of a European servant is to be thought of. There is a romance, all too true, of governmental interference, and the dismissal from his office of regent, of the native prince who wished to marry a European girl whose parents fully consented to the alliance. The laws allow a European to put away his native wife, to legally divorce her, upon the slightest pretexts, and to abandon her and her children with little redress; but fear of Malay revenge, the chilling tales of slow, mysterious deaths overtaking those who desert Malay wives or return to Europe without these jealous women, act as restraining forces.

The Dutch do not pose as philanthropists, nor pretend to be in Java "for the good of the natives." They have found the truth of the old adage after centuries of obstinate experiment in the other line, and honesty in all dealings with the native is much the best policy and conduces most to the general prosperity and abundant crops. Fear of the Malay spirit of revenge, and the terrible series of conspiracies and revolts of earlier times, have done much, perhaps, to bring about this era of kindness, fair dealing, and justice. The native is now assured his rights almost more certainly than in some freer countries, and every effort is made to prevent the exercise of tyrannical authority by village chiefs, the main oppressors. He can always appeal to justice and be heard; the prestige of the native aristocracy is carefully maintained; the Oriental ideas of personal dignity and the laws of caste are strictly regarded, and, if from prudential and economic reasons only, no omissions in such lines are allowed to disturb the even flow of the florin Hollandward.

Already the spirit of the age is beginning to reach Java, and it is something to make all the dead Hollanders turn in their graves when it can be openly suggested that there should be a separate and independent budget for Netherlands India, and that there should be some form of popular representation—a deliberative assembly of elected officials to replace the close Council of India. In fact, suggestions for the actual autonomy of Java have been uttered aloud. There are ominous signs everywhere, and the government finds its petty remnant of coffee-culture and grocery business a more vexing and difficult venture each year. The Samarang "Handelsblad," in commenting on it, says:

"The Javanese are no longer as easily led and driven as a flock of sheep, however much we may deplore that their character has changed in this respect. The Javanese come now a great deal into contact with Europeans, the education spread among them has had an effect, and communication has been rendered easy. They do not fear the European as they did formerly. The time is gone when the entire population of a village could be driven to a far-off plantation with a stick; the pruning-knife and the ax would quickly be turned against the driver in our times. The Javanese to-day does not believe that you are interested in his welfare only; he is well aware that he is cheated out of a large proportion of the value of the coffee that is harvested. Some people may think it a pity that the time of coercion is coming to an end in Java, but that cannot change the facts. The dark period in the history of Java is passing away, and every effort to prevent reforms will call forth the enmity of the natives."

The state committee on government coffee-plantations says in its latest reports:

"It cannot be denied that the intellectual status of the Javanese at the present day is very different from that during the time when the coffee monopoly was introduced. The reforms which we have introduced

JAVANESE COOLIES GAMELANG

in the administration of justice, the education according to Western methods, and the free admission of private enterprise have all brought about a change. If the native has not become more progressive and more sensible, he is at least wiser in matters about which he had best be kept in the dark, unless the government means to remove coercion at the expense of the exchequer."

The Amsterdam "Handelsblad" remarks that, "as far as the Dutch possessions are concerned, coercion and monopoly indeed must go. People who cannot see this betimes will find out their mistake rather suddenly."

That sage socialist, Élisée Reclus, remarks that "once more it appears that monopoly ends in the ruin not only of the despoilers, but of the state."

X

SINAGAR

SCIENTISTS and lay tourists have equally exhausted their adjectives in laudations of Java, Miss Marianne North calling it "one magnificent garden of luxuriance, surpassing Brazil, Jamaica, and Sarawak combined"; and Alfred Russel Wallace epitomizing it after this fashion: "Taking it as a whole, and surveying it from every point of view, Java is probably the very finest and most interesting tropical island in the world. . . . The most fertile, productive, and populous island in the tropics." Lesser folk have been as sweeping in their superlatives, and all agree that, of all exiled cultivators in the far parts of the world, the Java planter is most to be envied, leading, as he does, the ideal tropical life, the one best worth living, in a land where over great areas it is always luxurious, dreamy afternoon, and in the beautiful hill-country is always the fresh, breezy, dewy summer forenoon of the rarest June.

The most favored and the most famous plantations

are those around Buitenzorg and in the Preanger regencies, which lie on the other side of Gedeh and Salak, those two sleeping volcanoes that look down upon their own immediate foot-hills and valleys, to see those great, rolling tracts all cultivated like a Haarlem tulip-bed. Above the cacao limit, tea-gardens, coffee-estates, and kina-plantations cover all the land lying between the altitudes of two thousand and four thousand feet above the level of the sea. The owners of these choicest bits of "the Garden of the East" lead an existence that all other planters of growing crops, and most people who value the creature comforts, the luxuries of life, and nature's opulence, may envy. The climate of the hills is all that Sybarite could wish for,—a perpetual 70° by day, with light covering required at night,—the warm sun of the tropics tempering the fresh mountain air to an eternal mildness, in which the human animal thrives and luxuriates quite as do all the theobromas and caffein plants in the ground. In the near circle of these two great peaks there is no really dry season, despite the southeast monsoon of the conventional summer months. Every day in the year enjoys its shower, swept from one mountain or the other; and the heavy thunder-storms at the change of the monsoons and during the winter rainy season are the joy of the planter's heart, shaking out myriads of young tea-leaves by their jar and rushing winds, and freshening the coffee-trees like a tonic. As every day has its shower, each day has its tea-crop gathered and cured in this favorable region; and that profitable industry is as continuous and unchanging as the seasons on the

Preanger hillsides, and paramount there, now that coffee is no longer king.

The two great plantations of Sinagar and Parakan Salak, principalities of twelve and fifteen thousand acres respectively, that lie in the valley between Salak and Gedeh, are the oldest and the model tea-gardens of Java, the show-places of the Preangers. Parong Koeda and Tjibitad, an hour beyond Buitenzorg, are practically private railway-stations for these two great estates. The post-road from Tjibitad to Sinagar follows the crest of a ridge, and gives magnificent views between its shade-trees over twenty miles of rolling country, cultivated to the last acre. Blue vapors were tumbling in masses about the summit of Salak the afternoon we coursed along the avenues of shade-trees, and the low growls of distant thunder gave promise of the regular afternoon benefit shower to the thirsty plants and trees that ridged every slope and level with lines of luxuriant green. The small ponies scampered down an avenue of magnificent kanari-trees, with a village of basket houses like to those of Lilliput at the base of the lofty trunks, and, with a rush and a sudden turn around tall shrubbery, brought up before the low white bungalow, where the master of Sinagar sat in his envied ease under such vines and trees as would form a *mise en scène* for an ideal, generally acceptable paradise. A sky-line of tall areca-palms, massed flame-trees, and tamarinds, with vivid-leafed bougainvillea vines pouring down from one tree-top and mantling two or three lesser trees, filled the immediate view from the great portico-hall, or living-room, where the welcoming cups of afternoon tea were at once served.

With the nearest neighbor ten miles away, and the thousand workmen employed upon the place settled with their families in different villages within its confines, Sinagar is a little world or industrial commune by itself, its master a patriarchal ruler, whose sway over these gentle, childlike Javanese is as absolute as it is kindly and just. The "master" has sat under his Sinagar palms and gorgeous bougainvilleas for twenty-six out of the thirty-three years spent in Java, and his sons and daughters have grown up there, gone to Holland to finish their studies, and, returning, have made Sinagar a social center of this part of the Preangers. The life is like that of an English country house, with continental and tropical additions that unite in a social order replete with pleasure and interest. Weekly musicales are preceded by large dinner-parties, guests driving from twenty miles away and coming by train; and, with visitors in turn from all parts of the world, the guest-book is a polyglot and cosmopolitan record of great interest. Long wings have been added to the original bungalow dwelling, inclosing a spacious court, or garden, all connected by arcades and all illuminated by electric lights. The ladies' boudoir at the far end of the buildings opens from a great portico, or piazza, furnished with the hammocks, the ratan furniture, and the countless pillows of a European or American summer villa, but looking out on a marvelous flower-garden and an exquisite landscape view. To that portico were brought the rarest flowers and fruits for our inspection,—such lilies and orchids and strangely fragrant things!— and we cut apart cacao-pods, and those "velvety, cream-colored peaches" inclosing the nutmeg, and dissected clove-buds with a zeal that amused the young hostesses, to whom these had all been childhood toys. The telephone and telegraph connect all parts of the estate with virtually all parts of the world; and with the great news of Europe clicking in from Batavia, or "helloed" over by some friend at Buitenzorg, one could quite forget the distance from the older centers of civilization, and wonder that all the world did not make Java its playground and refuge of delight, and every man essay the rôle of Java planter.

While we sat at tea that first afternoon, two brilliant scarlet minivers flashed across the screen of shrubbery like tongues of flame, followed by crimson-and-black orioles; while at the master's call a flock of azure-and-iris-winged pigeons came whirling through the air and settled before us in all the sheen and beauty of their plumage. A great wire house full of rare tropic birds was the center of attraction for all the wild birds of the neighborhood, and gorgeously feathered and strangely voiced visitors were always on wing among the shrubbery. In that big aviary lived and flew and walked in beauty the crested Java pigeon, a creature flashing with all intense prismatic blues, and wearing on its head an aigret of living sapphires trembling on long, pliant stems—one of the most graceful and beautiful birds in the world. Other birds of brilliant plumage, wonderful cockatoos, parrots, long-tailed pheasants, and beauties of unknown name, lived as a happy family in the one great cage, around which prowled and sat licking its whiskers a cat of most enterprising and sagacious mien—a cat that had come all the way from Chicago, only to have its lakeside appetite tormented by this Barmecide feast of rainbow birds.

We were led past flower-beds nodding with strange lilies, past rose-gardens and oleander-hedges, down a paved path that was a steep tunnel through dense shrubbery and overarching trees, to a great white marble tank, or swimming-pool, as large as a ball-room; though few ball-rooms can ever have such lavish decorations of palms, bamboos, and tree-ferns as screen that pool around, with the purple summit of Salak showing just above the highest plumes and fronds—a landscape study just fitted for a theatrical drop-curtain. We might swim or splash, dive or float, or sit on marble steps and comfortably soak at will in that great white tank, the clear spring water warmed by the sun to a soothing temperature for the long, luxurious afternoon bath, and cooled sufficiently through the night to give refreshing shock to early morning plungers. Only the approaching storm, the nearer rumbles of thunder, and finally the first small raindrops induced us to leave that fairy white pool, deep sunk in its tropic glen.

After a half-hour of soft rain, accompanied by three sharp thunder-claps, the climate had done its perfect work: every tree, bird, flower, and insect rejoiced, and all nature literally sang. The warm red earth breathed pleasant fragrance, every tree had its aroma, and the perfumed flowers were overpowering with fresh sweetness. Then the master led the house party for a long walk, first through the oldest tea-gardens, where every leaf on every plant was erect, shining, as if ready for dress-parade, and more intensely, softly green than ever after the daily shower-bath and wind toilet. We strolled on through a toy village under a kanari avenue, where all the avocations and industries of Javanese life were on view, and the little people, smiling their welcome, dropped on their heels in the permanent courtesy of the *dodok*, the squatting attitude of humility common to all Asiatics. The servants who had brought notes to the master, as he sat on the porch, crouched on their heels as they offered them, and remained in that position until dismissed; and the villagers and wayfarers, hastily dropping on their haunches, maintained that lowly, reverent attitude until we had passed—an attitude and a degree of deference not at all comfortable for an American to contemplate, ineradicable old Javanese custom as it may be. The tiny brown babies, exactly matching the brown earth in tone, crawled over the warm lap of nature, crowing and gurgling their pleasure, their plump little bodies free from all garments, and equally free from any danger of croups or colds from exposure to the weather. We took a turn through the great cement-floored *fabrik* with its ingenious machines all silent for that night, and only the electric-light dynamos whirling to illuminate the great settlement of outbuildings around the residence. The stables were another great establishment by themselves, and fifty odd Arabian and Australian thoroughbreds, housed in a long, open-fronted stable, were receiving their evening rub and fare from a legion of grooms. Morphine, Malaria, Quinine, Moses, and Aaron, and other cup-winners, arched their shining necks, pawed to us, and nibbled their reward of tasseled rice-heads, brought on carrying-poles from the granaries, where legions of rice-sparrows twittered in perpetual residence. We sat on a bank near the little race-course, or manège, where the colts are trained, and the favorites were led past and put through their paces and accomplishments one by one. It was almost dusk, with the swiftness with which day closes in the tropics, when the banteng, or wild cow (*Bos sondaicus*), was trotted out—a clumsy, dun-colored creature, with a strange, musky odor, that was brought as a calf from the wild south-coast country, and was at once mothered and protected by a fussy little sheep, "the European goat," as the natives call the woolly animal from abroad, that was still guiding and driving it with all the intelligence of a collie.

The bachelor planter partner showed us his bungalow, full of hunting-trophies—skulls and skins of panthers, tigers, and wild dogs; tables made of rhinoceros-hide resting on rhinoceros and elephant skulls, and tables made of mammoth turtle-shells resting on deer-antlers. The great prizes were the nine huge banteng skulls, trophies of hunting-trips to the South Preanger, the lone region bordering on the Indian Ocean. There were also chandeliers of deer-antlers, and a frieze-like wall-bordering of python-skins, strange tusks and teeth, wings and feathers galore, and dozens of kodak pictures as witnesses and records of the many camps and battues of this sportsman—all gathered in that same wild region of big game, as much as fifty or a hundred miles away, but referred to in the Buitenzorg neighborhood as New York sportsmen used to speak of the buffalo country—"the south coast" and "out West," equally synonyms for all untamed, far-away wildness. Elephant-hunting must be enjoyed in Sumatra, since that animal has never existed in a wild state in Java.

With the younger people of the master's family, his young managers and assistants, fresh from Amsterdam schools and European universities, speaking English and several other languages, *au courant* with all the latest in the world's music, art, literature, and drama, plantation life and table-talk were full of interest and varied amusements. By a whir of the telephone, two of the assistants were bidden ride over from their far corner of the estate for dinner, and afterward a quartet of voices and instruments made the marble-floored music-room ring, while the elder men smoked meditatively, or clicked the billiard-balls in their deliberate, long-running tourney. The latest books and the familiar American magazines strewed boudoir and portico tables, and naturally there was talk of them.

"Ah, we like so much your American magazines— the 'Century' and the others. We admire so much the pictures. And then all those stories of the early Dutch colonists at Manhattan! We like, too, your great American novelists—Savage, Howells, Gunter— 'The Rise of Silas Lapham,' 'Mr. Potter of Texas,' and all those. We read them so much."

They were undoubtedly disappointed that we did not speak Dutch, or at least read it, since all Hollanders know that Dutch is the language of the best families in New York, of the cultivated classes and all polite society in the United States, since from the mynheers of Manhattan came the first examples of refined living in the New World. "The English colonists were of all sorts, you know, like in Australia," said our informants at Buitenzorg and everywhere else on the island, "and that is why you Americans are all so proud of your Dutch descent."

XI

PLANTATION LIFE

AFTER the sunrise cup of coffee at Sinagar—such coffee as we had dreamed of and confidently expected to enjoy, but never did encounter anywhere else in Java—all the men of the household appeared in riding-gear, and were off to inspect and direct work in the many gardens and sections of the estate. The ladies took us for a walk across the tea-fields to the great landmark of a Sinagar palm, which gave the name to the estate, and from which lookout we could view the miles of luxuriant fields between it and Parakan Salak's group of white houses, and also, chief feature in every view, the splendid blue slopes and summit of Salak clear cut against a sky of the palest, most heavenly turquoise. It was a very dream of a tropic morning, and a Java tea-garden seemed more than ever an earthly paradise.

Tea-bushes covered thousands of acres around and below us, as the ground dropped away from that commanding ridge, their formal rows decreasing in perspective until they shaded the landscape like a fine line-engraving. For mile after mile one could walk in direct line between soldierly files of tea-bushes—Chinese, Assam, and hybrids. The Chinese plant, descended by generations from that same wild bush discovered in Assam near the Yunnan frontier by English botanists in 1834, has, by centuries of cultivation, been brought to grow in low, compact little mats, or mere rosettes of bushes. It has a thick, woody stem, gnarled and twisted like any dwarf tree, and some of the Chinese tea-bushes at Sinagar are fifty or sixty years of age, the pioneers and patriarchs of their kind in Java, original seedlings and first importations from China. The Assam or wild Himalayan tea-plant is a tall spindling bush with large, thin leaves, and grafted on Chinese stock produces the tall hybrid commonly grown in the tea-gardens of Java. The red soil of these gardens is always being raked loose around the tea-plants, and at every dozen or twenty feet a deep hole, or trench, is dug to admit air and water more freely to the roots. Constant care is given lest these little open graves, or air-holes, fill up after heavy rains, and not a weed nor a stray blade of grass is allowed to invade these prim, orderly gardens and rob the soil of any of its virtues. Each particular bush is tended and guarded as if it were the rarest ornamental exotic, and the tea-gardens, with their broad stripings of green upon the red ground, and skeleton lines of palms outlining the footpaths and the divisional limits of each garden, are like a formal exhibit of tea-growing, an exposition model on gigantic scale, a fancy farmer's experimental show-place.

In the unending summer of the hill-country there

is no "tea season," no "spring leaf," "first pickings," or "fire-fly crop," as in China and Japan. Two years after the young seedling has been transplanted to the formal garden rows its leaves may be gathered; and there are new leaves every day, so that picking, curing, firing, and packing continue the year round. The tea-pickers, mostly women, gather the leaves only when the plants are free from dew or rain. They pick with the lightest touch of thumb and finger, heaping the leaves on a square cloth spread on the ground, and then tying up the bundle and "toting" it off on their heads, for all the world like the colored aunties of our southern states. The bright colors of their jackets and sarongs, and of their bundles, that look like exaggerated bandana turbans, give gay and picturesque relief to the green-striped gardens, whose exact lines converge in long, monotonous perspective whichever way one looks. There is great fascination in watching these bobbing figures among the bushes gradually converge to single lines, and the procession of lank, slender sarongs file through the gardens, down the avenues of palm and tamarind, to the fabrik.

The long, red-tiled buildings of the fabrik, in their order and speckless neatness, with the array of ingenious and intelligent machines, seem yet more like part of an exposition exhibit—a small machinery hall of some great international industrial aggregation. The picking and the processes of converting the tea-leaves into the green, oolong, and black teas of commerce, and of packing them into large and small, air-tight, leaded packages for export, occupy, at the most, but

JAVANESE DANCING-GIRL.

two days in ordinary working seasons. Less green tea is sold each year, and soon the entire Java crop of tea will be cured to the half black, or oolong, and the standard black tea, which alone can find sale in England or in Russia, the largest and most critical tea-consuming countries of Europe. An especially fine black tea is made at these Preanger tea-fabriks, and for this the green leaves are first exposed to the sun in wicker trays for wilting, then rolled by machinery to free the juices in the leaf-cells, and fermented in heaps for four or eight hours, until by their turning a dark reddish brown there is evidence that the rank theine, the active principle or stimulating alkaloid in the leaves, has been oxidized, and so modified into something less injurious to human nerves and the digestive system. The bruised red leaves are dried in a machine where hot blasts and revolving fans make quick, clean work of the "firing," that perspiring coolies do by hand over charcoal pans in China and Japan. All the sifting, sorting, packing, and labeling, the pressing of the broken leaves and dust into bricks, go on as neatly, swiftly, and surely; and the cases are hauled away to the railway-station and shipped from Batavia to their special markets. The leaves to be made into green teas are given a first toasting, almost as they come in from the bushes, are rolled on great trays ranged on tables in an open court, and fired again, and more thoroughly, before packing. As the taste of the world's tea-drinkers becomes more cultivated, green tea will lose favor, and the Java tea-fabriks will be employed in directly competing with the factories of India and Ceylon, from whose culture experiments they have profited, and whose ingenious machines they have so generally adopted for curing and preparing black teas. Often the profuse "flushing" of the tea-bushes forces the fabrik to run all night to dispose of the quantity of fresh leaves; and one gets an idea of the world's increasing consumption of tea in this quarter of a century since Java, India, and Ceylon entered into competition in the tea-trade with China and Japan. Parakan Salak teas are advertised and sold in Shanghai and Yokohama, and the appeal to those great tea-marts is significant of a progressive spirit in Java trade, that is matched by the threat that petroleum from Java's oil-wells will soon compete seriously with American and Russian oil.

The coffee harvest is a fixed event in the plantation's calendar, and occurs regularly in April and May, at the close of the rainy season. Now that the finer Arabian shrub has been so largely replaced by the hardy Liberian tree, coffee-culture is a little less arduous than before. The berries are brought to the mill, husked by machinery, washed, dried on concrete platforms in the sun, sacked, and shipped to Batavia, and nothing more is heard of that crop until the next spring comes around. The trees are carefully tended and watched, of course, throughout the year, and scrutinized closely for any sign of scale or worm, bug or blight. The glowing red volcanic soil is always being weeded and raked and loosened, the trees trimmed, young plants from the great nursery of seedlings set out in place of the old trees, and the coffee area extended annually by clearings.

The Sundanese who live in their ornamental little

fancy baskets of houses beneath Sinagar's tall tamarinds and kanari-trees are much to be envied by their people. The great estate is a world of its own, an agricultural Arcadia, where life goes on so happily that it is most appropriate that they should have presented model Javanese village life at the Chicago Exposition in 1893. These little Sinagar villagers have their frequent passers on one side or the other of the demesne by turn, with theater and *wayang-wayang*, or puppet-shows, lasting far into the night. Professional raconteurs thrill them with classic tales of their glorious past, while musicians make sweet, sad melodies to rise from *gamelan*, or *gambang kayu*, from fiddle, drum, bowls, bells, and the sonorous *alang-alang*—a rude instrument of most ancient origin, made of five or eight graduated bamboo tubes, cut like organ-pipes, and hung loosely in a frame, which, shaken by a master hand, or swinging in the breeze from some tree-branch, produces the strangest, most weird and fascinating melodies in all the East.

The play of village life about Sinagar is so prettily picturesque, so well presented and carried out, that it seems only a theatrical representation—a Petit Trianon sort of affair at the least. The smiling little women, who rub and toss tea-leaves over the wilting-trays at the fabrik, seem only to be playing with the loose leaves like a larger sort of intelligent, careful children. In the same way the plucking in the tea-gardens and the march to the fabrik in long, single file, with bundles balanced on their heads, are mere kindergarten exercises to develop the muscles of the back and secure an erect and graceful carriage—the secret, perhaps, of their splendid bearing, although all Javanese walk as kings and queens are supposed to walk, as the result of not being hampered by useless garments, and thus having control of every member and muscle of the body from earliest years. The same supple ease and grace distinguish their manners too, and one young planter said: "After living a few years among these gentle, graceful, winning natives, you cannot know how Europe jarred upon me. All the hard, sad, scowling faces and the harsh, angry voices oppressed me and made me so homesick for Java that I was really glad to turn away from it. I never before was so aware of the poverty, misery, distress, and vice of Europe."

Visitors to the Paris Exposition of 1889 and the Chicago Exposition of 1893 had a typical model Javanese village set before them, and all were unstinted in their praises of the *mise en scène* and the human features of the exhibit. The Chicago village was peopled by families from the Sinagar and Parakan Salak estates, and, as a purely ethnological exhibit, was the one success of that kind among the many trifling side-shows that detracted from the character of the Midway Plaisance. The trip to America was the prize and reward allotted to the most industrious and deserving villagers, who with their properties and industrial accessories filled two sailing-ships from Batavia to Hong Kong, whence they took steamer to San Francisco and railway across the continent to Chicago. There was a large outlay required at the start, and the best workmen were away from the estates for a year; and between a dishonest shipping-agent at Batavia and the heavy commissions upon all receipts levied by the exposition's managers at Chicago, and the free admissions which those same generous American managers bestowed so widely, the village did not nearly pay its current expenses, and the venture stands as an entire loss, or a gift to the American people from the two public-spirited Preanger planters who paid for it.

The good little Javanese who went to Chicago returned from their great outing as simple and unspoiled as before, settled down contentedly under their kanari-trees, and resumed their routine life in field and fabrik. And what tales they had to tell to open-mouthed villagers and neighbors, who sat around the traveled ones, to the neglect of wayang-wayang and provincial professional story-tellers, listening to their accounts of the very remarkable things on that other side of the world! For the first time ever in their lives these Javanese saw white men at work in the fields, drudging in city streets, and doing every kind of menial, coolie labor. They saw a few black men, blacker than Moormen, but they were great personages, wearing fine uniforms and having command of the railway-trains, and riding in the most magnificently gilded cars—individuals treated always with great respect, who came to the Midway Plaisance in rich clothing, with gold watch-chains, jeweled scarf-pins, and much loose money in their pockets—a superior and a moneyed, if not the ruling class, in that topsy-turvy country, America.

A striped cat of the common roof-and-fence variety was given to one of the village managers, and made the journey back to Java with the party. Everything else in Chicago had been paid for so dearly that this tabby could be fairly said to represent the entire profit and result of the Chicago village venture. The cat was named "Chicago," and soon became the pet of the whole plantation, roaming freely everywhere, and feasting on small rice-mice and tropical birds. "Chicago" came to us on our arrival, rubbed in friendly fashion against one and another American knee, and purred loudly, as if recognizing us for compatriots. The morning we left Sinagar there was hubbub and running to and fro in the great quadrangle of the residence. "Chicago," while walking the well-curb with gesticulating tail, had lost her balance, and with frightful cries and a splash ended her existence—by unpleasant coincidence, just as we were making our farewells to our kindly host. "In despair at being unable to return to America with you," said one mourner, "she has thrown herself in the well. It is plainly suicide." And this domestic tragedy saddened our leave-taking from those charming people, the fine flavor of whose hospitality, courtesy and kindliness took the edge from many of our disagreeable experiences in Java, and gave us pleasant memories with which to offset those of the other kind.

XII

ACROSS THE PREANGER REGENCIES

ONE may ride all day by train from Buitenzorg before reaching the limits of the Preanger regencies, where native princes still hold pretended sway; and it is a continuous landscape feast from the sunrise start to the sunset halt of the through-train. The railway line, after curving around the shoulder of Salak, runs through the vaunted hill-country, the region of the great tea, coffee, and kina estates; and from Soekaboemi to Bandong, the two great headquarters for planters, one perceives that the planter is paramount, the cultivator is king. The new cultures have not dispossessed the old, however, and the *sawas*, or flooded rice-fields, break the level of plain and valley floor with their myriad waving lines of division, and climb by terraces to the very hilltops —a system of cultivation and irrigation as old as the human race, and followed in these same valleys by these same Sundanese since the beginning of their recorded time. To them rice is a holy grain, the offspring of a god, and the gods' best gift to man; a grain both cultivated and worshiped. It argues for the industry of a tropical race that they should grow this troublesome grain at all, the grain that demands more back-breaking toil and constant attention from planting to harvest-time than any other grain which grows. It would seem discouraging to rice-cultivation, too, when in old times the natives were taxed according to the area of their rice-lands only, and mulcted of a fifth of their rice when it was harvested —all in this happy land, where they might sit under the breadfruit- and banana-trees and doze at their ease, while those kindly fruits dropped in their laps. These picturesque rice-fields have won for Java the name of "the granary of the East," and enabled it to export that grain in quantities, besides supporting its own great population, one of the densest in the world, and averaging four hundred and fifty inhabitants to each square mile. No fertilizer of any kind is applied to these irrigated rice-fields, save to burn over and plow under the rich stubble, after the *padi*, or ripe ears of grain, have been cut singly with a knife and borne away in miniature sheaves strung on carrying-poles across the peasants' shoulders.

Beyond the region of the great plantations, where every hillside is cleared and planted up to the kina limit, and only the summits and steepest slopes are left to primeval jungle, there succeed great stretches of wild country, where remarkable engineering feats were required of the railway-builders. With two heavy engines the train climbs to Tjandjoer station, sixteen hundred feet above the sea; and there, if one has telegraphed the order ahead, he may lunch at ease in his compartment as the train goes on. He may draw from the three-storied lunch-basket handed in either a substantial *riz tavel*, consisting of a little of everything heaped upon a day's ration of boiled rice, or a "tiffin," whose *pièce de résistance* is a huge *bifstek mit ard appelen*, that would satisfy the cravings of any three dragoons. Either feast is followed by bread or bananas, with a generous section of a cheese, with mangosteens or other fruits, and one feels that he has surely reached the land of plenty and solid, solid comforts, where fate cannot harm him—when all this may be handed in to fleeting tourists at a florin and a half apiece.

After this station of abundant rations, all signs of cultivation and occupancy disappear, and the station buildings and the endless lantana-hedges along the railway-track are the only signs of human habitation or energy in the wilderness of hills covered with alang-alang or bamboo-grass, and the coarse *glagah* reeds which cattle will not touch. The banteng, the one-horned rhinoceros, and the tigers that used to roam these moors, fled when the shriek of the locomotive was heard in the cañons, and the sportsmen have to seek such big game in the jungles and grass-lands of the south coast. The streams that come cascading down from all these green heights have carved out some beautiful scenery, and the Tjitaroem River, foaming in sight for a while, disappears, runs through a mountain by a natural tunnel, and reappears in a deep gorge, of which one has an all-too-exciting view as the train crosses on a spidery viaduct high in air.

A great, fertile green plain surrounds the native

capital of Bandong, and on its confines rises the Tangkoeban-Praoe, the Ararat of the natives, who see in its square summit-lines the reversed *praoe* in which their ancestors survived the flood, and, turning their boat over carefully to dry, descended, as the waters fell, to people the Malay universe. One may ascend the butte-like peak, passing up first through a belt of old coffee-plantations, whose product ranked first in the good old days before the blight, and by the villa and experimental grounds of Herr Junghuhn, the botanist, who first succeeded with the kina-culture and introduced so many other economic plants and trees to the island. At Lembang, ten miles from Bandong, the mountain-climber gives up his pony or carriage, and is carried in a *djoelie*, or sedan-chair, through a magnificent jungle to the edge of the open crater, where bubbling sulphur-pools in an ashy floor, and a wide view over the fertile valley, are sufficient reward for all exertion on the climber's part.

Bandong itself, as the capital of the Preanger regencies and the home of the native regent and the Dutch resident, is a place of great importance to both races. The regent, as a mere puppet and pensioner of the colonial government, supports the shadow of his old state and splendor in a large *dalem*, or palace, in the heart of the town. He has also a suburban villa in European style, to which are attached large racing-stables, and this progressive regent is a regular cup-winner at the Buitenzorg and Bandong races at every summer, or dry-season, meet, when the "good monsoon" inspires all the islanders to their greatest social exertions.

As one gets farther into the center of the island, native life becomes more picturesque, and every station platform offers one more diverting study. There is more color in costume, and the wayside and platform groups are kaleidoscopic with their gay sarongs and kerchiefs. More men are seen wearing the military jacket of rank with the native sarong, and the boat-handled kris thrust in the belt at the back. The little children, who ride astride of their mothers' hips and cling and cuddle so confidingly in the slandang's folds, seem of finer mold, and their deep, dark Hindu eyes tell of a different strain in the Malay blood than we had seen on the coast—these the Javanese, as distinguished from the Sundanese. The clumsy buffalo, or water-ox, is everywhere, plowing the fields, wallowing in mud, or browsing the stubble patch after the gleaners, always with a patient, statuesque, nude little brown boy on his blue-gray back, the fine, polished skins of these small herders glowing in the sun as if they were inanimate bronze figurines.

The train climbs very slowly from Bandong to Kalaidon Pass, and, after toiling with double engines up the steep grades, it rests at a level, and there bursts upon one the view of the plain of Leles—the fairest of all tropical landscapes, a vision of an ideal promised land, and such a dream of beauty that even the leaden blue clouds of a rainy afternoon could not dim its surpassing loveliness. The railway follows a long shelf hewn high on the mountain wall, that encircles an oval plain set with two conical mountains that rise more than two thousand feet above the level of this plain of Leles, itself two thousand feet above the level of the sea. The finely wrought surface of the plain—networked with the living green dikes and terraces of rice-fields, which, flooded, gleam and glitter in the fitful sun-rays, or, sown and harvested, glow with a mosaic of green and gold—is one exquisite symphony in color, an arrangement in greens that holds one breathless with delight. All the golden greens of rice seed-beds, the intense, vivid greens of young rice transplanted, the opaque and darker greens of advanced crops, and the rich tones of stubble are relieved by the clumps and masses of palms and fine-leaved trees, which, like islands or mere ornamental bits of shrubbery, are disposed with the most admirable effect to be attained by landscape art. Each of these tufted clumps of trees, foregrounded with broad, translucent banana-leaves, declares the presence of toy villages, where the tillers of the plain, the landscape-farmers, and the artist-artisans have woven and set up their pretty basketry homes. A masterpiece, a central ornament or jewel, to which the valley is but the fretted and appropriate setting, a very altar of agriculture, a colossal symbol and emblem of abundance, is the conical Goenong-Kalaidon, a mountain which rises three thousand feet from the level of the plain, and is terraced all the way from base to summit with narrow ribbons of rice-fields—the whole mountain mass etched with myriad fine green lines of verdure, wrinkled around and around with the curving parapets and tiny terraces that retain the flooded hanging gardens. Beyond this amazing piece of agricultural sculpture stands Goenong-Haroeman, a more perfect pyramid, a still rarer trophy of the landscape-farmer's art, even more finely carved in the living green lines of ancient terrace-culture. The rush of the thousand rills, dropping from one tiny terrace to another, fills the air with a peculiar singing undertone, an eerie accompaniment that adds the last magic touch to the fascination of the plain of Leles. Hardly the miles of sculptured bas-reliefs on Boro Boedor and Brambanam temple walls make them any more impressive as monuments and records of human toil than these great green pyramids of Kalaidon and Haroeman, on which human labor has been lavished for all the seasons of uncounted generations—the ascending lines, the successive steps of the great green staircases of rice-terraces, recording ages of toil as plainly as the rings within a tree-trunk declare its successive years of growth.

The railway, dipping nearly to the level of the plain as it describes a great curve around the gloriously green Kalaidon, again ascends along the side of the mountain wall, loops itself around the Haroeman pyramid, and halts at the station of Leles. From that point one has a backward view over the enchanting picture (a line of white bridges and culverts marking the path of the railway along the mountain-side) and he looks directly across at the soft green slopes of Haroeman, which faces him—that vast green dome or pyramid, which is a little world in itself, with uncounted villages nestling under clumps of palm-trees that break the lines of singing terraces, and those peasants of the hanging gardens looking down upon the most pleasing prospect, the most beautiful landscape in all Java, which should be world-famous, and whose charm it is as impossible to exaggerate as to describe.

The sesquipedalian names of the railway-stations throughout the Preanger regencies, are something to fill a traveler's mind between halts, and almost explain why the locomotives not only toot and whistle nearly all the time they are in motion, but stand on the track before station sign-boards and shriek for minutes at a time, like machines demented. Radjamendala is an easy arrangement in station names for the early hours of the trip, and all that family of names—Tjitjoeroek, Tjibeber, Tjirandjang, Tjipenjeum, Tjitjalenka, and also Tagoogapoe—will slip from the tongue after a few trials; but when one strains his eyes toward the limits of the plain of Leles, he may almost see the houses of Baloeboer-Baloeboer-Limbangan. People actually live there and pay taxes, and it is my one regret that I did not leave the train, drive over, and have some letters postmarked with that astonishing aggregation of sound-symbols. Only actual sight, too, could altogether convince one, that one small village of metal-workers could really support so much nomenclature together with any amount of profitable trade. In the intervals of practising the pronunciation of that particular geographic name, the artisans of Baloeboer-Baloeboer-Limbangan do hammer out serviceable gongs, bowls, and household utensils of brass and copper. In earlier times Baloeboer-Baloeboer-Limbangan was the Toledo of the isles, and the kris-blades forged there had finer edge than those from any other place in the archipelago. In these railroad and tramp-steamer days of universal, wholesale trade rivalry, the blade of the noble kris more often comes from abroad, and the chilled edges from Birmingham or those made in Germany have displaced the blades made at the edge of the plain of Leles, and the glory of Baloeboer-Baloeboer-Limbangan has departed.

XIII

"TO TISSAK MALAYA!"

THE sun fell at six o'clock, and in the fast-gathering twilight of the tropics the train shrieked past Tjihondje and Radjapolah, stopped but a minute at Indihiang, and panted into Tissak Malaya like an affrighted creature, to put up for the night. We were whirled through avenues of pitch-darkness, with illuminated porticos gleaming through splendid shrubberies, to the *passagrahan*, or government rest-house. At first we thought the Parthenon had been restored and whitened, and leased to some colonial landlord, or at least that we had come to the deserted summer palace of some great sovereign, so lofty were the columns, so enormous the shining white portico before which the sadoes halted. Quite feudal and noble we felt ourselves, too, when the sadoe-drivers crouched on their heels in that abject position of the dodok, or squatting obeisance, and when they raised the coins to their foreheads in a reverent *simbah*, or worshipful thanksgiving. Truly we were reaching the heart of a strange country, and experiences were thickening!

The passagrahan was an object for sight-seers by itself. The great open space under the portico was the usual living-room, with huge tables, reading-lamps, and lounging- and arm-chairs fitted for a giant's ease. A grand hallway running straight through the center of the building held the scattered and massive furniture of a banquet-hall. Bedrooms with latticed doors opened from either side of this noble hall, the least of these chambers twenty feet square, with ceilings twenty feet high; while the beds, measuring seven by nine feet, suggested Brobdingnagian nightmares to match.

At nine o'clock we followed a silent, beckoning Malay with a lantern off into pitch-darkness, down a deserted street, around a hedge, to a smaller white portico with lamps and rocking-chairs and center-tables. We were dazed as we came suddenly into the glare of lights; and the other guests at the *table d'hôte* of the little hotel viewed us as they would have viewed sudden arrivals by balloon.

"From America! To Tissak Malaya!" they all exclaimed, and we almost apologized for having come so far. There was an amiable and charming young Dutch woman in the company, who, speaking English, benefited all her compatriots with the details of our present itinerary, our past lives and mutual relationships, after each little conversational turn she took with us.

Having commanded a sunrise breakfast for the next morning, we followed the lantern and the silent Malay back through blackness to our illuminated Parthenon of a passagrahan, and had entomological excitement and entertainment for an hour, while all the strange flying things filled the air and strewed the table beneath the lamps. The usual lizards chuck-chucked and called for "Becky" in the shadows, and thin wraiths of lizards ran over the great columns and walls; but a house-front that was not decorated with lizards would be the strangest night sight in Java. When we had laid ourselves out on the state catafalques in the great bedrooms, stealthy whisperings and rustlings of palm-trees beyond the latticed windows, other strange sounds, and startled bird-calls throughout the night suggested the great snakes we had expected to encounter daily and nightly in Java. The tiny light floating in a tumbler of cocoanut-oil threw weird shadows over the walls, and within the bed-curtains one had space to dance a quadrille or arrange a whole set of ordinary bedroom furniture, while the open construction of the upper partition-walls let one converse at will with the occupant of the farthest apartment.

In the first clear light of the dewy morning we saw that a beautiful garden surrounded the passagrahan, and our vast Parthenon of the darkness did not seem so colossal when seen in the shadow of the magnificent kanari-trees that shaded the street before it. While lost in admiration of this splendid aisle of shade-trees, I saw a solitary pedestrian coming down the green avenue, just the pygmy touch of human life needed to complete the picture and give one measure for the soaring tree-trunks and vast canopy of leaves. The slender figure, advancing with the splendid, slow stride of these people, was visible now in a glorifying

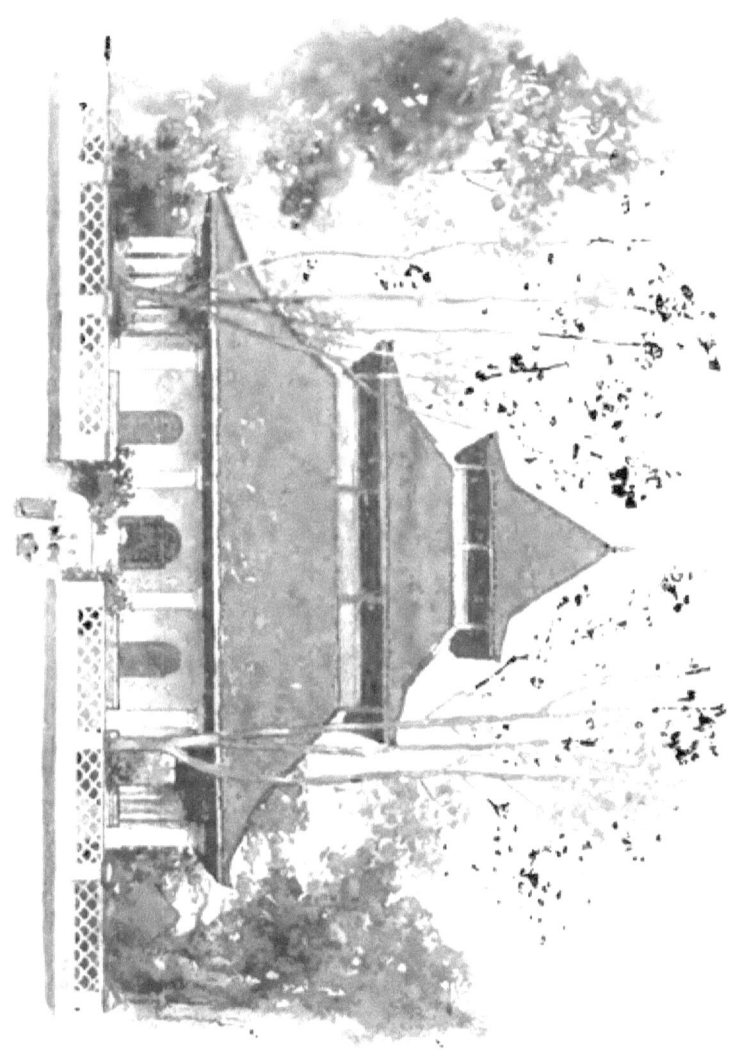

A MOHAMMEDAN MOSQUE.

shaft of earliest, level yellow sunlight, and then almost invisible against the tall hibiscus-hedges or the green shadows of tree-trunks. A nearer flash of sunlight gilded a tray he was carrying—a tray furnished with three small cups of coffee and a plate with six thin wafers of toast, which, well cooled by the long promenade in the fresh air of the morning, constituted the breakfast of three able-bodied travelers, who were to pass the rest of the day on the train, with only opportunity for a sandwich lunch before the evening's nine-o'clock dinner. We sent back those thimble cups, and they were refilled with the same lukewarm, indefinite, muddy gray fluid; but finally, by personal exertions and a hasty trip down the magnificent avenue, some solid additions were secured to the usual scant, skeleton, impressionist breakfast of the country—some marmalade, some eggs, and a bit of the cold blue meat of the useful buffalo. Everywhere in Java one's first, best instincts and finer feelings of the day are hurt and the appetite affronted by just such early morning incidents; protest and prevision are alike useless, and travel on the island is beset with unnecessary hardships.

The semi-weekly passer of Tissak Malaya was then beginning in a park, or open market-place, in front of the passagrahan, and picturesque processions of venders and buyers came straggling down the arched avenues, and filled the shady quadrangle with a holiday hum. There were double panoramas and stages of living pictures along each path in the passer encampment, that grew like magic; and the glowing colors of the fruit-, the flower-, and the pepper-markets, the bright sarongs and turbans, and, above all, the cheerful chatter, were quite inspiring. We bought everywhere—fruits, and a queer three-story basket to hold them; yards of jasmine garlands, bunches of roses, and great double handfuls of the green, lindenish ylang-ylang flowers, pinned with a thorn in a plantain-leaf cornucopia—this last lot of perpetual fragrance for three gulden cents only. Odd bottles of home-made attars of rose and jasmine were sold as cheaply. and gums in straw cases, ready for burning. There was a dry-goods district, where booths were piled high and hung round with Cheribon and other gay sarongs of Middle Java, slandangs and kerchiefs of strongest colors and intricate borderings. We were distracted with the wide choice offered, but could not rouse the phlegmatic dealers to any eagerness or excitement in bargaining; the whole overcharge, reductions, and slow-descending fall in prices proceeding, on the part of the dealers, with a well-assumed indifference, an uninterrupted betel-chewing, a bored and lethargic manner that wore one sadly. A long row of country tailors, thirty or forty of them in a line, sat like so many sparrows around the edges of the passer in the comforting shade of the kanari-trees. All were spectacled like owls, and sat cross-legged before their little American sewing-machines. The customers brought their cloth, the tailors measured them with the eye, and in no time at all the machines were humming up and down the seams of the jackets, that needed no fitting nor trying on, and were made while the candidates sat and smoked and chatted with the sartorial artists. From the chatter-chatter along this tailors' row one might conclude that what the barbers are to Seville, as purveyors of news, the tailors are to Tissak Malaya.

All too soon we had to tear ourselves away from the fascinating passer, and, loaded down with our mixed marketing, fly by sadoe to the station at the far end of town. We saw then the magnificent aisle of kanari-trees we had passed through in darkness the night before—an avenue more fitted for an emperor's triumphal procession than for our queer little two-wheeled carts, drawn each by a mite of a pony, that was all but lifted from the ground by the shafts when I stepped on the after foot-board untimely, the driver dodoking like a hop-toad on the ground in respectful humility. The natives were streaming down the great *allée* and in from all the side streets and by-paths toward the passer, and we half wished we might miss the train when we realized what a spectacle that Tissak Malaya passer was about to be.

In Middle Java, where the railway descends from the Preanger hills to the *terra ingrata's* succession of jungle and swamp at the coast-level, one experiences the same dull, heavy, sickening, depressing heat as in Batavia. After the clear, fresh, mildly cool air, the eternal southern-California climate of the hills, this sweltering atmosphere gave full suggestion of the tropics' deadly perils. Hour after hour the train followed a raised embankment across an endless swamp, the brilliantly flowered lantana-hedges still accompanying the tracks, and a dense forest wall, tangled and matted together with ratans and other creepers, shutting off the view on either side. The malaria and the deadly fever-germs that haunt this region were almost visible, so dense was the air. While this section of the railway was building, even the native workmen were carried back each day to sleep in camps in safer neighborhoods. No white man could work, nor remain there directing work, and Chinese, who are germ-, bacillus-, microbe-, and miasma-proof in every climate, superintended work between the flying visits of European engineers. Beside these tangled and noisome swamps there are quicksand regions, into which car-loads of solid materials were dumped for week after week, and where the track is still always being raised and rebuilt, and the floating earth-crust trembles with each passing train.

As we coursed along past those miles of rankest vegetation, not a waft of perfume reached us, nor did any mass of color or cloak of blossoms delight the eye —a green monotony of uninteresting vegetation, save for the ratan-palms which decorated every tree with their beautiful pinnate leaves. There was one luxuriant vine, half covering a tall tree, which bore clusters of large white blossoms and pendent red berries; but that was the one ideal vine of the imagined tropical jungle's mad riot of stranger and more gorgeous things than bougainvillea. No clouds, cascades, or festoons of gorgeous flowers, no waves of overpowering perfume, no masses of orchids, rewarded eager scrutiny; no birds of brilliant plumage flashed across the jungle's front; no splendidly striped tigers licked their chops and snarled in the jungle's shade; no rhinoceros snorted at the iron horse; and not a serpent raised a hissing head, slid away through dank grass, or looped itself from tree-top to tree-top in proper tropical fashion, as we steamed across the deadly, uninhabitable *terra ingrata*. Nor had even the first construction gangs of railway-builders met with any such sensational incidents, so the chief engineer of the railways afterward informed us. Seeing our disappointment and dejection, this obliging official racked his memory and at last recalled that he himself had once seen a wild peacock walking the track in the *terra ingrata*.

"And yes! so there was. I remember now that one of our engineers, who was running a special locomotive along there, did see a tiger sitting on the track. He whistled loudly, and the tiger trotted up the track until he found the engine gaining on him, and then the royal beast bounded off into the jungle, snarling and spitting like an angry cat."

"But there are great snakes in the swamps surely? You must run over them often?" we persisted.

"Doubtless; but we rarely see snakes here in Java. There are many in Borneo, Sumatra, and the other islands that are so wild yet. But you will see them all at the zoölogical garden in Batavia."

Closer questioning could only elicit the statement that, while all the terrible Java snake-stories we had read might be true, we had no need in this modern day to shake the pillows gently each night and morning to dislodge the sleeping cobra or python; nor to draw the bed-curtains closely at sounds like dry leaves blowing over the floor; nor to regard the harmless hop-toad as the certain pilot and advance-guard of a snake. I almost began to doubt, to discredit that standard favorite, that typical tropical snake-story of the man who fell asleep on the edge of a Java sawa, or rice-field, and waking with a sensation of great dampness around one knee, found that a huge but harmless sawa snake had swallowed his leg to that point. I was ready even to hear that there never had been any skeleton-strewn, deadly upas-tree valley on Papandayang's slope, since every expected sensation had fled my approach—had removed to Borneo, to Sulu, to more remote and impossible islands.

All travel, though, is only such disillusionment and disappointment, and he who would believe and enjoy blood-curdling things should stay by his own fireside. The disillusioned traveler has but to choose, on his return, whether he will truthfully dispel others' fondest illusions, or, joining that nameless club of so many returned travelers, continue to clothe the more distant parts of the world with the glamour of imagination.

XIV

PRISONERS OF STATE AT BORO BOEDOR

HE fact is not generally appreciated that there are ruins of Buddhist and Brahmanic temples in Middle Java surpassing in extent and magnificence anything to be seen in Egypt or India. There, in the heart of the steaming tropics, in that summer land of the world below the equator, on an island where volcanoes cluster more thickly and vegetation is richer than in any other region of the globe, where earthquakes continually rock and shatter, and where deluges descend during the rainy half of the year, remains nearly intact the temple of Boro Boedor, covering almost the same area as the Great Pyramid of Gizeh. It is ornamented with hundreds of life-size statues and miles of bas-reliefs presenting the highest examples of Greco-Buddhist art—a sculptured record of all the arts and industries, the culture and civilization, of the golden age of Java, of the life of the seventh, eighth, and ninth centuries in all the farther East—a record that is not written in hieroglyphs, but in plainest pictures carved by sculptor's chisel. That solid pyramidal

temple, rising in magnificent sculptured terraces, that was built without mortar or cement, without column or pillar or arch, is one of the surviving wonders of the world. On the spot it seems a veritable miracle.

It is one of the romances of Buddhism that this splendid monument of human industry, abandoned by its worshipers as one cult succeeded another, and forgotten after the Mohammedan conquest imposed yet another creed upon the people, should have disappeared completely, hidden in the tangle of tropical vegetation, a formless, nameless, unsuspected mound in the heart of a jungle, lost in every way, with no part in the life of the land, finally to be uncovered to the sight of the nineteenth century. When Sir Stamford Raffles came as British governor of Java in 1811, the Dutch had possessed the island for two centuries, but in their greed for gulden had paid no heed to the people, and knew nothing of that earlier time before the conquest when the island was all one empire, the arts and literature flourished, and, inspired by Hindu influence, Javanese civilization reached its highest estate; nor did the Hollander allow any alien investigators to peer about this profitable plantation. Sir Stamford Raffles, in his five years of control, did a century's work. He explored, excavated, and surveyed the ruined temples, and searching the voluminous archives of the native princes, drew from the mass of romantic legends and poetic records the first "History of Java." His officers copied and deciphered inscriptions, and gradually worked out all the history of the great ruins, and determined the date of their erection at the beginning of the seventh century.

At this time Sir Stamford wrote: "The interior of Java contains temples that, as works of labor and art, dwarf to nothing all our wonder and admiration at the pyramids of Egypt." Then Alfred Russel Wallace said: "The number and beauty of the architectural remains in Java . . . far surpass those of Central America, and perhaps even those of India." And of Boro Boedor he wrote: "The amount of human labor and skill expended on the Great Pyramid of Egypt sinks into insignificance when compared with that required to complete this sculptured hill-temple in the interior of Java." Herr Brumund called Boro Boedor "the most remarkable and magnificent monument Buddhism has ever erected"; and Fergusson, in his "History of Indian and Eastern Architecture," finds in that edifice the highest development of Buddhist art, an epitome of all its arts and ritual, and the culmination of the architectural style which, originating at Barhut a thousand years before, had begun to decay in India at the time the colonists were erecting this masterpiece of the ages in the heart of Java.

There is yet no Baedeker, or Murray, or local red book to lead one to and about the temples and present every dry detail of fact. The references to the ruins in books of travel and general literature are vague or cautious generalities, absurd misstatements, or guesses. In the great libraries of the world's capitals the archaeologists' reports are rare, and on the island only Dutch editions are available. Fergusson is one's only portable guide and aid to understanding; but as he never visited the stupendous ruin, his is but a formal record of the main facts. Dutch scientists criticize

Sir Stamford Raffles's work and all that Von Humboldt and Lassen deduced from it concerning Javanese religion and mythology. They entirely put aside all native histories and traditions, searching and accepting only Chinese and Arabic works, and making a close study of ancient inscriptions, upon the rendering of which few of the Dutch savants agree.

We had applied for new toelatings-kaarten, or admission tickets, to the interior of the island; and as they had not arrived by the afternoon before we intended leaving Buitenzorg, we drove to the assistant resident's to inquire. "You shall have them this evening," said that gracious and courtly official, standing beside the huge carriage; "but as it is only the merest matter of form, go right along in the morning, ladies, anyhow, and I shall send the papers after you by post. To Tissak Malaya? No? Well, then, to Djokjakarta."

Upon that advice we proceeded on our journey, crossed the Preangers, saw the plain of Leles, and made our brief visit to Tissak Malaya. We rode for a long, hot day across the swamps and low-lying jungles of the *terra ingrata* of Middle Java, and just before sunset we reached Djokjakarta, a provincial capital, where the native sultan resides in great state, but poor imitation of independent rulership. We had tea served us under the great portico of the Hotel Toegoe, our every movement followed by the uncivilized piazza stare of some Dutch residents—that gaze of the summer hotel that has no geographic or racial limit, which even occurs on the American littoral, and in Java has a fixedness born of stolid Dutch ancestry, and an intensity due to the tropical fervor of the thermometer, that put it far beyond all other species of unwinking scrutiny. The bovine, ruminant gaze of those stout women, continued and continued past all provincial-colonial curiosity as to the cut and stuff of our gowns, drove us to the garden paths, already twinkling with fireflies. The landlord joined us there, and strolled with us out to the street and along a line of torch-lighted booths and shops, where native products and native life were most picturesquely presented. Our landlord made himself very agreeable in explaining it all, walked on as far as the gates of the sultan's palace, plying us with the most pointblank personal questions, our whence, whither, why, for how long, etc.; but we did not mind that in a land of stares and interrogative English. He showed us the carriage we could have for the next day's twenty-five-mile drive to Boro Boedor—"if you go," with quite unnecessary emphasis on the phrase of doubt. He finally brought us back to the portico, disappeared for a time, and returning, said: "Ladies, the assistant resident wishes to meet you. Will you come this way?" And the courteous one conducted us through lofty halls and porticos to his own half-office parlor, all of us pleased at this unexpected attention from the provincial official.

A tall, grim, severe man in the dark cloth clothes of ceremony, with uniform buttons, waved a semi-military cap, and said curtly: "Ladies, it is my duty to inform you that you have no permission to visit Djokja."

It took some repetitions for us to get the whole sensation of the heavens suddenly falling on us, to learn that a telegram had come from official headquarters at Buitenzorg to warn him that three American ladies would arrive that afternoon, without passports, to visit Djokja.

"Certainly not, because those Buitenzorg officials told us not to wait for the passports—that they would mail them after us." Then ensued the most farcical scene, a grand burlesque rendering of the act of apprehending criminals, or rather political suspects. The assistant resident tried to maintain the stern, judicial manner of a police-court magistrate, cross-examining us as closely as if it were testimony in a murder trial we were giving, and was not at all inclined to admit that there could be any mistake in the elaborately perfect system of Dutch colonial government. Magnificently he told us that we could not remain in Djokja, and we assured him that we had no wish to do so, that we were leaving for Boro Boedor in the morning. The Pickwickian message from Buitenzorg had not given any instructions. It merely related that we should arrive. We had arrived, and the assistant resident evidently did not know just what to do next. At any rate, he intended that we should stand in awe of him and the government of Netherlands India. He "supposed" that it was intended that we should be sent straight back to Buitenzorg. We demurred, in fact refused—the two inflammable, impolitic ones of us, who paid no heed to the gentle, gray-haired elder member of our party, who was all resignation and humility before the terrible official. We produced our United States passports, and quite as much as told him that he and the noble army of Dutch officials might finish the discussion with the American consul; we had other affairs, and were bound for Boro Boedor. He waved the United States passports aside, curtly said they were of "no account," examined the letters of credit with a shade more of interest, and gave his whole attention to my "Smithsonian passport," or general letter "to all friends of science." That beautifully written document, with its measured phrases, many polysyllabic words in capital letters, and the big gold seal of Saint-Gaudens's designing, worked a spell; and after slowly reading all the commendatory sentences of that great American institution "for the increase and diffusion of knowledge among men," he read it again:

"Hum-m-m! Hum-m-m! The Smithsonian Institution of Washington—National Geographic Society —scientific observation and study—anthropology— photography—G. Brown Goode, acting secretary! Ah, ladies, since you have such credentials as *this*," —evidently the Smithsonian Institution has better standing abroad than the Department of State, and G. Brown Goode, acting secretary of the one, was a better name to conjure with away from home than Walter Q. Gresham, actual secretary of the other,— "since you come so highly commended to us, I will allow you to proceed to Boro Boedor, and remain there while I report to Buitenzorg and ask for instructions. You will go to Boro Boedor as early as possible in the morning," he commanded, and then asked, "How long had you intended to remain there?"

"That depends. If it is comfortable, and the rains keep off, we may stay several days. If not, we return to-morrow evening."

"No, no, no!" he cried in alarm; "you must stay there at Boro Boedor. You have no permission to visit Djokja, and I cannot let you stay in my residency. You must stay at Boro Boedor or go back to Buitenzorg."

To be ordered off to the Buddhist shrine at sunrise put the pilgrimage in quite another light; to be sentenced to Nirvana by a local magistrate in brass buttons was not like arriving there by slow stages— meditation and reincarnation; but as the assistant resident seemed to be on the point of repenting his clemency, we acquiesced, and the great man and his minions drove away, the bearer of the *pajong*, or official umbrella of his rank, testifying to the formal character of the visit he had been paying. The landlord mopped his brow, sighed, and looked like one who had survived great perils; and we then saw that his sight-seeing stroll down the street with us had been a ruse, a little clever scouting, a preliminary reconnaissance for the benefit of the puzzled magistrate.

We left Djokja at sunrise, with enthusiasm somewhat dampened from former anticipations of that twenty-five-mile drive to Boro Boedor, "the aged thing" in the Boro district of Kedu Residency, or Bára Budha, "Great Buddha." We had expected to realize a little of the pleasure of travel during the barely ended posting days on this garden island, networked over with smooth park drives all shaded with tamarind-, kanari-, teak-, and waringen-trees, and it proved a half-day of the greatest interest and enjoyment. Our canopied carriage was drawn by four little rats of ponies, driven by a serious old coachman in a gay sarong and military jacket, with a huge lacquered vizor or crownless hat tied on over his battek turban, like a student's exaggerated eye-shade. This gave the shadow of great dignity and owlish wisdom to his wrinkled face, ornamented by a mustache as sparsely and symmetrically planted as walrus whiskers. He held the reins and said nothing. When there was anything to do, the running footman did it—a lithe little creature who clung to a rear step, and took to his heels every few minutes to crack the whip over the ponies' heads, and with a frenzied "Gree! G-r-r-ee! *Gr-r-r-e-e-e!*" urge the mites to a more breakneck gallop in harness. He steered them by the traces as he galloped beside them, guided them over bridges, around corners, past other vehicles, and through crowds, while the driver held the reins and chewed betel tobacco in unconcerned state. We rocked and rolled through beautiful arched avenues, with this bare-legged boy in gay petticoat "gr-r-ree-ing" us along like mad, people scattering aside like frightened chickens, and kneeling as we passed by. The way was fenced and hedged and finished, to each blade of grass, like some aristocratic suburb of a great capital, an endless park, or continuous estate, where fancy farming and landscape-gardening had gone their most extravagant lengths. There was not a neglected acre on either side for all the twenty-five miles; every field was cultivated like a tulip-bed; every plant was as green and perfect as if entered in a horticultural show. Streams, ravines, and ditches were solidly bridged, each with its white cement parapet and smooth concrete flooring, and each numbered and marked with

Dutch preciseness; and along every bit of the road were posted the names of the kampongs and estates charged to maintain the highway in its perfect condition. Telegraph- and telephone-wires were strung on the rigid arms of cotton-trees, and giant creepers wove solid fences as they were trained from tree-trunk to tree-trunk—the tropics tamed, combed, and curbed, hitched to the cart of commerce and made man's abject servant.

Every few miles there were open red-tiled pavilions built over the highways as refuges for man and beast from the scorching sun of one season and the cloudburst showers of the rainy half of the year. Twice we found busy passers going on in groves beside these rest-houses—picturesque gatherings of men, women, and children, and displays of fowls, fruits, nuts, vegetables, grain, sugar, spices, gums, and flowers, that tempted one to linger and enjoy, and to photograph every foot of the passer's area. The main road was crowded all the way like a city street, and around these passers the highway hummed with voices. One can believe in the density of the population—450 to the square mile[1]—when he sees the people trooping along these country roads; and he can well understand why every foot of land is cultivated, how even in the benevolent land of the banana every one must produce something, must work or starve. The better sanitary condition of the native kampongs is given as

---

[1] Holland has a population of 359 to the square mile (December 31, 1892), and Belgium a population of 540 to the square mile. French statisticians are confident that Java will soon surpass Belgium in the density of its population.

WAYSIDE PAVILION ON POST-ROAD.

a great factor in the remarkable increase of population in the last half-century; but it took many years of precept and example, strict laws, and a rating of native rulers and village chiefs according to the cleanliness of their kampongs, before the native hamlets became tropical counterparts of Broek and the other absurdly clean towns of Holland. These careless children of the tropics are obliged to whitewash their houses twice a year, look to their drains and debris, and use disinfectants; and with the dainty little basket houses, one of which may be bought outright for five dollars, and the beautiful palms and shrubberies to serve as screens from rice-field vapors, each little kampong is a delight in every way.

Men and boys toiled to the passer, bent over with the weight of one or two monstrous jack-fruits or durians on their backs. A woman with a baby swinging in the slandang over her shoulder had tied cackling chickens to the back of her belt, and trudged on comfortably under her umbrella; and a boy swung a brace of ducks from each end of a shoulder-pole, and trotted gaily to the passer. The kampongs, or villages, when not hidden in palm- and plantain-groves behind fancy bamboo fences, were rows of open houses on each side of the highway, and we reviewed native life at leisure while the ponies were changed. The friendly, gentle little brown people welcomed us with amused and embarrassed smiles when our curiosity as to sarong-painting, lacquering, and mat-weaving carried us into the family circle. The dark, round-eyed, star-eyed babies and children showed no fear or shyness, and the tiniest ones—their soft little warm brown bodies bare of ever a garment save the cotton slandang in which they cuddle so confidingly under the mother's protecting arm—let us lift and carry and play with them at will.

We left the main road, and progressed by a narrower way between open fields of pepper, manioc, indigo, and tobacco, with picturesque views of the three symmetrical and beautiful mountains, Soembung, Merbaboe, and Merapi—the first and largest one as pure in line, as exquisite and ideal a peak, as Fujiyama, and the others sloping splendidly in soft volcanic outlines. Soembung is the very center of Java, and native legends cling to the little hill of Tidar at its base—the "spike of the universe," the nail which fastens the lovely island to the face of the earth. Merbaboe, the "ash-ejecting," has wrought ruin in its time, and a faint white plume of steam waves from its summit still. The capitulations which delivered the Napoleonic possessions of the Dutch East Indies to England in 1811 were signed at the base of Merbaboe, and in our then frame of mind toward the Dutch government we wished to make a pilgrimage of joyous celebration to the spot. The third of the graceful peaks, Merapi, the "fire-throwing," was a sacred peak in Buddhist times, when cave-temples were hewn in its solid rock and their interiors fretted over with fine bas-reliefs. A group of people transplanting rice, a little boy driving a flock of geese down the road, a little open-timbered temple of the dead in a frangipani-grove—all these, with the softly blue-and-purple mountains in the background, are pictures in enduring memory of that morning's ride toward Nirvana.

A gray ruin showed indistinctly on a hilltop, and after a run through a long, arched avenue we came out suddenly at the base of the hill-temple. Instead of a mad, triumphant sweep around the great pyramid, the ponies balked, rooted themselves past any lashing or "gr-r-ree-ing," and we got out and walked under the noonday sun, around the hoary high altar of Buddha, down an avenue of tall kanari-trees, lined with statues, gargoyles, and other such *recha*, or remains of ancient art, to the passagrahan, or government rest-house.

XV

BORO BOEDOR

THE deep portico of the passagrahan commands an angle and two sides of the square temple, and from the mass of blackened and bleached stones the eye finally arranges and follows out the broken lines of the terraced pyramid, covered with such a wealth of ornament as no other one structure in the world presents. The first near view is almost disappointing. In the blur of details it is difficult to realize the vast proportions of this twelve-century-old structure—a pyramid the base platform of which is five hundred feet square, the first terrace walls three hundred feet square, and the final dome one hundred feet in height. Stripped of every kindly relief of vine and moss, every gap and ruined angle visible, there was something garish, raw, and almost disordered at the first glance, almost as jarring as newness, and the hard black-and-white effect of the dark lichens on the gray trachyte made it look like a bad photograph of the pile. The temple stands on a broad platform, and rises first in five square terraces, inclos-

ATHENS: THE PARTHENON FROM THE PASSAGEWAY

ing galleries, or processional paths, between their walls, which are covered on each side with bas-relief sculptures. If placed in single line these bas-reliefs would extend for three miles. The terrace walls hold four hundred and thirty-six niches or alcove chapels, where life-size Buddhas sit serene upon lotus cushions. Staircases ascend in straight lines from each of the four sides, passing under stepped or pointed arches the keystones of which are elaborately carved masks, and rows of sockets in the jambs show where wood or metal doors once swung. Above the square terraces are three circular terraces, where seventy-two latticed *dagobas* (reliquaries in the shape of the calyx or bud of the lotus) inclose each a seated image, seventy-two more Buddhas sitting in these inner, upper circles of Nirvana, facing a great dagoba, or final cupola, the exact function or purpose of which as key to the whole structure is still the puzzle of archæologists. This final shrine is fifty feet in diameter, and either covered a relic of Buddha, or a central well where the ashes of priests and princes were deposited, or is a form surviving from the tree-temples of the earliest, primitive East when nature-worship prevailed. The English engineers made an opening in the solid exterior, and found an unfinished statue of Buddha on a platform over a deep well-hole; and its head, half buried in debris, still smiles upon one from the deep cavern. M. Freidrich, in "L'Extrême Orient" (1878), states that this top dagoba was opened in the time of the resident Hartman (1835), and that gold ornaments were found; and it was believed that there were several stories or chambers to this well, which reached to the lowest level of the structure. M. Désiré de Charnay, who spent an afternoon at Boro Boedor in 1878 in studying the resemblance of the pyramid temples of Java to those of Central America, believed this wellhole to be the place of concealment for the priest whose voice used to issue as a mysterious oracle from the statue itself.

A staircase has been constructed to the summit of this dagoba, and from it one looks down upon the whole structure as on a ground-plan drawing, and out over finely cultivated fields and thick palm-groves to the matchless peaks and the nearer hills that inclose this fertile valley of the Boro Boedor—"the very finest view I ever saw," wrote Marianne North.

Three fourths of the terrace chapels and the upper dagobas have crumbled; hundreds of statues are headless, armless, overturned, missing; tees, or finials, are gone from the bell-roofs; terrace walls bulge, lean outward, and have fallen in long stretches; and the circular platforms and the processional paths undulate as if earthquake-waves were at the moment rocking the mass. No cement was used to hold the fitted stones together, and another Hindu peculiarity of construction is the entire absence of a column, a pillar, or an arch. Vegetation wrought great ruin during its buried centuries, but earthquakes and tropical rains are working now a slow but surer ruin that will leave little of Boro Boedor for the next century's wonder-seekers, unless the walls are soon straightened and strongly braced.

All this ruined splendor and wrecked magnificence soon has an overpowering effect on one. He almost hesitates to attempt studying out all the details, the intricate symbolism and decoration lavished by those Hindus, who, like the Moguls, "built like Titans, but finished like jewelers." One walks around and around the sculptured terraces, where the bas-reliefs portray all the life of Buddha and his disciples,

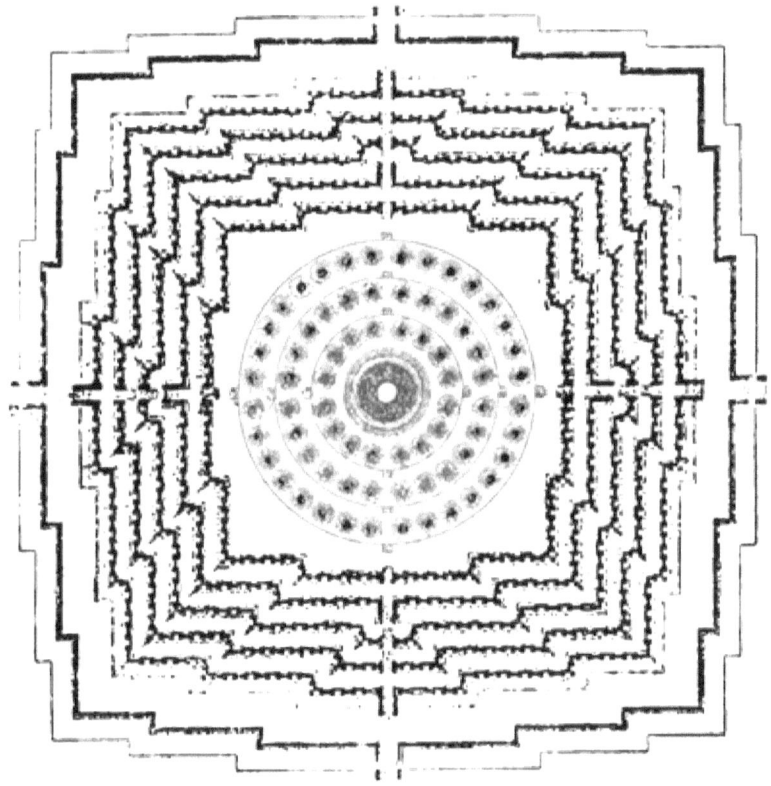

GROUND PLAN OF BORO BOEDOR.

and the history of that great religion—a picture-Bible of Buddhism. All the events in the life of Prince Siddhartha, Gautama Buddha, are followed in turn: his birth and education, his leaving home, his meditation under Gaya's immortal tree, his teaching in the deer-park, his sitting in judgment, weighing even the birds in his scales, his death and entrance into Nirvana. The every-day life of the seventh and eighth century is pictured, too—temples, palaces, thrones and tombs, ships and houses, all of man's constructions, are portrayed. The life in courts and palaces, in fields and villages, is all seen there. Royal folk in wonderful jewels sit enthroned, with minions offering gifts and burning incense before them, warriors kneeling, and maidens dancing. The peasant plows the rice-fields with the same wooden stick and ungainly buffalo, and carries the rice-sheaves from the harvest-field with the same shoulder-poles, used in all the farther East to-day. Women fill their water-vessels at the tanks and bear them away on their heads as in India now, and scores of bas-reliefs show the unchanging customs of the East that offer sculptors the same models in this century. Half the wonders of that great three-mile-long gallery of sculptures cannot be recalled. Each round disclosed some more wonderful picture, some more eloquent story, told in the coarse trachyte rock furnished by the volcanoes across the valley. Even the humorous fancies of the sculptors are expressed in stone. In one rilievo a splendidly caparisoned state elephant flings its feet in imitation of the dancing-girl near by. Other sportive elephants carry fans and state umbrellas in their trunks; and the marine monsters swimming about the ship that bears the Buddhist missionaries to the isles have such expression and human resemblance as to make one wonder if those primitives did not occasionally pillory an enemy with their chisels, too. In the last gallery, where, in the progress of the religion, it took on many features of Jainism, or advancing Brahmanism, Buddha is several times represented as the ninth avatar, or incarnation, of Vishnu, still seated on the lotus cushion, and holding a lotus with one of his four hands. Figure after figure wears the Brahmanic cord, or sacrificial thread, over the left shoulder; and all the royal ones sit in what must have been the pose of high fashion at that time—one knee bent under in tailor fashion, the other bent knee raised and held in a loop of the girdle confining the sarong skirt. There is not a grotesque nor a nude figure in the whole three miles of sculptured scenes, and the costumes are a study in themselves; likewise the elaborate jewels which Maia and her maids and the princely ones wear. The trees and flowers are a sufficient study alone; and on my last morning at Boro Boedor I made the whole round at sunrise, looking specially at the wonderful palms, bamboos, frangipani-, mango-, mangosteen-, breadfruit-, pomegranate-, banana-, and bo-trees—every local form being gracefully conventionalized, and, as Fergusson says, "complicated and refined beyond any examples known in India." It is such special rounds that give one a full idea of what a monumental masterpiece the great Buddhist *vihara* is, what an epitome of all the arts and civilization of the eighth century A. D. those galleries of sculpture hold, and turn one to dreaming of the builders and their times.

No particularly Javanese types of face or figure are represented. All the countenances are Hindu, Hindu-Caucasian, and pure Greek; and none of the objects or accessories depicted with them are those of an uncivilized people. All the art and culture, the highest standards of Hindu taste and living, in the tenth century of triumphant Buddhism, are expressed in this sculptured record of the golden age of Java. The Boro Boedor sculptures are finer examples of the Greco-Buddhist art of the times than those of Amravati and Gandahara as one sees them in Indian museums; and the pure Greek countenances show sufficient evidence of Bactrian influences on the Indus, whence the builders came.

Of the more than five hundred statues of Buddha enshrined in niches and latticed dagobas, all, save the one mysterious figure standing in the central or summit dagoba, are seated on lotus cushions. Those of the terrace rows of chapels face outward to the four points of the compass, and those of the three circular platforms face inward to the hidden, mysterious one. All are alike save in the position of the hands, and those of the terrace chapels have four different poses accordingly as they face the cardinal points. As they are conventionally represented, there is Buddha teaching, with his open palm resting on one knee; Buddha learning, with that hand intently closed; Buddha meditating, with both hands open on his knees; Buddha believing and convinced, expounding the lotus law with upraised hand; and Buddha demonstrating and explaining, with thumbs and index-fingers touching. The images in the lotus bells of the circular platforms hold the right palm curved like a shell over the fingers of the left hand—the Buddha who has comprehended, and sits meditating in stages of Nirvana. It was never intended that worshipers should know the mien of the

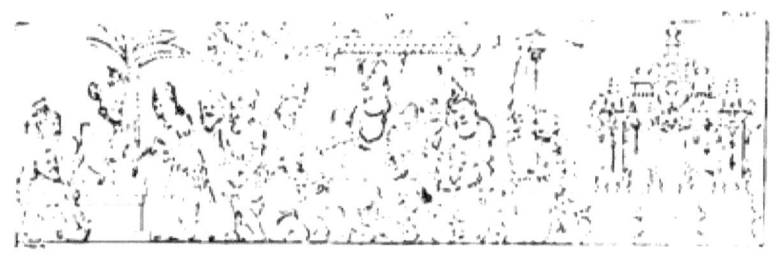

FOUR BAS-RELIEFS FROM BORO BOEDOR.
After Wilson's drawings.

great one in the summit chalice, the serene one who, having attained the supreme end, was left to brood alone, inaccessible, shut out from, beyond all the world. For this reason it is believed that this standing statue was left incomplete, the profane chisel not daring to render every accessory and attribute as with the lesser ones.

Humboldt first noted the five different attitudes of the seated figures, and their likeness to the five Dhyani Buddhas of Nepal; and the discovery of a tablet in Sumatra recording the erection of a seven-story vihara to the Dhyani Buddha was proof that the faith that first came pure from the mouth of the Oxus and the Indus must have received later bent through missionaries from the Malay Peninsula and Tibet. The Boro Boedor images have the same lotus cushion and aureole, the same curls of hair, but not the long ears of the Nepal Buddhas, who in the Mongol doctrine had each his own paradise or quarter of the earth. The first Dhyani, who rules the paradise of the Orient, is always represented in the same attitude and pose of the hands as the image in the latticed bells of these upper, circular or Nirvana terraces of Boro Boedor. The images on the east side of Boro Boedor's square terraces correspond to the second Dhyani's conventional pose; those on the south walls, to the third Dhyani; the west-facing ones, to the fourth Dhyani; and the northern ones, to the fifth Dhyani of Nepal.

There are no inscriptions visible anywhere in this mass of picture-writings, no corner-stone or any clue to the exact year of its founding. We know certainly that the third great synod of Buddhists in Asoka's time, 264 B. C., resolved to spread Buddhism abroad, and that the propaganda begun in Ceylon was carried in every direction, and that Asoka opened seven of the eight original dagobas of India enshrining relics of Buddha's body, and, subdividing, put them in eighty-four thousand vases or precious boxes, that were scattered to the limits of that religious world. Stupas, or dagobas, were built over these holy bits, and all the central dagoba of Boro Boedor is believed to have been the original structure built over some such reliquary, and afterward surrounded by the great sculptured terraces. Fa Hian, the Chinese pilgrim who visited Java in 414 A. D., remarked upon the number of "heretics and Brahmans" living there, and noted that "the law of Buddha is not much known." Native records tell that in 603 A. D. the Prince of Gujerat came, with five thousand followers in one hundred and six ships, and settled at Mataram, where two thousand more men of Gujerat joined him, and a great Buddhist empire succeeded that of the Brahmanic faith. An inscription found in Sumatra, bearing date 656 A. D., gives the name of Maha Raja Adiraja Adityadharma, King of Prathama (Great Java), a worshiper of the five Dhyani Buddhas, who had erected a great seven-storied vihara, evidently this one of Boro Boedor, in their honor. This golden age of the Buddhist empire in Java lasted through the seventh, eighth, and ninth centuries. Arts and religion had already entered their decline in the tenth century, when the Prince Dewa Kosoumi sent his daughter and four sons to India to study religion and the arts. The princelings returned with artists, soldiers, and many trophies and products; but

ON THE SECOND TERRACE.

this last fresh importation did not arrest the decay of the faith, and the people, relapsing peaceably into Brahmanism, deserted their old temples. With the Mohammedan conquest of 1475–79 the people in turn forsook the worship of Siva, Durga, and Ganesha, and abandoned their shrines at Brambanam and elsewhere, as they had withdrawn from Boro Boedor and Chandi Sewou.

When the British engineers came to Boro Boedor, in 1814, the inhabitants of the nearest village had no knowledge or traditions of this noblest monument Buddhism ever reared. Ever since their fathers had moved there from another district it had been only a tree-covered hill in the midst of forests. Two hundred coolies worked forty-five days in clearing away vegetation and excavating the buried terraces. Measurements and drawings were made, and twelve plates from them accompany Sir Stamford Raffles's work. After the Dutch recovered possession of Java, their artists and archæologists gave careful study to this monument of earlier civilization and arts. Further excavations showed that the great platform or broad terrace around the temple mass was of later construction than the body of the pyramid, that a flooring nine feet deep had been put entirely around the lower walls, presumably to brace them, and thus covering many inscriptions the meanings of which have not yet been given, not to English readers at least. Dutch scientists devoted many seasons to the study of these ruins, and Herr Brumund's scholarly text, completed and edited by Dr. Leemans of Leyden, accompanies and explains the great folio volumes of four hundred plates, after Wilsen's drawings, published by the Dutch government in 1874. Since their uncovering the ruins have been kept free from vegetation, but no other care has been taken. In this comparatively short time legends have grown up, local customs have become fixed, and Boro Boedor holds something of the importance it should in its immediate human relations.

For more than six centuries the hill-temple was lost to sight, covered with trees and rank vegetation; and when the Englishmen brought the great sculptured monument to light, the gentle, easily superstitious Javanese of the neighborhood regarded these recha—statues and relics of the ancient, unknown cult—with the greatest reverence. They adopted them as tutelary divinities, as it were, indigenous to their own soil. While Wilsen lived there the people brought daily offerings of flowers. The statue on the first circular terrace at the right of the east staircase, and the secluded image at the very summit, were always surrounded with heaps of stemless flowers laid on moss and plantain-leaves. Incense was burned to these recha, and the people daubed them with the yellow powder with which princes formerly painted, and even humble bridegrooms now paint, themselves on festal days, just as Burmese Buddhists daub gold-leaf on their shrines, and, like the Cingalese Buddhists, heap champak and tulse, jasmine, rose, and frangipani flowers, before their altars. When questioned, the people owned that the offerings at Boro Boedor were in fulfilment of a vow or in thanksgiving for some event in their lives—a birth, death, marriage, unexpected good fortune, or recovery from illness. Other

worshipers made the rounds of the circular terraces, reaching to touch each image in its latticed bell, and many kept all-night vigils among the dagobas of the Nirvana circles. Less appealing was the custom, that grew up among the Chinese residents of Djokjakarta and its neighborhood, of making the temple the goal of general pilgrimage on the Chinese New Year's day. They made food and incense offerings to the images, and celebrated with fireworks, feasts, and a general May-fair and popular outdoor fête.

After the temple was uncovered the natives considered it a free quarry, and carried off carved stones for door-steps, gate-posts, foundations, and fences. Every visitor, tourist or antiquarian, scientist or relic-hunter, helped himself; and every residency, native prince's garden, and plantation lawn, far and near, is still ornamented with Boro Boedor's sculptures. In the garden of the Magelang Residency, Miss Marianne North found a Chinese artist employed in "restoring" Boro Boedor images, touching up the Hindu countenances with a chisel until their eyes wore the proper Chinese slant. The museum at Batavia has a full collection of recha, and all about the foundation platform of the temple itself, and along the path to the passagrahan, the way is lined with displaced images and fragments, statues, lions, elephants, horses; the *hansa*, or emblematic geese of Buddhism; the *Garouda*, or sacred birds of Vishnu; and giant genii that probably guarded some outer gates of approach. A captain of Dutch hussars told Herr Brumund that, when camping at Boro Boedor during the Javanese war, his men amused themselves by striking off the heads of statues with single lance- or saber-strokes. Conspicuous heads made fine targets for rifle and pistol practice. Native boys, playing on the terraces while watching cattle, broke off tiny heads and detachable bits of carving, and threw them at one another; and a few such playful shepherds could effect as much ruin as any of the imaginary bands of fanatic Moslems or Brahmans. One can better accept the plain, rural story of the boy herders' destructiveness than those elaborately built up tales of the religious wars, when priests and people, driven to Boro Boedor as their last refuge, retreated, fighting, from terrace to terrace, hurling stones and statues down upon their pursuers, the last heroic believers dying martyrs before the summit dagoba. Fanatic Mohammedans in other countries doubtless would destroy the shrines of a rival, heretic creed; but there is most evidence in the history and character of the Javanese people that they simply left their old shrines, let them alone, and allowed the jungle to claim at its will what no longer had any interest or sacredness for them. To this day the Javanese takes his religion easily, and it is known that at one time Buddhism and Brahmanism flourished in peace side by side, and that conversion from one faith to the other, and back again, and then to Mohammedanism, was peaceful and gradual, and the result of suasion and fashion, and not of force. The old cults faded, lost prestige, and vanished without stress of arms or an inquisition.

XVI

BORO BOEDOR AND MENDOET

WITH five hundred Buddhas in near neighborhood, one might expect a little of the atmosphere of Nirvana, and the looking at so many repetitions of one object might well produce the hypnotic stage akin to it. The cool, shady passagrahan at Boro Boedor affords as much of earthly quiet and absolute calm, as entire a retreat from the outer, modern world, as one could ever expect to find now in any land of the lotus. This government rest-house is maintained by the resident of Kedu, and every accommodation is provided for the prilgrim, at a fixed charge of six florins the day. The keeper of the passagrahan was a slow-spoken, lethargic, meditative old Hollander, with whom it was always afternoon. One half expected him to change from battek pajamas to yellow draperies, climb up on some vacant lotus pedestal, and, posing his fingers, drop away into eternal meditation, like his stony neighbors. Tropic life and isolation had reduced him to that mental stagnation, torpor, or depression so common with single Europeans in far Asia, isolated from all social friction, active, human interests, and natural sympathies, and so far out of touch with the living, moving world of the nineteenth century. Life goes on in placidity, endless quiet, and routine at Boro Boedor. Visitors come rarely; they most often stop only for riz tavel, and drive on; and not a half-dozen American names appear in the visitors' book, the first entry in which is dated 1869.

I remember the first still, long lotus afternoon in the passagrahan's portico, when my companions napped, and not a sound broke the stillness save the slow, occasional rustle of palm-branches and the whistle of birds. In that damp, heated silence, where even the mental effort of recalling the attitude of Buddha elsewhere threw one into a bath of perspiration, there was exertion enough in tracing the courses and projections of the terraced temple with the eye. Even this easy rocking-chair study of the blackened ruins, empty niches, broken statues, and shattered and crumbling terraces, worked a spell. The dread genii by the doorway and the grotesque animals along the path seemed living monsters, the meditating statues even seemed to breathe, until some "chuck-chucking" lizard ran over them and dispelled the half-dream.

In those hazy, hypnotic hours of the long afternoon one could best believe the tradition that the temple rose in a night at miraculous bidding, and was not built by human hands; that it was built by the son of the Prince of Boro Boedor, as a condition to his receiving the daughter of the Prince of Mendoet for a wife. The suitor was to build it within a given time, and every detail was rigidly prescribed. The princess came with her father to inspect the great work of art, with its miles of bas-reliefs and hundreds of statues fresh from the sculptor's chisel. "Without doubt these images are beautiful," she said coldly, "but they are dead. I can no more love you than they can love you"; and she turned and left her lover to brood in eternal sorrow and meditation upon that puzzle of all the centuries—the Eternal Feminine.

At last the shadows began to stretch; a cooler breath came; cocoanut-leaves began to rustle and lash with force, and the musical rhythm of distant, soft Malay voices broke the stillness that had been that of the Sleeping Beauty's enchanted castle. A boy crept out of a basket house in the palm-grove behind the passa-grahan, and walked up a palm-tree with that deliberate ease and nonchalance that is not altogether human or two-footed, and makes one rub his eyes doubtingly at the unprepared sight. He carried a bunch of bamboo tubes at his belt, and when he reached the top of the smooth stem began letting down bamboo cups, fastening one at the base of each leaf-stalk to collect the sap.

Everywhere in Java we saw them collecting the sap of the true sugar-palm and the toddy-palm, that bear such gorgeous spathes of blossoms; but it is only in this region of Middle Java that sugar is made from the cocoa-palm. Each tree yields daily about two quarts of sap that reduce to three or four ounces of sugar. The common palm-sugar of the passers looks and tastes like other brown sugar, but this from cocoa-palms has a delicious, nutty fragrance and flavor, as unique as maple-sugar. We were not long in the land before we learned to melt cocoa-palm sugar and pour it on grated ripe cocoanut, thus achieving a sweet supreme.

The level valley about Boro Boedor is tilled in such fine lines that it seems in perspective to have been etched or hatched with finer tools than plow and hoe. There is a little Malay temple surrounded by graves in a frangipani-grove near the great pyramid, where the ground is white with the fallen "blossoms of the dead," and the tree-trunks are decked with trails of white and palest pink orchids. The little kampong of Boro Boedor hides in a deep green grove—such a pretty, picturesque little lot of basket houses, such a carefully painted village in a painted grove,—the village of the Midway Plaisance, only more so,—such a set scene and ideal picture of Java, as ought to have wings and footlights, and be looked at to slow music. And there, in the early summer mornings, is a busy passer in a grove that presents more and more attractive pictures of Javanese life, as the people come from miles around to buy and to sell the necessaries and luxuries of their picturesque, primitive life, so near to nature's warmest heart.

All the neighborhood is full of beauty and interest, and there are smaller shrines at each side of Boro Boedor, where pilgrims in ancient times were supposed to make first and farewell prayers. One is called Chandi Pawon, or more commonly Dapor, the kitchen, because of its empty, smoke-blackened interior resulting from the incense of the centuries of living faith, and of the later centuries when superstitious habit, and not any surviving Buddhism, led the humble

THE EIGHT-HAND IMAGE AT MENDOET.

people to make offerings to the recha, the unknown, mysterious gods of the past.

Chandi Mendoet, two miles the other side of Boro Boedor, is an exquisite pyramidal temple in a green quadrangle of the forest, with a walled foss and bridges. Long lost and hidden in the jungle, it was accidentally discovered by the Dutch resident Hartman in 1835, and a space cleared about it. The natives had never known of or suspected its existence, but the investigators determined that this gem of Hindu art was erected between 750 and 800 A. D. The workmanship proves a continued progress in the arts employed at Boro Boedor, and the sculptures show that the popular faith was then passing through Jainism back to Brahmanism. The body of the temple is forty-five feet square as it stands on its walled platform, and rises to a height of seventy feet. A terrace, or raised processional path, around the temple walls is faced with bas-reliefs and ornamental stones, and great bas-reliefs decorate the upper walls. The square interior chapel is entered through a stepped arch or door, and the finest of the Mendoet bas-reliefs, commonly spoken of as the "Tree of Knowledge," is in this entrance-way. There Buddha sits beneath the bo-tree, the trunk of which supports a pajong, or state umbrella, teaching those who approach him and kneel with offerings and incense. These figures, as well as the angels overhead, the birds in the trees, and the lambs on their rocky shelf, listening to the great teacher, are worked out with a grace and skill beyond compare. Three colossal images are seated in the chapel, all with Buddha's attributes, and Brahmanic cords as well, and the long Nepal ears of the Dhyani ones. They are variously explained as the Hindu trinity, as the Buddhist trinity, as Buddha and his disciples, and local legends try to explain them even more romantically. One literary pilgrim describes the central Adi Buddha as the statue of a beautiful young woman "counting her fingers," the mild, benign, and sweetly smiling faces of all three easily suggesting femininity.

One legend tells that this marvel of a temple was built by a rajah who, when once summoned to aid or save the goddess Durga, was followed by two of his wives. To rid himself of them, he tied one wife and nailed the other to a rock. Years afterward he built this temple in expiation, and put their images in it. An avenging rival, who had loved one of the women, at last found the rajah, killed him, turned him to stone, and condemned him to sit forever between his abused partners.

A legend related to Herr Brumund told that "once upon a time" the two-year-old daughter of the great Prince Dewa Kosoumi was stolen by a revengeful courtier. The broken-hearted father wandered all over the country seeking his daughter, but at the end of twelve years met and, forgetting his grief, demanded and married the most beautiful young girl he had ever seen. Soon after a child had been born to them, the revengeful courtier of years before told the prince that his beautiful wife was his own daughter. The priests assured Prince Dewa that no forgiveness was possible to one who had so offended the gods, and that his only course of expiation lay in shutting himself, with the mother and child, in a walled cell, and there ending their days in penitence and prayer. As a last divine favor, he was told that the crime would be forgiven if within ten days he could construct a Boro Boedor. All the artists and workmen of the kingdom were summoned, and working with zeal and frenzy to save their ruler, completed the temple, with its hundreds of statues and its miles of carvings, within the fixed time. But it was then found that the pile was incomplete, lacking just one statue of the full number required. Prayers and appeals were useless, and the gods turned the prince, the mother, and the child to stone, and they sit in the cell at Mendoet as proof of the tale for all time.

With such interests we quite forgot the disagreeable episode in the steaming, provincial town beyond the mountains, and cared not for toelatings-kaart or assistant resident. Nothing from the outer world disturbed the peace of our Nirvana. No solitary horseman bringing reprieve was ever descried from the summit dagoba. No file of soldiers grounded arms and demanded us for Dutch dungeons. Life held every tropic charm, and Boro Boedor constituted an ideal world entirely our own. The sculptured galleries drew us to them at the beginning and end of every stroll, and demanded always another and another look. A thousand Mona Lisas smiled upon us with impassive, mysterious, inscrutable smiles, as they have smiled during all these twelve centuries, and often the realization, the atmosphere of antiquity was overpowering in sensation and weird effect.

Boro Boedor is most mysterious and impressive in the gray of dawn, in the unearthly light and stillness of that eerie hour. Sunrise touches the old walls and statues to something of life; and sunset, when all the palms are silhouetted against skies of tenderest rose, and the warm light flushes the hoary gray pile, is the time when the green valley of Eden about the temple adds all of charm and poetic suggestion. Pitch-darkness so quickly follows the tropic sunset that when we left the upper platform of the temple in the last roselight, we found the lamps lighted, and huge moths and beetles flying in and about the passagrahan's portico. Then lizards "chuck-chucked," and ran over the walls; and the invisible gecko, gasping, called, it seemed to me, "*Becky! Becky! Becky! Becky! Becky! Becky!*" and Rebecca answered never to those breathless, exhausted, appealing cries, always six times repeated, slowly over and over again, by the fatigued soul doomed to a lizard's form in its last incarnation. There was infinite mystery and witchery in the darkness and sounds of the tropic night—sudden calls of birds, and always the stiff rustling, rustling of the cocoa-palms, and the softer sounds of other trees, the shadows of which made inky blackness about the passagrahan; while out over the temple the open sky, full of huge, yellow, steadily glowing stars, shed radiance sufficient for one to distinguish the mass and lines of the great pyramid. Villagers came silently from out the darkness, stood motionless beside the grim stone images, and advanced slowly into the circle of light before the portico. They knelt with many homages, and laid out the cakes of palm-sugar, the baskets and sarongs, we had bought at their toy village. Others brought frangipani blossoms that they heaped in mounds at our feet. They sat on their heels, and with muttered whispers watched us as we dined and went about our affairs on the raised platform of the portico, presenting to them a living drama of foreign life on that regularly built stage without footlights. One of the audience pierced a fresh cocoanut, drank the milk, and then rolling kanari and benzoin gum in corn-fiber, lighted the fragrant cigarette, and puffed the smoke into the cocoa-shell. "It is good for the stomach, and will keep off fever," they answered, when we asked about this incantation-like proceeding; and all took a turn at puffing into the shell and reinhaling the incense-clouds. The gentle little Javanese who provided better dinners for passagrahan guests than any island hotel had offered us, came into the circle of light, with her mite of a brown baby sleeping in the slandang knotted across her shoulder. The old landlord could be heard as he came back far enough from his Nirvana to call for the boy to light a fresh pipe; and one felt a little of the gaze and presence of all the Dhyani Buddhas on the sculptured terraces in the strange atmosphere of such far-away tropic nights by the Boedor of Boro.

WHEN we came "gree-ing" back by those beautiful roads to Djokja, and drew up with a whirl at the portico of the Hotel Toegoe, the landlord of beaming countenance ran to meet us, greet us with effusion, and give us a handful of mail—long, official envelops with seals, and square envelops of social usage.

"Your passports are here. They came the next day. They are so chagrined that it was all a stupid mistake. The assistant resident at Buitenzorg telegraphed to the resident here to tell the three American ladies who were to arrive in Djokja that he had posted their passports, and to have every attention paid you. He wished to commend you and put you *en rapport* with the Djokja officials, that you might enjoy their courtesies. Then the telegraph operator changed the message so as not to have to send so many words on the wire, and he made them all think you were some very dangerous people whom they must arrest and send back. The assistant resident knew there was some mistake as soon as he saw you." (Did he?) "He is so chagrined. And it was all the telegraph operator's fault, and you must not blame our Djokja Residency."

Instead of mollifying, this rather irritated us the more, and the assistant resident's long, formal note was fuel to the flame.

"Ladies: This morning I telegraphed to the secretary-general what in heaven's name could be the reason you were not to go to Djokja. I got no answer from him, but received a letter from the chief of the telegraph, who had received a telegram from the telegraph office of Buitenzorg, to tell me there had been a mistake in the telegram. Instead of 'The permission is not given,' there should have been written, 'The papers of permission I have myself this moment posted. Do all you can in the matter,' etc. Perhaps you will have received them the moment you get this my letter.

"So I am so happy I did not insist upon your returning to Buitenzorg, and so sorry you had so long stay at Boro Boedor; and I hope you will forget the fatal mistake, and feel yourself at ease now," etc.

Evidently the little episode was confined to the

bureau of telegraphs entirely, the messages to the American consul, secretary-general, and Buitenzorg resident all suppressed before reaching them. Certainly this was no argument for the government ownership and control of telegraphs in the United States. There were regrets and social consolations offered, but no distinct apology; and we were quite in the mood for having the American consul demand apology, reparation, and indemnity, on pain of bombardment, as is the foreign custom in all Asia. Pacification by small courtesies did not pacify. Proffered presentation to native princes, visits to their bizarre palaces, and attendance at a great performance by the sultan's actors, dancers, musicians, and swordsmen, would hardly offset being arrested, brought up in an informal police-court, cross-questioned, bullied, and regularly ordered to Boro Boedor under parole. We would not remain tacitly to accept the olive-branch—not then. The profuse landlord was nonplussed that we did not humbly and gratefully accept these amenities.

"You will not go back to Buitenzorg now, with only such unhappy experience of Djokja! Every one is so chagrined, so anxious that you should forget the little contretemps. Surely you will stay now for the great *topeng* [lyric drama], and the wedding of Pakoe Alam's daughter!"

"No; we have our toelatings-kaarten, and we leave on the noon train."

And then the landlord knew that we should have been locked up for other reasons, since sane folk are never in a hurry under the equator. They consider the thermometer, treat the zenith sun with respect, and do not trifle with the tropics.

XVII

BRAMBANAM

"In the whole course of my life I have never met with such stupendous and finished specimens of human labor and of the science and taste of ages long since forgot, crowded together in so small a compass, as in this little spot [Brambanam], which, to use a military phrase, I deem to have been the headquarters of Hinduism in Java." (Report to Sir Stamford Raffles by Captain George Baker of the Bengal establishment.)

THERE are ruins of more than one hundred and fifty temples in the historic region lying between Djokjakarta and Soerakarta, or Djokja and Solo, as common usage abbreviates those syllables of unnecessary exertion in this steaming, endless midsummer land of Middle Java. As the train races on the twenty miles from Djokja to Brambanam, there is a tantalizing glimpse of the ruined temples at Kalasan; and one small temple there, the Chandi Kali Bening, ranks as the gem of Hindu art in Java. It is entirely covered, inside as well as outside, with bas-reliefs and ornamental carvings which surpass in elaboration and artistic merit everything else in this region, where re-

TEMPLE OF LORO JONGGRAN AT BRAMBANAM.

fined ornament and lavish decoration reached their limit at the hands of the early Hindu sculptors. The Sepoy soldiers who came with the British engineers were lost in wonder at Kalasan, where the remains of Hindu art so far surpassed anything they knew in India itself; while the extent and magnificence of Brambanam's Brahmanic and Buddhist temple ruins amaze every visitor—even after Boro Boedor.

We had intended to drive from Boro Boedor across country to Brambanam, but, affairs of state obliging us to return from our Nirvana directly to Djokja, we fell back upon the railroad's promised convenience. In this guide-bookless land, where every white resident knows every crook and turn in Amsterdam's streets, and next to nothing about the island of Java, a kind dispenser of misinformation had told us that the railway-station of Brambanam was close beside the temple ruins; and we had believed him. The railway had been completed and formally opened but a few days before our visit, and our Malay servant was also quite sure that the road ran past the temples, and that the station was at their very gates.

When the train had shrieked away from the lone little station building, we learned that the ruins were a mile distant, with no sort of a vehicle nor an animal nor a palanquin to be had; and archæological zeal suffered a chill even in that tropic noonday. The station-master was all courtesy and sympathy; but the choice for us lay between walking or waiting at the station four hours for the next train on to Solo.

We strolled very slowly along the broad, open country road under the deadly, direct rays of the midday sun,—at the time when, as the Hindus say, "only Englishmen and dogs are abroad,"—reaching at last a pretty village and the grateful shade of tall kanari-trees, where the people were lounging at ease at the close of the morning's busy passer. Every house, shed, and stall had made use of carved temple stones for its foundations, and the road was lined with more such recha—artistic remains from the inexhaustible storehouse and quarry of the neighboring ruins. Piles of tempting fruit remained for sale, and brown babies sprawled content on the warm lap of earth, the tiniest ones eating the green edge of watermelon-rind with avidity, and tender mothers cramming cold sweet potato into the mouths of infants two and four months old. There was such an easy, enviable tropical calm of abundant living and leisure in that Lilliput village under Brobdingnag trees that I longed to fling away my "Fergusson," let slip life's one golden, glowing, scorching opportunity to be informed on ninth-century Brahmanic temples, and, putting off all starched and unnecessary garments of white civilization, join that lifelong, happy-go-lucky, care-free picnic party under the kanari-trees of Brambanam; but—

A turn in the road, a break in the jungle at one side of the highway, disclosed three pyramidal temples in a vast square court, with the ruins of three corresponding temples, all fallen to rubbish-heaps, ranged in line facing them. These ruined piles alone remain of the group of twenty temples dedicated to Loro Jonggran, "the pure, exalted virgin" of the Javanese, worshiped in India as Deva, Durga, Kali, or Parvati. Even the three temples that are best preserved have crumbled

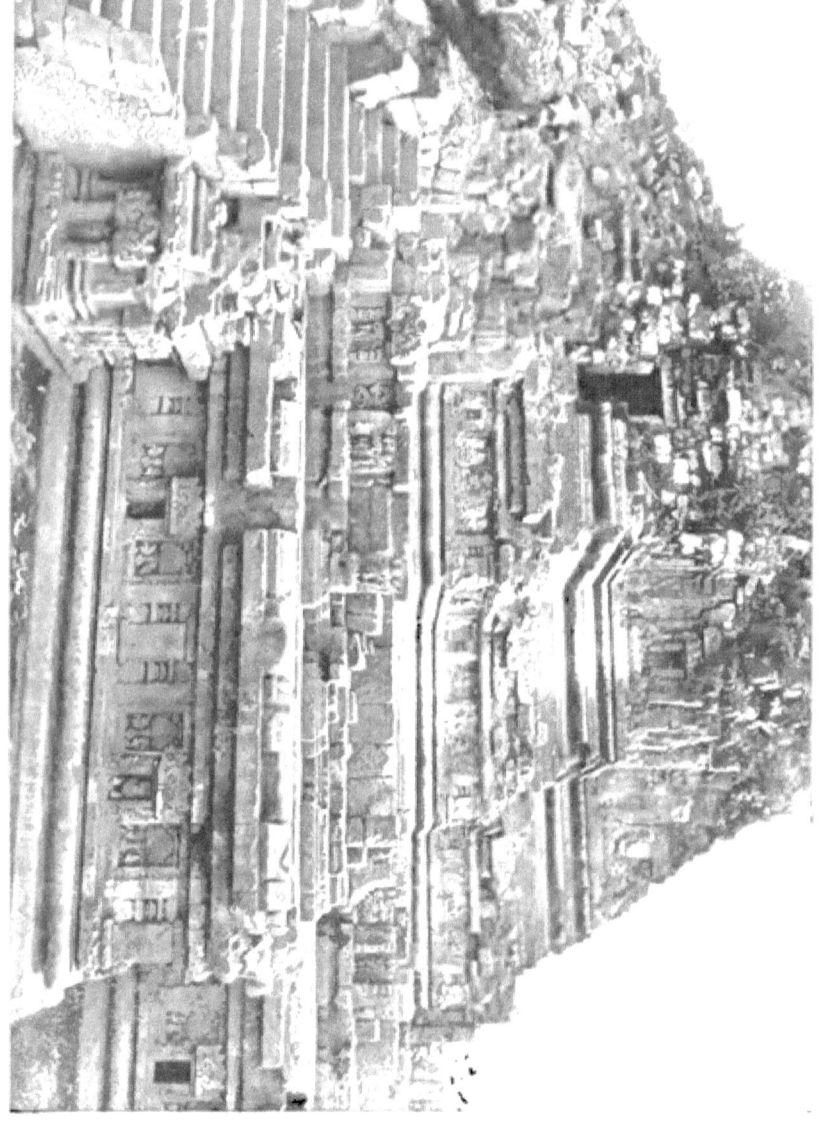

CLEARING AWAY RUBBISH AND VEGETATION AT BRAMBANAM TEMPLES

at their summits and lost their angles; but enough remains for the eye to reconstruct the symmetrical piles and carry out the once perfect lines. The structures rise in terraces and broad courses, tapering like the Dravidian gopuras of southern India, and covered, like them, with images, bas-reliefs, and ornamental carvings. Grand staircases ascend from each of the four sides to square chapels or alcoves half-way up in the solid body of the pyramid, and each chapel once contained an image. The main or central temple now remaining still enshrines in its west or farther chamber an image of Ganesha, the hideous elephant-headed son of Siva and Parvati. Broken images of Siva and Parvati were found in the south and north chambers, and Brahma is supposed to have been enshrined in the great east chapel. An adjoining temple holds an exquisite statue of Loro Jonggran, "the maiden with the beautiful hips," who stands, graceful and serene, in a roofless chamber, smiling down like a true goddess upon those who toil up the long carved staircase of approach. Her particular temple is adorned with bas-reliefs, where the *gopis*, or houris, who accompany Krishna, the dancing youth, are grouped in graceful poses. One of these bas-reliefs, commonly known as the "Three Graces" has great fame, and one and two thousand gulden have been vainly offered by British travelers anxious to transport it to London. Another temple contains an image of Nandi, the sacred bull; but the other shrines have fallen in shapeless ruins, and nothing of their altar-images is to be gathered from the rubbish-heaps that cover the vast temple court.

The pity of all this ruined splendor moves one strongly, and one deplores the impossibility of reconstructing, even on paper, the whole magnificent place of worship. The wealth of ornament makes all other temple buildings seem plain and featureless, and one set of bas-reliefs just rescued and set up in line, depicting scenes from the Ramayan, would be treasure enough for an art museum. On this long series of carved stones disconsolate Rama is shown searching everywhere for Sita, his stolen wife, until the king of the monkeys, espousing his cause, leads him to success. The story is wonderfully told in stone, the chisel as eloquent as the pen, and everywhere one reads as plainly the sacred tales and ancient records. The graceful figures and their draperies tell of Greek influences acting upon those northern Hindus who brought the religion to the island; and the beautifully conventionalized trees and fruits and flowers, the mythical animals and gaping monsters along the staircases, the masks, arabesques, bands, scrolls, ornamental keystones, and all the elaborate symbols and attributes of deities lavished on this group of temples, constitute a whole gallery of Hindu art, and a complete grammar of its ornament.

These temples, it is believed, were erected at the beginning of the ninth century, and fixed dates in the eleventh century are also claimed; but at least they were built soon after the completion of Boro Boedor, when the people were turning back to Brahmanism, and Hindu arts had reached their richest development at this great capital of Mendang Kumulan, since called Brambanam. The fame of the Javanese empire had

KRISHNA AND THE THREE GRACES

then gone abroad, and greed for its riches led Khublai
Khan to despatch an armada to its shores; but his
Chinese commander, Mengki, returned without ships
or men, his face branded like a thief's. Another expedition was defeated, with a loss of three thousand
men, and the Great Khan's death put an end to further
schemes of conquest. Marco Polo, windbound for
five months on Sumatra, then Odoric, and the Arab
Ibn Batuta, who visited Java in the fourteenth century, continued to celebrate the riches and splendor of
this empire, and invite its conquest, until Arab priests
and traders began its overthrow. Its princes were
conquered, its splendid capitals destroyed, and with
the conversion of the people to Mohammedanism the
shrines were deserted, soon overgrown, and became
hillocks of vegetation. The waringen-tree's fibrous
roots, penetrating the crevices of stones that were
only fitted together, and not cemented, have done most
damage, and the shrines of Loro Jonggran went fast
to utter ruin.

A Dutch engineer, seeking to build a fort in the disturbed country between the two native capitals, first
reported these Brambanam temples in 1797; but it
was left for Sir Stamford Raffles to have them excavated, surveyed, sketched, and reported upon. Then
for eighty years—until the year of our visit—they had
again been forgotten, and the jungle claimed and covered the beautiful monuments. The Archæological
Society of Djokja had just begun the work of clearing
off and rescuing the wonderful carvings, and groups
of coolies were resting in the shade, while others pottered around, setting bas-reliefs in regular lines around

the rubbish-heaps they had been taken from. This salvage corps chattered and watched us with well-contained interest, as we, literally at the very boiling-point of enthusiasm, at three o'clock of an equatorial afternoon, toiled up the magnificent staircases, peered into each shrine, made the rounds of the sculptured terraces, or processional paths, and explored the whole splendid trio of temples, without pause.

Herr Perk, the director of the works, and curator of this monumental museum, roused by the rumors of foreign invasion, welcomed us to the grateful shade of his temporary quarters beside the temple, and hospitably shared his afternoon tea and bananas with us, there surrounded by a small museum of the finest and most delicately carved fragments, that could not safely be left unprotected. While we cooled, and rested from the long walk and the eager scramble over the ruins, we enjoyed too the series of Cephas's photographs made for the Djokja Society, and in them had evidence how the insidious roots of the graceful waringen-trees had split and scattered the fitted stones as thoroughly as an earthquake; yet each waringen-gripped ruin, the clustered roots streaming, as if once liquid, over angles and carvings, was so picturesque that we half regretted the entire uprooting of these lovely trees.

When the director was called away to his workmen, we bade our guiding Mohammedan lead the way to Chandi Sewou, the "Thousand Temples," or great Buddhist shrine of the ancient capital. "Oh," he cried, "it is far, far from here — an hour to walk. You must go to Chandi Sewou in a boat. The water is

LORO JONGGRAN AND HER ATTENDANTS.

up to here," touching his waist, "and there are many, many snakes." Distrusting, we made him lead on in the direction of Chandi Sewou; perhaps we might get at least a distant view. When we had walked the length of a city block down a shady road, with carved fragments and overgrown stones scattered along the way and through the young jungle at one side, we turned a corner, walked another block, and stood between the giant images that guard the entrance of Chandi Sewou's great quadrangle.

The "Thousand Temples" were really but two hundred and thirty-six temples, built in five quadrilateral lines around a central cruciform temple, the whole walled inclosure measuring five hundred feet either way. Many of these lesser shrines—mere confessional boxes in size—are now ruined or sunk entirely in the level turf that covers the whole quadrangle, and others are picturesque, vine-wreathed masses, looking most like the standing chimneys of a burnt house. This Buddhist sanctuary of the eleventh century has almost the same general plan as Boro Boedor, but a Boro Boedor spread out and built all on the one level. The five lines of temples, with broad processional paths between them, correspond to the five square terraces of Boro Boedor; and the six superior chapels correspond to the circles of latticed dagobas near Boro Boedor's summit. The empty central shrine at Chandi Sewou has crumbled to a heap of stones, with only its four stepped-arch entrance-doors distinct; and the smaller temples, each of them eleven feet square and eighteen feet high, with inner walls covered with bas-reliefs, are empty as well. When the British officers surveyed Chandi Sewon, five of the chapels contained cross-legged images seated on lotus pedestals—either Buddha, or the *tirthankars*, or Jain saints; but even those headless and mutilated statues are missing now. Every evidence could be had of wilful destruction of the group of shrines, and the same mysterious well-hole was found beneath the pedestal of the image in each chapel— whether as receptacle for the ashes of priests and princes; a place for the safe keeping of temple treasures; as an empty survival of the form of the earliest tree-temples, when the mystery of animate nature commanded man's worship; or, as M. de Charnay suggests, the orifice from which proceeded the voice of the concealed priest who served as oracle.

With these Brambanam temples, when Sivaism or Jainism had succeeded Buddhism, and even before Mohammedanism came, the decadence of arts and letters began. The Arab conquest made it complete, and the art of architecture died entirely, no structures since that time redeeming the people and religion which in India and Spain have left such monuments of beauty.

The ruins of the "Thousand Temples" are more lonely and deserted in their grassy, weed-grown quadrangle, more forlorn in their abandonment, than any other of the splendid relics of Java's past religions. The glorious company of saintly images are vanished past tracing, and the rows of little sentry-box chapels give a different impression from the soaring pyramids of solid stone, with their hundreds of statues and figures and the wealth of sculptured ornament, found elsewhere. The vast level of the plain around it is a lake or swamp in

the rainy season, and the damp little chapels, with
their rubbish-heaps in dark corners and the weed-
grown well-hole, furnish ideal homes for snakes. As
our Mohammedan had suggested snakes, we imagined
them everywhere, stepping carefully, throwing stones

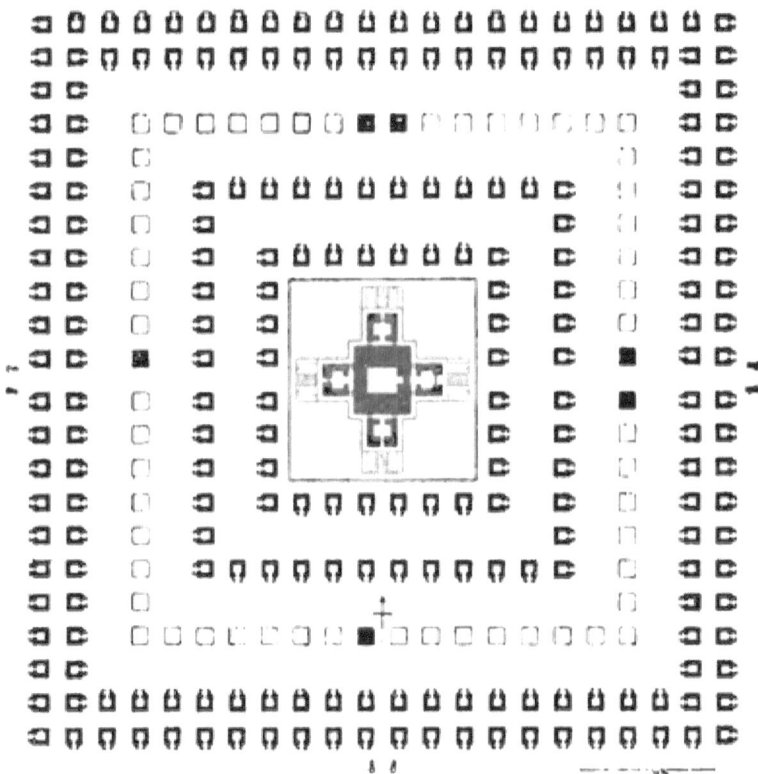

PLAN OF CHANDI SEWOU ("THOUSAND TEMPLES").
From Sir Stamford Raffles's "History of Java."

ahead of us, and thrusting our umbrellas noisily into
each chapel before we ventured within; but the long-
anticipated, always expected great snake did not ma-
terialize to give appropriate incident to a visit to such
complete ruins. Only one small wisp of a lizard gave

the least starting-point for a really thrilling traveler's tale. The only other moving object in sight at Chandi Sewou was a little girl, with a smaller sister astride of her hip, who followed us timidly and sat for a time resting on the knee of one of the hideous gate guardians—one of the Gog and Magog stone monsters, who, although kneeling, is seven feet in height, and who, with a club in his right hand, a snake wound around his left arm, and a ferocious countenance, should frighten any child into spasms rather than invite familiarity.

Herr Perk pointed out to us, on the common between the two great temples, a formless green mound which he would excavate the following week, and showed us also the Chandi Lompang, a temple cleared off eighty years ago, but covered with a tangle of underbrush and a few tall trees—a sufficient illustration of what all the Loro Jonggran temples had been when the Djokja Society began its work of rescue and preservation. The British engineers could see in 1812 that Chandi Lompang had been a central shrine surrounded by fourteen smaller temples, whose carved stones have long been scattered to fence fields and furnish foundation-stones for the neighborhood. It was hoped that the kind mantle of vegetation had preserved a series of bas-reliefs of Krishna and the lovely gopis, wrought with an art equal to that employed by the sculptors of the "Three Graces" at Loro Jonggran which the British surveyors uncovered. Every one must rejoice that a period of enlightenment has at last come to the colony, and that steps are being taken to care for the antiquities of the island.

FRAGMENT FROM LORO JONGGRAN TEMPLE.

There are other regions of extensive temple ruins in Java, but none where the remains of the earlier civilization are so well preserved, the buildings of such extent and magnificence, their cults and their records so well known, as at Boro Boedor and Brambanam. The extensive ruins of the Singa Sari temples, four miles from Malang, near the southeastern end of the island, are scattered all through a teak and waringen forest, half sunk and overgrown with centuries of vegetation. Images of Ganesha, and a colossal Nandi, or sacred bull of Siva, with other Brahmanic deities, remain in sight; and inscriptions found there prove that the Singa Sari temples were built at about the same time as the Loro Jonggran temples at Brambanam. The mutilation and signs of wanton destruction of the recha suggest that it was not a peaceful conversion from Brahmanism to Mohammedanism in that kingdom either.

On the Dieng plateau, southwest of Samarang, and not far from Boro Boedor, there are ruins of more than four hundred temples, and the traces of a city greater than any now existing on the island. This region has received comparatively little attention from archæologists, although it has yielded rich treasures in gold, silver, and bronze objects, a tithe of which are preserved in the museum of the Batavian Society. For years the Dieng villagers paid their taxes in rough ingots of gold melted from statuettes and ornaments found on the old temple sites, and more than three thousand florins a year were sometimes paid in such bullion. The Goenoeng Praoe, a mountain whose summit-lines resemble an inverted praoe, or boat, is the fabled home of the gods; and the whole sacred height was once built over with temples, staircases of a thousand steps, great terraces, and embankment walls, now nearly lost in vegetation, and wrecked by the earthquakes of that very active volcanic region. These Dieng temples appear to have been solid structures, whose general form and ornamentation so resemble the ruins in Yucatan and the other states of Central America that archæologists still revolve the puzzle of them, and hazard no conjectures as to the worshipers and their form of worship, save that the rites or sacrifices were very evidently conducted on the open summits or temple-tops. I could not obtain views of these ruined pyramid temples from any of the Batavia photographers, to satisfy me as to their exact lines even in decay. There are other old Siva temples in that region furtively worshiped still, and the "Valley of Death," where the fabled upas grew, was long believed to exist in that region, where the cult of the destroyer was observed.

M. de Charnay did not visit these pyramid temples of the Dieng plateau; but after seeing the temple of Boro Boedor, and those at Brambanam, he summed up the resemblances of the Buddhist and Brahmanic temples of Java to those at Palenque and in Yucatan as consisting: in the same order of gross idols; the pyramid form of temple, with staircases, like those of Palenque and Yucatan; the small chapels or oratories, with subterranean vaults beneath the idols; the same interior construction of temples; the stepped arches; the details of ornamentation, terraces, and esplanades,

GANESHA, THE ELEPHANT-HEADED GOD.

as in Mexico and Yucatan; and the localization of temples in religious centers far from cities, forming places of pilgrimage, as at Palenque, Chichen-Itza, and, in a later time, at Cozumel.[1]

---

[1] Vide "Six Semaines à Java," par Désiré de Charnay ("Le Tour du Monde," volume for 1880).

XVIII

SOLO: THE CITY OF THE SUSUNHAN

AS the two native states of Middle Java, the *Vorstenlanden*, or "Lands of the Princes," were last to be brought under Dutch rule, Djokjakarta and Soerakarta are the capitals and head centers of native supremacy, where most of Javanese life remains unchanged. The Sultan of Djokja, and the so-called emperor, or *susunhan*, of Solo, were last to yield to oversea usurpers, and, as tributary princes enjoying a "protected and controlled independence," accept an "advisory elder brother," in the person of a Dutch resident, to sit at their sovereign elbows and by "suggestions" rule their territories for the greater good of the natives and the Holland exchequer. All the region around Djokja and Solo is classic ground, and the oldest Javanese myths and legends, the earliest traditions of native life, have their locale hereabout. These people are the Javanese, and show plainly their Hindu descent and their higher civilization, which distinguish them from the Sundanese of West Java; yet the Sundanese call themselves the "sons of the soil," and the

Javanese "the stranger people." The glories of the Hindu empire are declared by the magnificent ruins so lately uncovered, but the splendor of the Mohammedan empire barely survives in name in the strangely interesting city of the susunhan set in the midst of the plain of Solo—a plain which M. Désiré de Charnay described as "a paradise which nothing on earth can equal, and neither pen, brush, nor photography can faithfully reproduce."

At this Solo, second city of the island in size, one truly reaches the heart of native Java—the Java of the Javanese—more nearly than elsewhere; but Islam's old empire is there narrowed down to a kraton, or palace inclosure, a mile square, where the present susunhan, or object of adoration, lives as a restrained pensioner of the Dutch government, the mere shadow of those splendid potentates, his ancestors.

The old susunhans were descended from the Moormen or Arab pirates who harried the coast for a century before they destroyed the splendid Hindu capital of Majapahit, near the modern Soerabaya. They followed that act of vandalism with the conquest of Pajajaran, the western empire, or Sundanese end of the island; and religious conversion always went with conquest by the followers of the prophet. There was perpetual domestic war in the Mohammedan empire, which by no means held the unresisting allegiance of the Javanese at any time, and the Hindu princes of Middle Java were never really conquered by them or the Dutch. The Java war of the last century between the Mohammedan emperor, the Dutch, and the rebellious native prince, Manko Boeni, lasted for thirteen years; and in this century the same sort of a revolt cost the Dutch as imperial allies more than four millions of florins, and made the British rejoice that their statesmen had wisely handed back such a troublesome and expensive possession as Java proved to be. The great Mataram war of the last century, however, established the family of the present susunhan on the throne, after dividing his empire with a rebellious younger brother, who then became Sultan of Djokjakarta, and a new capital was built on the broad plain cut by the Bengawan or Solo River, which is the largest river of the island. At the death of the susunhan, Pakoe Bewono II ("Nail of the Universe"), in 1749, his will bequeathed his empire to the Dutch East India Company, and at last gave Holland control of the whole island. Certain lands were retained for the imperial family, and its present head, merely nominal, figurehead susunhan that he is, receives an annuity of one hundred thousand florins—a sum equal to the salary of the governor-general of Netherlands India.

The present susunhan of Solo is not the son of the last emperor, but a collateral descendant of the old emperors, who claims descent from both Mohammedan and Hindu rulers, the monkey flag of Arjuna and the double-bladed sword of the Arab conquerors alike his heirlooms and insignia. His portraits show a gentle, refined face of the best Javanese type, and he wears a European military coat, with the native sarong and Arab fez, a court sword at the front of his belt, and a Solo kris at the back. Despite his trappings and his sovereign title, he is as much a puppet and a prisoner as any of the lesser princes, sultans, and regents

THE SUSUHAN

whom the Dutch, having deposed and pensioned, allow to masquerade in sham authority. He maintains all the state and splendor of the old imperialism within his kraton, which is confronted and overlooked by a Dutch fort, whose guns, always trained upon the kraton, could sweep and level the whole imperial establishment at a moment's notice. The susunhan may have ten thousand people living within his kraton walls; he may have nine hundred and ninety-nine wives and one hundred and fifty carriages, as reported; but he may not drive beyond his own gates without informing the Dutch resident where he is going or has been, with his guard of honor of Dutch soldiers, and he has hardly the liberty of a tourist with a toelatings-kaart. He may amuse himself with a little body-guard of Javanese soldiers; but there is a petty sultan of Solo, an ancient vassal, whose military ambitions are encouraged by the Dutch to the extent of allowing him to drill and command a private army of a thousand men that the Dutch believe would never by any chance take arms against them, as allies of the susunhan's fancy guard. Wherever they have allowed any empty show of sovereignty to a native ruler, the Dutch have taken care to equip a military rival, with the lasting grudge of an inherited family feud, and establish him in the same town. But little diplomacy is required to keep such jealousies alive and aflame, and the Dutch are always an apparent check, and pacific mediators between such rivals as the susunhan and the sultan at Solo, and the sultan and Prince Pakoe Alam at Djokja.

The young susunhan maintains his empty **honors**

with great dignity and serenity, observing all the European forms and etiquette at his entertainments, and delighting Solo's august society with frequent court balls and fêtes. Town gossip dilates on his marble-floored ball-room, the fantastic devices in electric lights employed in illuminating the palace and its maze of gardens on such occasions, and on the blaze of heirloom jewels worn by the imperial ladies and princesses at such functions. The susunhan sometimes grants audiences to distinguished strangers, and one French visitor has told of some magnificent Japanese bronzes and Chinese porcelains in the kraton, which were gifts from the Dutch in the early time when the Japanese and Javanese trade were both Holland monopolies. No prostrations or Oriental salaams are required of European visitors at court, although the old susunhans obliged even the crown prince and prime minister to assume the dodok, and sidle about like any cup-bearer in his presence. The princes and petty chiefs were so precisely graded in rank in those days that, while the highest might kiss the sovereign's hand, and those of a lower rank the imperial knee, there were those of lesser pretensions who adoringly kissed the instep, and, last of all, those who might only presume to kiss the sole, of the susunhan's foot. The susunhan is always accompanied on his walks in the palace grounds, and on drives abroad, by a bearer with a gold pajong, or state umbrella, spreading from a jeweled golden staff. The array of pajongs carried behind the members of his family and court officials present all the colors of the rainbow, and all the variegations a fancy umbrella is capable of showing—each striped, banded, bordered, and vandyked in a different way, that would puzzle the brain of any but a Solo courtier, to whom they speak as plainly as a door-plate.

Solo has the same broad streets and magnificent shade-trees as the other towns of Java, and some of the streets have deep ditches or moats on either side of the drive, with separate little bridges crossing to each house-front, which give those thoroughfares a certain feudal quaintness and character of their own. At the late afternoon hour of our arrival we only stopped for a moment to deposit the luggage at the enormously porticoed Hotel Sleier, and then drove on through and about the imperial city. The streets were full of other carriages,—enormous barouches, "milords," and family carryalls, drawn by big Walers,— with which we finally drew up in line around the park, where a military band was playing. We had seen bewildering lines of palace and fort and barrack walls, marching troops, and soldiers lounging about off duty, until it was easy to see that Solo was a vast garrison, more camp than court. Later, when we had returned to the hotel portico, to swing at ease in great broad-armed rocking-chairs,—exactly the Shaker piazza-chairs of American summer life,—there was still sound of military music off beyond the dense waringen shade, and the fanfare of bugles to right and to left.

Solo's hotel, with its comforts, offered more material inducements for us to make a long stay, than any hotel we had yet encountered in Java; and the clear-headed, courteous landlady was a hostess in the most kindly sense. The usual colonial table d'hôte assembled at nine o'clock in the vast inner hall or pavilion, looking on a garden; and in this small world, where every one knows every one, his habitat and all his affairs, the new-comers were given a silent, earnest attention that would have checked any appetites save those engendered by our archæological afternoon at Brambanam. When beefsteak was served with a sauce of pineapple mashed with potato, and the succeeding beet salad was followed by fried fish, and that by a sweet pudding flooded with a mixture of melted chocolate and freshly ground cocoanut, we were oblivious to all stares and whispers and open comments in Dutch, which these colonials take it for granted no alien understands or can even have clue to through its likeness to German. While we rocked on the great white portico we could see and hear that Solo's lizards were as gruesome and plentiful as those of other towns. While tiny fragilities flashed across white columns and walls, and arrested themselves as instantaneous traceries and ornaments, a legion of toads came up from the garden, and hopped over the floor in a silence that made us realize how much pleasanter companions were the croaking and bemoaning geckos, who keep their ugliness out of sight.

At sunrise we set out in the company of an American temporarily in exile at Solo, and drove past the resident's great garden of palms and statues and flower-beds, into the outer courts of the emperor's and the sultan's palaces, watching in the latter the guard-mount and drill of a fine picked body of his troops. The palace of one of the younger princes of the imperial house was accessible through kind favor, as the owner is pleased to let uitlanders enjoy the many for-

THE DODOK.

eign features of these pleasure-grounds. This foreign garden did not, however, make us really homesick by any appealing similarity to the grounds of citizens or presidents on the American side of the globe; for the progressive prince has arranged his demesne quite after the style of the gardens of the cafés chantants of the lower Élysée in Paris—colored-glass globes and all, marble-rimmed flower-beds, and a cascade to be turned on at will and let flow down over a marble staircase set with colored electric bulbs. Colored globes and bulbs hang in festoons and arches about the bizarre garden, simulate fruits and flowers on the trees and bushes, glow in dark pools and fountain basins, and play every old fantastic trick of al-fresco cafés in Europe. A good collection of rare beasts and birds is disposed in cages in the grounds, and there are countless kiosks and pavilions inviting one to rest. In one such summer-house, with stained-glass walls, the attendants showed photographs of the prince, his father and family, the solemn old faces and the costumes of these elders almost the only purely Javanese things to be seen in this fantastic garden, since even the recha, gray old images from Boro Boedor and Brambanam, have been brightened with red, white, and blue paint and made to look cheerful and decorative—have been restored, improved, brought down to modern times, and made to accord better with their café-chantant surroundings.

Quite unexpectedly, we saw the princely personage himself receive his early cup of coffee—attracted first to the ceremony by noticing a man carrying a gold salver and cup, and followed by an umbrella-bearer and two other attendants, enter an angle of the court in whose shady arcade we were for the moment resting. Suddenly all four men dropped to their heels in the dodok, and, crouching, sidled and hopped along for a hundred feet to the steps of a pavilion. The cup-bearer insinuated himself up those four steps, still squatting on his heels, and at the same time balancing his burden on his two extended hands, and proffered the gold salver to a shadowy figure half reclining in a long chair. We stood motionless, unseen in our dark arcade, and watched this precious bit of court comedy through, and saw the cup-bearer retire backward down the steps, across the court, to the spot where he might rise from his ignoble attitude and walk like a human being again. While exacting this much of the old etiquette, this prince of European education and tastes has the finest ball-room in Solo—a vast white-marble-floored *pringitan*, or open-sided audience-hall, which is lighted with hundreds of electric lights, and on whose shining surface great cotillions are danced, and rich favors distributed to companies blazing with diamonds.

XIX

THE LAND OF KRIS AND SARONG

THE stir of camp and court, the state and pomp and pageantry of three such grandees as emperor, sultan, and resident in the one city, made such street-scenes in Solo as tempted the kodaker to constant play while the sun was high. Bands and marching troops were always to be seen in the street, and the native officials of so many different kinds made pictures of bewildering variety. The resident, returning from an official call, dashed past in a coach and four, with pajong-bearers hanging perilously on behind, and a mounted escort clattering after. Members of the imperial household staff were distinguished by stiff sugar-loaf caps or fezzes of white leather; and such privileged ones stalked along slowly, magnificently, each with a kris at the back of his belt, and always followed by one or two lesser minions. Those of superior rank went accompanied by a pajong-bearer balancing the great flat umbrella of rank above the distinguished one's head; and the precision with which the grandee kept his head within the halo of shadow, or the bearer managed to keep such a true angle on the sun, were something admirable, and only to be accomplished by generations of the two classes practising their respective feats. The emperor's mounted troops were objects of greater interest, these dragoons wearing huge lacquered vizors or crownless caps over their turbaned heads, the regulation jackets, sarongs, and heavy krises, and bestriding fiery little Timor ponies. The native stirrup is a single upright bar of iron, which a rider holds between the great toe and its neighbor; and these troopers seemed to derive as much support from this firm toe-grip as booted riders do from resting the whole ball of the foot on our stirrups.

There is a labyrinthine passer at Solo, where open sheds and rustic booths have grown upon one another around several open court spaces, which are dotted with the huge mushrooms of palm-leaf umbrellas, and whose picturesqueness one cannot nearly exhaust in a single morning's round. The pepper- and fruit- and flower-markets are, of course, the regions of greatest attraction and richest feasts of color. The horn of plenty overflowed royally there, and the masses of bananas and pineapples, durians, nankos, mangosteens, jamboas, salaks, dukus, and rambutans seemed richer in color than we had ever seen before; and the brass-, the basket-, the bird-, the spice-, and the gum-markets had greater attractions too. The buyers were as interesting as the venders, and a frequent figure in these market groups that tempted the kodaker to many an instantaneous shot, regardless of the light,—better any muddy impression of that than none at all,—was the Dutch housewife on her morning rounds. I braved

JAVA, BALI, AND MADURA KRISES.
From Sir Stamford Raffles's "History of Java."

sunstroke and apoplexy in the hot sunshine, and trailed my saronged subjects down crowded aisles to open spots, to fix on film the image of these sockless matrons in their very informal morning dress. I lurked in booths and sat for endless minutes in opposite shops, with focus set and button at touch, to get a good study of Dutch ankles, when certain typical Solo *hausfraus* should return to and mount their carriage steps—only to have some loiterer's back obscure the whole range of the lens at the critical second.

We found pawnshops galore in this city full of courtiers and hangers-on of greatness, and such array of krises and curious weapons that there was embarrassment of choice. We left the superior shops of dealers in arms, where new blades, fresh from Sheffield or German works, were pressed upon us, and betook ourselves to the junk-shops and pawnshops, where aggregations of discarded finery and martial trappings were spread out. Books, silver, crystal, cutlery, jeweled decorations, medals, epaulets, swords, and krises in every stage of rust and dilapidation were found for sale.

The kris is distinctively the Malay weapon, and is a key to much of Malay custom and lore; and if the Japanese sword was "the soul of the Samurai," as much may be said for the kris of the Javanese warrior. The cutler or forger of kris-blades ranked first of all artisans. There are more than one hundred varieties of the kris known, the distinctive Javanese types of kris differing from those of the Malay Peninsula and the other islands, and forty varieties of kris being used in Java and its immediate dependencies. The kris used in Bali differs from that of Madura or Lombok, and that of Solo from that used in West or Sundanese Java. These differences imply many curiously fine distinctions of long-standing importance in etiquette and tradition; yet the kris is a comparatively modern weapon—modern as such things go in Asia. No kris is carved on Boro Boedor or Brambanam walls, and its use cannot be traced further back than the thirteenth century, despite the legends of mythical Panji, who, it is claimed, devised the deadly crooked blade and brought it with him from India. When it was introduced from the peninsula it was instantly adopted, and all people wearing the kris were counted by that badge as subjects of Java. The kris is worn by all Javanese above the peasant class and over fourteen years of age, and is a badge of rank and station which the wearer never puts aside in his waking hours. Great princes wear two and even four krises at a time, and women of rank are allowed to display it as a badge. It is always thrust through the back of the girdle or belt, a little to the left, and at an angle, that the right hand may easily grasp the hilt; and its presence there, ready for instant use, has proved a great restraint to the manners of a spirited, hot-blooded people, and lent their intercourse that same exaggerated formality, mutual deference, and high decorum that equally distinguished the old two-sworded men of Japan. The kris is the warrior's last refuge, as the Javanese will run amuck, like other Malays, when anger, shame, or grief has carried him past all bounds, and, stabbing at every one in the way, friend or enemy alike, is ready then to take his own life.

The Javanese are still the best metal-workers in the

archipelago, and long displayed wonderful skill in tempering steel, in welding steel and iron together, and in giving the wavy blade fine veinings and damascenings. Those beautiful veinings, grained and knotted in wood, and other curious patternings of the blade, were obtained by soaking the blades, welded of many strips of hard and soft metal, in lime-juice and arsenic until the surface iron was eaten out. A wound from such a weapon is, of course, as deadly as if the kris were dipped in poison for that purpose solely; and from this arises the common belief that all kris-blades are soaked in toxic preparations. With the more general use of firearms, and the arming of the troops with European rifles, the kris remains chiefly a personal adornment, an article of luxury, and a badge of rank.

Solo has always been considered a later Toledo for its blades, and in the search for a really good, typical Solo kris I certainly looked over enough weapons to arm the sultan's guard. The most of them were disappointingly plain as to sheath and hilt, the boat-shaped wooden hilts having only enough carving on the under part to give the hand a firm grasp. We could not find a single Madura kris, with the curious totemic carvings on the handle; and all the finely ornamental krises, with gold, silver, or ivory handles inlaid with jewels, have long since gone to museums and private collections. One may now and then chance upon finely veined blades with mangosteen handles in plain, unpromising wood, and brass Sundanese sheaths; but after seeing the treasures of krises in the Batavia museum, one is little satisfied with such utilities, mere every-day serviceable weapons. Increasing tourist travel will soon encourage the manufacture of ornamental krises, and in numbers to meet the certain fixed demand, so that later tourists will have better souvenirs than can be had now.

There is one whole street of sarong-shops in Solo, each little shop or open booth glowing with cloths of brilliant colors, and each shop standing in feudal dignity behind a tiny moat, with a mite of a foot-bridge quite its own. Solo sarongs presented many designs quite new to us, and the sarong-painters there employ a rich, dull, dark red and a soft, deep green in the long diamonds and pointed panels of solid color, relieved with borders of intricate groundwork, that tempt one to buy by the dozen. There were many sarongs, painted with four and five colors in fine, elaborate designs, that rose to ten and twenty United States gold dollars in value; but one's natural instincts protested against paying such prices for a couple of yards of cotton cloth, mere figured calico, forsooth, despite its artistic and individual merits. Our landlady at the Sleier had inducted us into much of the sarong's mysteries, qualities, and details of desirability, and we had the museum's rare specimens in mind; but we were distracted in choice, and the thing I desired, just any little scrap as an example of the *prang rusa*, or deer-fight, pattern, which only the imperial ones may wear, was not to be had anywhere in Solo. We looked in upon many groups of little women tracing out fine, feathery, first-outline designs in brown dye with their tiny funnel arrangements that are the paint-brushes of their craft; and we found one great cement-floored fabrik of sarongs, a regular factory or wholesale establishment, with many Chinese and native workmen. There whole sections of the sarong pattern were stamped at a stroke by lean Chinese, who used the same kind of tin stamping-blocks as are used in stamping embroidery patterns in Western lands. We knew there was such a factory for block-printed sarongs on Tenabang Hill in Batavia, but it was a shock, a disillusionment, to come upon such an establishment of virtually ready-made, "hand-me-down" sarongs in Solo.

There is a large Chinese population in Solo; and one has sufficient evidence of the wealth and prosperity of these Paranaks as one sees them driving past in handsome victorias, wearing immaculate duck suits, patent-leather shoes, and silk hose, with only the ignoble pigtail, trailing away from the derby hat and disappearing shamefully inside the collar, to betray them. These rich Paranaks sit rigid and imperturbable, with folded arms, the very model of good form, smoking long black cheroots, and viewing all people afoot with undisguised scorn. One need not possess a Californian's bitter anti-Chinese sentiments to have this spectacle irritate him, and to almost wish to see the plutocrats pitched out of their "milords" and the Javanese Jehu drive over them. One easily understands the hatred that Dutch and natives alike entertain for these small traders, middlemen, and usurers, who have driven out all competitors, and fatten on the necessities of the people. Although these island-born Chinese have adopted so many European fashions in dress and luxurious living, they are still Celestials, never cutting the queue nor renouncing the tinseled household altars.

Solo's Chinatown, or Tjina kampong, is a little China complete, barring its amazing cleanliness and order without odors other than those of the cook-shops, where sesame-oil sizzles and smells quite as at home in "big China." There were three great weddings in progress on one "lucky day" in Solo, and each house-front was trimmed with flags, lanterns, garlands, and tinsel flowers; orchestras tinkled and thumped, and great feasts were spread in honor of the brides' coming to the new homes. Every one was bidden to enter and partake; and we were hospitably urged to enter at each gorgeous door, and rice-wine, champagne, painted cakes, and all the fruits of two zones were generously pressed upon us. The thumps of an approaching band drew us from one sarong-shop, and we saw a procession advancing, with banners and huge lanterns borne aloft. One felt sure the remarkable train must have issued from the palace gates until the faces were in range, and there followed the gorgeous red Chinese wedding-chair, and all the bride's jewels and gowns and gilded slippers, carried about on cushions like sovereign regalia. Men in uniform bore palanquins full of varnished pig, and mountains of the pies and cakes and nameless things of Chinese high-holiday appetites, that roused the gaping envy of the street crowds. Urchins cheered and danced and ran with the band much as they do elsewhere; and the strangers, captivated with the sights, drove beside the gaudy procession until sated with the Oriental splendors and Celestial opulence of a Solo marriage feast.

The street life of Solo could well entertain one for many days. Native life is but the least affected by foreign ways, and the local color is all one could wish. There are drives of great beauty about the town, with far views of those two lovely symmetrical peaks, Merapi and Merbaboe, on one side, and of the massive Mount Lawu on the other. The temple ruins at Suku, at the foot of Mount Lawu, twenty-six miles southeast of Solo, are the most puzzling to archæologists, least known and visited of all such remains in Java. They are of severe form and massive construction, without traces of any carved ornament, and the solid pylons, truncated pyramids, and great obelisks, standing on successive platforms or terraces, bear such surprising resemblance to the monuments of ancient Egypt and Central America that speculation is offered a wide range and free field. The images found there are ruder than any other island sculptures, and everything points to these strange temples having been the shrines of an earlier, simpler faith than any now observed or of which there is any record. These Suku temples were discovered in 1814 by Major Johnson, the British officer residing at the native court of Solo. They were then unknown to the natives; there were no inscriptions found, nothing in native records or traditions to lead to any solution of their mysteries; and no further attempts have been made toward discovering the origin of these vast constructions since Sir Stamford Raffles's day.

When M. Désiré de Charnay came to Java, in 1878, to study the temple ruins whose puzzling resemblance to Central American structures had puzzled archæologists, all of government assistance was lent him. He had driven only eight leagues from Solo toward Mount

Lawu, when his carriage broke down; he spent the night at a village, and returned the next morning to Solo, "sufficiently humiliated with" his "failure," he wrote. He did not repeat the attempt, as there was a great fête occurring at the emperor's palace which occupied his remaining days. He says that every one at Solo consoled him for his failure to reach the Suku temples by saying that the visible ruins there were only the attempted restorations of an epoch of decadence, and dated only from the fourteenth century. M. de Charnay quotes all that Sir Stamford Raffles and Fergusson urge as to the striking and extraordinary resemblance of these particular temples to those of Mexico and Yucatan; and as ethnologists admit that the Malays occupied the archipelagos from Easter Island to Madagascar, he thinks it easy to believe that they or a parent race extended their migrations to the American continent, and that if this architectural resemblance be an accident, it is the only one of its kind in the universe.[1]

The three-domed summit of the mountain is visited now by Siva worshipers, who make offerings and burn incense to the destroying god who manifests himself there, and the region is one to tempt a scientist across the seas to exploit it, and should soon invite the attention of the exploring parties which Mr. Morris K. Jesup has enlisted in the search for proofs of early Asiatic and American contact.

[1] "Le Tour du Monde," "Six Semaines à Java," par M. Désiré de Charnay, volume for 1880.

XX

DJOKJAKARTA

AS the heat of Solo was but little less than that of Batavia, and we had only worse accounts and solemn warnings given of the sickening, unendurable heat of Soerabaya, where fever and cholera most often abide, it seemed wisest to give up the visit to that east end of the island, to forego that torrid shore where first the Arabs landed and conquered the Hindu rulers of Majapahit, to be succeeded in their turn by the Portuguese, and then the Dutch. The ruins of Majapahit, and the tombs of its princes, and the graves of the Arab priests who were the first rulers of the conquered empire are attractions in Soerabaya's neighborhood; but the great object was the Mount Bromo of the Tengger plateau, where the exhausted residents may take refuge from the steaming plain and breathe again. Tosari, the great sanatorium, on one of the sharp spurs of the Tengger, is over five thousand feet in air, and commands one of the most famous views in Java, with the plains, the sea, and groups of islands in one direction, and the great Bromo, smoking splendidly, in another. The great crater of the Bromo, with several smoking cones rising from a level of rippling, wind-swept "sandy sea," is three miles in diameter, and is claimed, despite Kilauea, as the largest crater in the world, as it is certainly the largest in Java. A colony of Siva worshipers, who fled to the Tengger that they might pursue their religion unmolested by Arab rulers, live there in long communal houses, tend the sacred fire once brought from India, and sacrifice regularly to Brama, the "God of Fire," at his smoking temple. In this modern day living sacrifices are not offered, save of fowl; and priests and people content themselves with offerings of fruit and foods, and make other great ceremonies of burning lumps of fragrant benzoin, the "Java frankincense," at the crater's edge.

The most serious sacrifices in the Bromo's neighborhood are of those unfortunate natives who are seized by tigers as they work in clearings or walk mountain paths alone. The briefest stay at Tosari equips a visitor with tiger stories fit for tropical regions; and my envy was roused when some Tosari tourists told of having seen a child who had been seized and slightly mangled by a tiger, but a day before, on a road near the village, over which they themselves had passed.

The short railway ride back from Solo to Djokja, past the familiar ground of Brambanam, was a morning's delight. We could see from the train that the railway did run close past the temple courts; and with the brief glimpse of the ruined pyramids, we viewed our exploit of walking to Loro Jonggran's fane at midday, and clambering over the temples through the

THE BEAMBANAM BABY.

long afternoon, with great complacency—a feat that nothing could induce us to repeat, however.

It is all historic and sacred soil in the region around Djokja, and we returned with the greater interest for our real visit to the city, where one touches the age of fable in even the geographic names of the place and its environs, since the modern Dutch rendering of Djokjakarta, and the older Yugya-Karta of Sir Stamford Raffles, are only variants of the native Ayogya-Karta, the Ayudya mentioned in the Javanese Parvas, or Ramayan, as the capital established by Rama. The exploits of Na-yud-ya, the earliest ruler of Djokja, are described in the same sacred Parvas, and this was the center of the early Hindu empire, whose princes were great builders and for ten centuries were busy erecting temples, palaces, and towers in the region around this their city of Mataram.

Na-yud-ya's descendants resisted the Arab invaders to the last, and the Hindu princes of Middle Java retained their independence long after Islam's susunhan had declared himself supreme over the eastern empire of Majapahit [1] and the western empire of Pajajaran.[2] These Hindu or native princes, as they were considered, resisted susunhan and Dutch alike, and the Java war of the last century against the two usurpers was a long and bitter struggle, lasting from 1745 to 1758. The susunhan's brother, the second prince, who had joined the native or Hindu princes, was won back to

[1] Majapahit, capital of the eastern empire, was near the modern Soerabaya.

[2] Pajajaran, capital of the western empire, was near the modern Batavia.

family allegiance by Dutch intrigue and influence; and the susunhan, dividing his eastern or Majapahit empire with his troublesome brother, made the latter a ruler, under the title of Sultan of Djokjakarta. The Dutch had been given the site of Samarang for their aid in such wars, and soon after the division of the eastern empire, the susunhan made that remarkable will of 1749, deeding his empire to the Dutch East India Company after his decease. The region between Djokja and Solo remained a seat of war for the rest of the century, the old princes, different heirs, claimants, and factions, always resorting to arms, and the Dutch always having an interest in the struggles. Marshal Daendels had his campaigns against and his sieges of Djokja, and the British had to besiege and bombard it before it admitted Sepoy occupation. After the restoration of Java to the Dutch there was a thirteen years' war with this eastern empire,—the Mataram or Majapahit war,—and then, by treaty, the Dutch gained final control of the whole island and became absolute masters of Java; susunhan and sultan accepted annuities; each paid a revenue in products of the soil, and admitted Dutch residents to "make recommendations." The Sultan of Djokja is only another of the puppet rulers. He maintains the outward show and trappings of his ancestors' estate, and, with fine irony, is termed one of the "independent princes."

The city of Djokja, fifth in size of the cities of the island, and reputed as more Javanese than Solo, less influenced by Chinese and European example, is in the center of the residency, and but twelve miles from the shores of the Indian Ocean. It is approached by railway from either side over a plain planted chiefly with indigo and tapioca, whose low, uninteresting plants in myriad rows, and the frequent roofs and tall chimneys of fabriks, speak of abundant prosperity for all classes. The broad streets of the provincial capital are beautifully shaded, and the residency, a great, low, white building with a classical portico, is set in a luxuriant garden, where Madagascar palms and splendid trees make halos and shadow for the grim stone images, the pensive Buddhas and fine bas-reliefs, brought from neighboring ruins. The government offices adjoin, and on any court day one may see the crowds of litigants and witnesses sitting around on their heels beneath a shadowing waringen-tree that would be fit bench for Druids' justice. The majority of the cases tried before the assistant resident, who there balances the scales, are of petty thieving; for notwithstanding the severity of the penalties for such offenses, the inherent bias of the Malay mind is toward acquiring something for nothing—transmuting *tuum* into *meum*. The death sentence is pronounced upon the burglar caught with a weapon on his person, and twenty years in chains is prescribed for the unarmed burglar; for in this eternal summer, where people must live and sleep with open doors and windows, or at most with flimsy lattices, some protection must be assured to those who own portable properties and valuables. But with the great advances made in the security of property, the innate propensities of the race are not to be eradicated by even three centuries of stern Dutch justice; and there is the same mass-meeting of witnesses and lookers-on squatting under the big waringen-tree at Djokja, when the scales are to be balanced by the blind lady, as before every petty court-room on the island. An ingenious little firefly lamp, taken from a Djokja burglar, was given me as a souvenir of one such a court day. It was a veritable fairy's dark lantern—a half of a nutshell, with a flat cover sliding on a pivot and concealing at will the light of two fireflies struggling in a dab of pitch. The burglar carried a reserve supply of fireflies in a bit of hollow bamboo stoppered at the ends, and added a fresh illuminator whenever the dark lantern's living glow diminished.

The Djokja passer is a large and important daily gathering, but corrugated-iron and tiled sheds in formal rows have pretty nearly robbed it of all a passer's picturesqueness. Model municipal government, Dutch system and order, are too pronounced to please one whose eye has seen what a few palm-thatched booths and umbrellas, and a few tons of scattered fruits and peppers, can produce in that picnic encampment by Boro Boedor's groves or in the open common at Tissak Malaya.

We had been promised great finds in the way of old silver and krises in a street of Chinese pawnshops opening from one corner of the passer; but the promises were not realized. The betel-boxes, buckles, and clasps in charge of these wily "uncles" of Djokja were plain and commonplace, and not a jeweled nor a fancy kris of any kind was to be seen, after all the repute of Djokja's riches in these lines of native metal-work. Hundreds of sarongs, each with a dangling ribbon of a ticket, were stowed away on the shelves of these pawnshops, proofs of the improvidence and small necessities of these easy-going, chance-inviting people; and while we were haggling over a veined kris-blade with the most obdurate Chinese that ever kept a pawnshop, a timid little woman stole in and offered her sarong to the arrogant, blustering old rascal. He scowled and scolded and stormed at the frightened little creature, shook out and snapped the finely patterned battek as if it were a dust-cloth, and still muttering as if making threats of blood and vengeance, made out a ticket, and threw it at her with a few silver cents. We wanted nothing more from that shop, save the head of the "uncle" on a trencher or impaled on a kris's point.

With a shameless eye to revenue only, the government has long continued to sell pawnbrokers' licenses at auction to the highest bidder, after a brief relapse from the year 1869 to 1880, when the experiment was tried of selling licenses to any one at a moderate rate. The great income from such licenses fell away so amazingly that the auctions were resumed, and the improvident natives handed over again to the merciless Chinese pawnbrokers, who charge interest even up to ninety per cent., and usually retain everything that crosses their counters. M. Emile Metzger, in a communication to the "Scottish Geographic Magazine" (vol. iv., 1888), gives fifty thousand florins a year as the annual revenue during the eleven years when the other system prevailed, which soon increased to as much as one million, sixty-five thousand florins a year when licenses were again auctioned to the highest bidder.

The Sultan of Djokja has a kraton, or palace inclosure, a mile square in the very heart of the city, the great entrance-gates fronting on a vast *plein* or *platz*, where waringen-trees have been clipped and trained to the shape of colossal state umbrellas, great green pajongs planted in permanence in the outer court or approach to the throne, as a badge of royalty. The huge Burmese elephants, that play an important part in state processions, trumpet in one corner; and strangely costumed retainers are coming and going, some of them as gaily uniformed as parrakeets, and others reminding one of the picadors and matadors in the chorus of "Carmen." Surrounded by this indoor army of gorgeous musicians, singers, dancers, bearers of fan and pajong, pipe and betel-boxes, the sultan's court is as splendidly staged as in the last century; and when this "regent of the world" and "vicegerent of the Almighty," as his titles translate, goes abroad in state procession, the spectacle is worth going far to see, the Djokjans assure one. Twenty different kinds of pajongs belong to this court—those flat umbrellas that are the oldest insignia of royalty in all the East, and are sculptured on Boro Boedor's walls through all the centuries pictured there. From the sultan's own golden pajong with orange border, the gold-bordered pajong of the crown prince, the white pajongs of sultanas and their children and of concubines' children, down to the green, red, pink, blue, and black pajongs of the lesser officials and nobles, all pajongs are exactly ordered by court heraldry—the pajong the definite symbol of rank, a visiting-card that announces its owner's consequence from afar. Strange accompaniments these, however, for a sultan who plays billiards at the club and a sultana who takes a hand at whist.

The old Taman Sarie, or Water Kastel, in the suburbs, built by a Portuguese architect in the middle of the last century for the great sultan Manko Boeni, is an Oriental Trianon, a paradise garden of the tropics, where former greatness spent its hours of ease in cool, half-underground chambers and galleries such as Hindu princes have made for themselves in every part of India. The Taman Sarie is sadly deserted now. The most important buildings were shaken to formless mounds by earthquakes—the last great Djokja earthquake of 1867, when so many lives were lost, making the complete ruins that are covered with vines and weeds. The ornamental waters are choked with weeds and rubbish; the carved stonework is black with mold and lichens; the caves, grottoes, tunnels, staircases, and galleries around the wells are dripping and slippery with green mosses; and the rose-gardens and shrubberies are fast going to jungle. A few pavilions remain, whose roof gables are as deeply recurved as those of Burmese temples, but for the most part all the once splendid carved and gilded constructions are but wrecks and refuges for bats and lizards. The Water Kastel in its better days stood in the midst of a lake, reached only by boat or a secret tunnel; and here the old sultan Hamanku Bewono IV and his harem whiled away their leisure hours, even when an army thundered at the gates.

On one unfortunate day he kept Marshal Daendels waiting in the outer court for an hour beyond the time appointed for an interview, while the sultan and his women made merry, and the gamelan sounded gaily from the Water Kastel's galleries. Daendels, growing weary, suddenly pushed through the retainers to the mouth of the tunnel, and appeared to the dallying sultan in the Water Kastel without announcement or further ceremony, and with still less ceremony seized the sultan by the arm and led him back to Dutch headquarters, where the interview took place. Another version of this Water Kastel tradition describes the mad marshal as making a dash down terraces and staircases to a water-pavilion sunk deep in foliage at the edge of a tank, where, in a shady cellar of a sleeping-room, shielded and cooled by a water curtain falling in front of it, he dragged the sultan from his bed, and carried him off to headquarters. The *opas* and the chattering old guardian, who led us about the Kastel's labyrinths, plunged into the green gloom of a long, mossy staircase that led to the platform on which the sultan's sleeping-room opened, to show us the "unlucky bed" and prove by it their particular or favored version of the irruption of Marshal Daendels. The bedstead or couch is an elaborately carved affair, and must once have been the chief ornament of this cool cave-like retreat; but in the reek and gloom of the late afternoon this water boudoir seemed too suggestive of rheumatism, malaria, and snakes by wholesale to invite one to linger, or to suggest repose on the "unlucky bed," which insures an early death to the one who touches it.

Another water-chamber was provided in the Sumoor Gamelan ("Musical Spring"), a deep circular well or tank near the ruined banquet-hall, with vaulted chambers opening around it—just such echoing places of green twilight, where it must be cool on the hottest noonday, as one may see in the old palaces at Lucknow, Futtehpore Sikri, and Ahmedabad, in the fatherland whence the ruling princes of Java came. There is, too, a great oval tank with beautiful walls, parapets, and pavilions, well worthy of a Hindu palace; and in this secluded place there lived for many decades a sacred white or dingy yellow turtle with red eyes, an albino to whom the people made offerings and paid homage. The Taman Sarie has great fascination for one, and at sunset something of romance seems to linger in the old gardens and grottoes, the picturesque courtyards and galleries; and one could imagine scores of legends and harem's mysteries belonging there— that anything and everything had happened there by that lake that burns a rose-red when the palms are silhouetted against the high sunset sky. A group of children played hide-and-seek about the once august court, supple, nimble little bronze fauns, with the carefully folded kerchiefs on their heads their only garments—kerchiefs that they arrange with the greatest care and deliberation many times a day, holding the ends of the cloth with agile toes while they pat and crease and coax the fine folds into the prescribed order of good form. These children dashed through the shrubberies, leaped balusters and walls as lightly and easily as wild creatures, and ran up tall trees like squirrels, to gather tasseled orchids and some strange blue flowers that we pointed to with suggestive coppers, and they hailed us as old friends when we came again.

There were delightful drives to be taken in and around Djokja in the cool of the afternoon, the tamarind- and waringen-shaded streets leading to bowery suburbs, that gave wider views out over the fertile plain with the winding Oepak River, or toward the beautiful blue mountain cones that slumbered to northward. There were always the most decorative palm-trees in the right place to outline themselves against the rosy sunset sky, and the drives back to the hotel through the quick twilight and sudden darkness gave many views into lamp-lighted huts and houses — genre pictures of native life, Dutch-Indies interiors, where candle-light or firelight illuminated family groups and women at their homely occupations, that should inspire a new, a tropical school of Dutch painters. The graves of the old Hindu princes of Mataram crown a beautiful wooded hill south of the city near the sea-shore, and are still worshiped and garlanded by their people.

Through our now near friend, august patron, and protector, the kindly assistant resident, we received word at sunrise that the independent Prince Pakoe Alam V ("Axis of the Universe") and his family would graciously receive us the next morning at nine o'clock; and that meanwhile our patronage was invited for a topeng, or lyric dance, to be given by Prince Pakoe Alam's palace troupe on that evening for the benefit of the widows and orphans of the soldiers killed in the Lombok war. This Lombok war had been brought to a close that week by the capture of the treacherous Balinese sultan who had so tyrannized over the Sassaks, and was then on his way to be paraded

TYING THE TURBAN.

with the victorious soldiers before the governor-general in a grand triumph or review at Batavia.

I had a long, quiet afternoon at the Hotel Toegoe to give again to the enormous folios of Wilsen's drawings of Boro Boedor, while my companions napped, the palm-branches hung motionless in the garden, and only a few barefooted servants moved without sound —that deathly silence of tropic afternoon life that is sometimes a boon, and sometimes an exasperation and irritation to one accustomed to doing his sleeping by dark and not turning day into night. Finally the pale skeleton of an invalid, who was my next neighbor on the long porch, lifted his pitiful voice, and was helped out to his chair, and then our imperturbable Amat stirred from his leisured sleep on the flags beyond, meditated for a while, twisted his kerchief turban anew, disappeared, and returned with the tea-tray, silent, impassive, and automatic, as if under some spell. A graceful little woman peddler came to the porch's edge—a pretty, gentle creature with dark, starry Hindu eyes, clear-cut features, even little white teeth, and crinkly hair. It was delight enough to watch this pretty creature's flash of eyes and teeth, and her manners were most beguiling as she proffered her sarongs —intricately figured batteks from Cheribon and Solo, silk plaided ones from Singapore, and those of Borneo shot through with glittering threads. Nothing could have been more graceful and charming than the naïve appeals of the little peddler woman, and nothing could have presented more extreme and unfortunate contrast than to have the sockless and waistless young Dutch matron of the opposite portico step down and run to the garden gate at sound of a military band. Few women since Atalanta's time have been able to run gracefully; and this thick-ankled young matron, with her flapping mule slippers, scant sarong, and shapeless jacket, outdid all descriptions and caricatures of "the woman who runs." A friendly cavalier in gaudy battek pajamas, who had been talking to the lady, and blowing clouds of pipe-smoke into her face the while, gaily danced an elephantine fandango as the band went sounding down the street to give its sunset concert in the park.

When tea was taken to the lady's porch after this divertisement, she took a banana to the edge, and called, "Peter! Peter!" There was a rustle and crash of boughs overhead, and a great ape, nearly the size of a man, swung from one tree-branch to another, snatched the banana, and bounded back into the tree, where it peered cunningly at us while he ate. After that every rustle in the shrubbery made us jump; we kept umbrellas at hand for defense, and made solemn compact that no one of us should be left asleep unguarded while doors and windows were open to this dreadful reminder of "The Murders in the Rue Morgue."

XXI

PAKOE ALAM: THE "AXIS OF THE UNIVERSE."

AS the lines of the topeng-players are always delivered in the ancient Kawi, or classic language of Java, one has need to brush up beforehand, and to wish for a libretto, a book of the opera, to keep in hand as the lyric drama progresses. Sir Stamford Raffles's "History of Java" furnishes one a general glimpse of the ancient literature of the island, and by many translations acquaints one with the great epics. This old literature is Hindu in form and origin; and Kawi, the classic or literary language of the past, in which all the history, early records, epic and legendary poems, and the books of religion and the law are written, is closely related to Sanskrit and Pali. The famous myths and legends of India are included in this literature, and the Ramayan and Mahabharata appear, incomplete but unaltered, in the Javanese epics known as the Kandas and the Parvas. Besides these two great works, there is the "Arjuna Vivaya," giving an account of the exploits of the Indian Arjuna, the real hero of the Mahabharata; and there is still another romantic legendary poem, the "Bharata Yuddha," in which many of the incidents and the heroes of the Mahabharata are presented in Javanese settings with Javanese names. All these Kawi books are known to the people by translations in modern Javanese, and by their frequent presentation in the common dramatic entertainments, the wayang-wayang, or shadow-plays, of even the smallest villages.

Many "Books of Wisdom" and of exhortation to pious and righteous living survive in Kawi literature; but with all that Hindu civilization brought, it bequeathed nothing that could be called Buddhist literature, and the bulk of ancient Javanese literature is decidedly secular and profane—sentimental and romantic poems, love-tales in verse, that continue to extreme lengths. The Arab conquest has left almost no impress upon the language. Although schools were established, and a considerable body of Arabic literature came with the Mohammedan conquerors, but little save *bababs*, romantic chronicles of the loves of imaginary princes and heroes, have been added to Javanese literature in the four centuries since Islam's conquest. The spoken language of the Javanese shows few traces of Arabic, and the written language is also unchanged—a neater, more beautiful and graceful system of ornamental characters than either Arabic or Persian.

The old Kawi epics are popularized by the theater, the topeng, and the common wayang-wayang, or shadow-dance of puppets, where a manager delivers the well-known lines. Of these three dramatic forms

WAYANG-WAYANG.

the topeng is the highest, the most classic and refined presentation, a lyric drama very like the No dance of Japan, and doubtless, like the No dance, had a religious origin. A topeng troupe has its *dalang*, or manager, who prompts, sometimes explains, and often delivers all the lines for the masked actors; and there is a gamelan, or orchestra, of four or more musicians, and a chorus which chants accompanying and explanatory verses as the action proceeds. Great princes maintain their own private topeng troupes, and in their palace presentations, and always in the presence of native royalties, the actors go without masks. The topeng's gamelan consists of two sets of the circles of tiny gongs (*gong* or *agong*, a pure Javanese word and instrument), that are struck with wooden sticks, and two wood and two metal gambang kayu (wood and metal bars of different length and thickness mounted on a boat-shaped frame), or native xylophones, to which single instrument the name "gamelan" is so often given in the West.

The common wayang-wayang of the people is a modification of the same masked or puppet drama that was in vogue long before the Mohammedan conquest. As the religion of Islam forbade the representation of the human figure, the susunhan ordered the puppets to be so distorted that the priests could not call them images of human beings, and that even then only their shadows, thrown on a curtain, should be seen. Hence the exaggerated heads, the beaks and noses, of the cardboard jumping-jacks which, pulled by unseen strings, serve to maintain an interest in the national history and legends, and by preludes and lines, chanted in classic Kawi, preserve acquaintance with the literary language among the common people. There is a form of wayang-wayang half-way between this puppet-show and the real drama, in which the actors themselves are visible, wearing distorted masks; but the plays are of modern times, in the common dialect, and the manager often improvises his lines and scenes as the play progresses. With these popular dramas there rank the performances of the graceful *bedaya*, or dancing-girl, whose tightly folded sarong, floating scarf-ends, measured steps, outward sweep of the hand, and charming play of arm and wrist recall the Japanese *maiko*. Although the winsome bedaya is sculptured on Boro Boedor's recording walls, there is nothing there to indicate the puppet-play, nor anything from which it might have evolved, although from other records ethnologists claim that the Javanese possessed this dramatic art when the Hindus came. A love of the drama in the form of the topeng and the wayang-wagang was so ingrained in the tastes and fixed in the customs of the people that the Mohammedan conquerors could not suppress those popular amusements, and were finally content to modify them in trifling points. The Dutch were also wise enough never to interfere with these harmless pleasures of the people, the greatest distraction and delight of these sensitive, emotional, innately esthetic and refined Javanese, who will sit through shadow-plays for half the night, and are moved to frenzy and tears by the martial and romantic exploits of their national heroes.

All of society,—the two hundred of Djokja's superior circle,—European and native together, gathered at the Societeit's marble hall on the night of the topeng. That exalted being, the resident, entered in his modestly gilded uniform; and all the company rose, and stood until he and Prince Pakoe Alam had advanced and seated themselves in the two arm-chairs placed in front of the chairs of the rest of the audience. "Our best people are all here to-night," said our amiable table d'hôte acquaintance of the Hotel Toegoe; and we looked around the lofty white hall, where row upon row of robust, prosperous-looking Europeans sat in state attire. All the men wore heavy cloth coats, either richly frogged military jackets or the civilian's frock or cutaway, only a few wearing conventional black dress-coats, and none the rational white duck clothes of the tropics. The Dutch ladies were dressed in rich silks, brocades, and even velvets, and fanned vigorously as a natural consequence, while more of mildew fumes than of sachet odors came from these heavy cloth and silk garments, whose care and preservation are so difficult in the tropics. One was reminded of those tropical burghers in crimson velvet coats who received Lord Macartney and Staunton in a red velvet council-room at Batavia just one century before. The native officers and their families were naturally more interesting to a stranger—splendid-looking Javanese men, who stood and walked like kings, all wearing the battek kerchief or turban folded in myriad fine plaitings, richly patterned sarongs, and the boat-handled kris showing at the back of the short black military jacket. Many of these native officials had constellations of stars and decorations pinned to their breasts, and their finely cut features, noble mien, and graceful manners declared them aristocrats and the fine flower of an old race. Their wives, shy, slender, graceful women in clinging sarongs and the disfiguring Dutch jacket, wore many clasps and buckles and jeweled knobs of ear-rings. They seemed to have inherited all the Hindu love of glittering, glowing jewels, and the Buddhist love of flowers and perfumes, each little starry-eyed, flower-like woman redolent of rose or jasmine attar, and wearing some brilliant blossom in the knot of satin-black hair. The women had thrust their pretty brown feet into gold-heeled mule slippers, that clicked musically on the tiles as they walked, while the children comfortably rubbed their bare feet on the cool white floor.

A few Chinese families, nearly all of them Paranaks, or half-castes, to the island born, were there; the women in gay embroidered satins, jeweled and diamonded out of all reason, and the children gay as cockatoos and parrakeets in their bright little coats and caps and talismanic ornaments. Rows of shadowy, silent natives, opas, lantern- and pajong-bearers, and attendants of every kind, crouched in rows among the great columns of the portico—gallery gods who squatted spellbound, rapt, and freely tearful in their enjoyment of the splendid topeng produced that night.

Prince Pakoe Alam's artists rendered for the sake of military charities a four-act lyric drama, dealing with the adventures of mythical Panji, a hero of Hindu times, who is said to have introduced the kris to Java. The gamelan's music was all soft harmonies, tender, weird, sad melodies in plaintive minor key, that accompanied the action throughout. The high-pitched

TORENG TROUPE WITH MASKS

nasal recitatives, the squeaks and squawks and stamps of fencing warriors, the slow posing, the stilted and automatic movements of all the actors, were enough like the No dance of Japan to confuse one greatly. All the actors were magnificently costumed and accoutred, their dresses, armor, and weapons being historic properties of the Pakoe Alam family, that had figured on festal occasions in the topengs of a century and more. In the first act four women in silk sarongs and velvet jackets did a regular Delsarte dance, with all those theatrical poses, sweeps, and gestures with the devitalized arm and wrist that the trainers of the would-be beautiful are teaching in America. Dark-robed attendants, identical with the mutes and invisible supers of the Japanese stage, crawled around behind the principals, arranging costumes, handing and carrying away weapons, as needed. Then deliberate mortal combat raged to slow music; and after it the harmless automatic dance was resumed. There was one tedious act where warriors in modern military jackets, worn with sarongs, indulged in long-drawn recitatives in Kawi; there were prolonged fan, spear, and bow drills; and one fine final act, where heroes, stripped to the waist in old style, with bodies powdered yellow, and half protected by gorgeously gilded breast-plates, fenced with fury and some earnest.

At the end of the first act nearly every man in the audience rose and went out, each mopping his brows and whewing great breaths of air from his lungs. Some few returned with cups of coffee, glasses of pink lemonade, and tall beakers of soda-water for the perspiring ladies wedged in their chairs. These men stayed outside after that act, declaring themselves only during intermissions, when they rushed cooling drinks to their partners at the front. At the end of three hours Panji triumphed over all his enemies, the performance ended, chairs scraped loudly as the audience stirred, the applause was long, and the sighs of relief profound.

After the resident had made the tour of the room and honored the most distinguished ones, and the European dancing was about to begin, the native ladies withdrew; and as we saw these most interesting figures leaving, we, who had risen at five o'clock that morning, and expected to repeat the act the next morning, followed the beauties in golden slippers out to the picturesque confusion of lantern- and pajong-bearers at the carriage entrance. Dancing as it is done in Djokja could not keep us longer awake that night, though we have regretted ever since that we did not wait to see how many of the broadcloth-coated men and their partners in winter gowns survived one vigorous continental waltz on a marble floor, or if an anteroom was converted into an emergency hospital for treating heat prostrations.

With the exemplary early rising the tropics enjoin, we had been up for hours—had enjoyed the dash of a dipper-bath, breakfasted, written letters, visited the passer, the pawnshops, and the photographer—before it was time to join the assistant resident's party and drive to the palace of Prince Pakoe Alam. The carriages went through several gateways, past a guard house and sentries, before they drew up in an inner court before an open pringitan, or audience-hall, eighty feet square, whose great, low-spreading roof, resting only on heavy teak columns, was all open to the air. The prince, his crown prince, and his second son, who is the father's aide-de-camp, were waiting to receive us as we alighted, all three dressed in conventional European military uniforms, with many medals and orders illuminating their coat fronts, and only the native turban on the old prince's head suggesting anything Javanese in attire. The prince spoke Dutch, his sons English and French as well as Dutch; and each gave us cordial welcome and courteous greetings before they offered an arm to conduct us back to the cool inner part of the pringitan, where the young princesses were waiting. We went far in over the shining marble floor, away from all glare and reflection of the vast sanded court, to a region of tempered shadow, where the wife, a daughter-in-law, and a granddaughter of the prince stood beside a formal semicircle of chairs. The ladies spoke only Dutch and Malay, but they did the honors most gracefully, and with the two princes to interpret, conversation moved along smoothly. These princesses wore sarongs and jackets and gilded mule slippers, but their simple costumes were brightened by many jeweled clasps and brooches and great, glittering knobs of ear-rings, and both had coronals of pale-yellow flowers around the knot of black hair drawn low at the back of the head, in foreign style. Their complexions were the pure pale yellow of the true Javanese aristocracy, not the pasty greenish yellow of the higher-class women of China. They had very pretty manners, combining gentleness and dignity, and they put the conventional questions as to our homes and journeys with great earnestness and seeming interest.

The old prince, whose high military rank makes him an offset and check upon the Sultan of Djokja, and who, by his lineage and connections with the imperial house of Solo, almost ranks the sultan, is very literally a serene highness, a most gracious and courtly host, whose dignity and charming address befit his rank and exalted name. His lands and mills and highly improved estates bring him a large private income; and progressive as he may be, I am sure his people speak of him admiringly as a gentleman of the old school—and that old school must have been an admirable one in Java, where the native manners are as fine as in Japan. Prince Pakoe Alam received a foreign military education in his youth, and his sons have enjoyed still greater advantages to fit them for the still newer order. They are the most charming, natural, and unaffected young men, unspoiled and with truly princely mien and manners. To be told hereafter that a young man has the manners of a prince will mean a great deal in simple courtesy, fine finish, and perfection, to those who remember these Javanese princes, the handsome young Pakoe Alams. The natural refinement and charm that one is sensible of in even the lowliest Javanese have their fullest and finest flowering in these princely ones; and that delightful hour spent in the vast shady white pringitan offset many misadventures in Java.

Rows of red-coated and -cowled servitors sat around the edges of the pringitan's shining floor, holding the state pajongs and hooded spears of ceremony; and a full gamelan and a group of singers, in the same bright court livery, squatted in rows facing us at the far front of the hall, awaiting the signal to begin. The artists of the previous night, all the singers and musicians of the full topeng troupe, lifted up their voices to the tinkling, softly booming, sonorous airs of the gamelan and delighted us with a succession of chants throughout our stay. The young princes led us "down front,"—for the whole strange scene in which we found ourselves was very like a theater,—and, in the strong glare of the footlights of daylight, explained the several instruments of the native orchestra. Then in from the wings—"enter right," as the play-books would say—came a procession of servants, swinging racks of decanters and glasses, and bearing bowls of ice, trays of fruits, wafers, and sweets. Abject minions sidled over the floor, and mutely offered us iced wines or aërated waters, moving awkwardly about in the ignominious attitude of the dodok, like so many land-crabs. "Light-boys" crouched and crawled behind each smoker, handing cigars, holding burning punk-sticks, or extending trays to receive the ashes, maintaining their abject position during all our stay. One never gets used to this abasement of the dodok, often as he may see it; and after the first absurdity and humor of it wears off, it is irritating and humiliating to see one human being thus belittle himself before another. One suspects that there was more of fear than reverence in its first observance, and that it comes from centuries of tyranny and oppression rather than from any spontaneous expressions of humility and admiration. This group of household retainers, sidling and jerking over the floor with something between the gait of a toad and a crab, seemed to mar the perfect dignity and decorum of the occasion. These same attendants strode into the sunlit court with the free, splendid tread of Javanese men, only to crouch to their heels at the pringitan's edge, make the simbah's imploring obeisance with clasped hands to the forehead, repeating the simbah if they caught a princely eye, while they sidled grotesquely over the pringitan floor and crouched like dogs at the master's feet.

There was a carved screen behind us, closing off an inner space, where broad divans invited to informal ease, and many beautiful objects were disposed. We were taken there by the old prince to see the great gold-bound "Menac," or family record of the Pakoe Alams —an immense volume with jeweled covers, resting on a yellow satin cushion. This family history was put in this splendid form a hundred years ago by Prince Pakoe Alam II, a literary highness who possessed considerable artistic talent, and maintained a staff of artists and writers in his palace, who were busied for years in tracing and illuminating, under his instructions, this one precious manuscript. Javanese calligraphy, which is even more decorative and ornamental than Arabic or Persian, makes beautiful pages; and each page, gracefully written in black, gold, or colors, is also bordered and illuminated more lavishly than any old Flemish missal. The beautiful ornamental letters, medallions, and miniatures, the tangle of graceful arabesques, and the glow of soft colors and gold, relieved with touches and dashes of black, make the Pakoe Alam's "Menac" a treasure of delight for a whole morning's inspection; but we had only time to turn its leaves, see the more remarkable pages, and obtain a general dazzling idea of its quality. The "Axis of the Universe" is a bibliophile and collector by inheritance, and there were many precious manuscript books, unique éditions de luxe in jeweled bindings, that we could have given hours to inspecting. There is one particular book of Arabian tales, rivaling the family "Menac" in the beautiful lettering and rich illumination, that was sent to the Amsterdam Colonial Exposition some years ago, and naturally excited surprise and admiration among European book-collectors.

Conversation never lagged during this morning call, and the little second prince was regretful that we had given up a trip to the sweltering end of the island, where the Bromo smokes. "The Bromo is the only 'lake of fire' in the world, you know," said the prince, proudly. And soon after, in answer to a question, he said, "No, I have never been in Europe, but I have been all over Java"—this last with an emphasis that became one to the island born, and appreciative of all its wonderful beauties.

When we praised and extolled the scenery of Java, he asked naïvely, "Is America not beautiful, then? Have you no mountains, no beautiful scenery there?" And when we answered patriotically to the facts,—Niagara, the Yellowstone, the Yosemite, Mount Rainier, and Alaska,—he asked in amazement, "Then why do you travel to other countries?"

The old prince announced the approaching marriage of his granddaughter to the son of the Prince of Malang, and asked that we would attend the fêtes which he would give in celebration of the affair a fortnight later; but with all of the other India beckoning, we could not prolong our stay in Java; and we took leave of our princely hosts then, to hasten to the train, promising, as one always does in every pleasant place, to come again when time would allow for a fuller enjoyment of this Javanese Djokja, that we had only begun to know as we were leaving.

XXII

"TJILATJAP," "CHALACHAP," "CHELACHAP"

"TJILATJAP! Tjilatjap!" Often as one may sound those syllables aloud, they seem absurd; and the very idea of spending the night in a town of such name, of buying a railway ticket with that name printed on it, and asking to have one's luggage labeled to that destination, was enough to tickle the fancy. Could there be solemn men and serious women living there? and had the station a sign-board? and could the pale, grave little Dutch children keep their faces straight and glibly pronounce the name of that town without sneezing?

Whether it is printed "Tjilatjap," "Chalachap," or "Chelachap," it at once suggests enough puns to spare one printing them, and surely no town on the north side of the equator could support such a name with any dignity.

But Tjilatjap is one of the oldest foreign settlements in Java, the one good harbor on the whole south coast; and the "Tjilatjap fever" is a distinguished specialty of the region that surpasses all the deadly forms of fever in Java. The place proved to be such a cemetery for European troops that the government was finally forced to abandon the extensive barracks, magazines, and fortifications it had once constructed there. A considerable white population remains, however, and the passer is one of great local importance to the natives. The completion of the railway brought new life to the old settlement; and with such easy access, Tjilatjap is well worth visiting, if it were only to see its shade-trees. All the post-roads running into the town, every street and lane, are such continuous isles, arcades, and tunnels of living green that one is repaid for coming, even after all the other teak and tamarind, kanari and waringen avenues he may have seen elsewhere in Java. Not the allées of Versailles, nor the *cryptomeria* avenues of Japan, can surpass these tree-lined streets of Tjilatjap, the endless vistas of straight trunks and arching branches, the lofty canopies of solid, impenetrable shade, rejoicing one in every part of the town. Tamarind may be the coolest and waringen the densest shade, but kanari-trees give the most splendid and inspiring effect, and Tjilatjap is the place of their greatest perfection.

We drove during the late afternoon and until dusk through kanari avenues, whose great green cathedral aisles, with fretted arches a hundred feet overhead, dwarfed everything that moved or stood beneath them; and then under cool, feathery tamarind bowers, and past arrays of noble teak, everywhere exclaiming with delight. The use of the big-leaved teak for street and post-road shade-trees seemed to me the acme of botanical extravagance,—as ill ordered as putting Pegasus to a cart,—since we of the temperate zone are used to even speaking of that expensive timber with respect. While we drove through the magnificent avenues in the late afternoon light, past parade-grounds and parks, over canals and along their embankments, the rising mists and the solid blue vapors massing in the distances were so much actual, visible evil—malaria almost in tangible form. One felt that he should dine on so many courses of quinine only, taking the saving sulphate first with a soup-spoon, if he expected to survive the mad venture into Tjilatjap's fever-laden air. A crowded, neglected cemetery gave one further creeps and gruesome thoughts; and the evil-smelling sugar and copra warehouses on the harbor front seemed to seal our doom—that old ignorant instinct or idea asserting itself that the bad smell must necessarily be the bad air. There is a beautiful view from the old military encampment out over the land-locked harbor, with a glimpse of the open ocean through a narrow entrance. The dark mass of Noesa Kambangan ("Floating Island") rises beyond the silvery waters—a tropical paradise deliberately depopulated by the Dutch as a strategic measure, that there might be no temptation of sustenance to induce an attack or siege from that quarter. The island is mountainous, and contains much fine scenery, many floral marvels, curious stalactite caverns of holy repute where Siva is secretly worshiped, hot springs, and even gold-mines, and is famous in the old Javanese poems and legends. The great surf of the Indian Ocean beats upon its precipitous south shore, where the clefts and caves in the bold cliffs are inhabited by myriads of sparrows, who build there their edible nests. Nest-hunting furnishes employment to the few islanders, and, like everything else, is strictly regulated and taxed by the colonial government. The nest-hunters only pursue their perilous quest after the young sparrows are well grown each season, as only new, fresh, one-season-old nests serve to make the "bad vermicelli" soup Celestial gourmets adore; and the hunters are often suspended over the cliffs by ropes in order to reach their carefully hidden homes. The glutinous white lumps are as much esteemed in Java as in China, and this rare dainty commands a high price from the moment it is secured.

There is a typical little country colonial hotel at Tjilatjap—a large building containing the offices, drawing-room, and dining-room in the center of a garden, with long, low buildings at either side of it, where rows of bedrooms open upon the long arcade or bricked porch, which is a general corridor, screened off into as many little open sitting-rooms, each with its table, lamp, and lounging-chairs. After our malarial drive we were served an excellent dinner, which concluded with a dessert course of kanari *ambon*, the "Java almond," or nut of the kanari-tree, soaked in brandy. The kanari ambon has the shape and shell of a butternut; but the long, solid white kernel is finer and firmer than even an almond, and of a richer, more distinct and delicate flavor. These nuts of the Tjilatjap region are superior to those grown elsewhere in Java, but we learned this too late, when we tried to buy them elsewhere.

After the sun fell the air grew heavier and hotter—

a stifling, sodden, steaming, reeking atmosphere of evil that one could hardly force in and out of the lungs. We gasped at intervals all through the long evening, and wondered if some vast vacuum bell had not been dropped down over Tjilatjap, while we batted flying things from our faces and swept them from the writing-table. Lizards ran over the walls, of course; and one pale-gray, clammy thing was picked from the bed-curtains, and thrown out with a sickening " ugh ! " The invisible one, in agony, called for " *Becky! Becky! Becky!* " and a hoarser voice cried for " *Tokee! Tokee! Tokee!* " of whom we had never heard before.

Wearily, without rustle of leaves, stir, or any provocation, a sullen rain began to fall, and saturating the atmosphere, made it that much heavier. The rain ceased as wearily as it had begun, and the awful, sodden stillness was only broken by the slow, heavy drip of the listless foliage, and the occasional thud of a falling mango. Far, far away, faintly in the air was heard a smothered booming, moaning sound—the ceaseless surf of the Indian Ocean. Overhead there was darkness, profound and intense, beyond even heat-lightning's illumining, with a more impenetrable blackness where the double rows of ancient kanari-trees shaded the street beyond the hotel garden. The possibilities of its effects, the awful, desperate depression that loneliness in such surroundings would surely cause, made me wonder how great was the proportion of suicides' graves in that damp, weedy cemetery we had driven past in the gloaming.

Then three guests came over from the other part of the hotel, and, spreading themselves out on chairs in the section of porch beyond our partition screen, began conversation, all in Dutch consonants and palatal garglings, with a volume and lung-power, a fervor and emphasis, that made the languid air vibrate and the mangos fall in showers. Their voices could have easily been heard at the harbor's edge or the railway-station, in a stamp-mill or in a boiler factory; and the humor of it—the three Dutchmen in the stilly night bellowing away as if conversing through a half-mile of fog—greatly relieved the sodden melancholy of the malarial evening. Clouds of dense, rank, Sumatra tobacco-smoke rose from the talkers' mouths in volumes to match their voices, and until long past midnight those three men on a silent porch conversed *more Hollandico*, the roar of voices and the pungent smoke sending us dreams of Chicago fires and riots, passing freight-trains, and burning forests.

We had been warned betimes that there would be no opportunity to lunch at wayside stations or from compartment baskets during the long ride from Tjilatjap to Garoet, and we planned accordingly. Our gentle Moslem, who made such inconsequent, irresponsible child's play at waiting on us, was shown the bread and the cold buffalo beef, and bidden make sandwiches in plenty. I even went into details as to salt and pepper, the "mustard" and "no mustard" varieties, and insisted on white paper only for wrapping, before leaving him to the task.

After all Tjilatjap's evil name, we never had any ill effects from venturing into it, and we had a sense of complacent rejoicing when we took train, that next morning, for Maos on the main line of the railway, and knew that a few hours would put us beyond the *terra ingrata*.

Nearly always, in our railway rides in Java, we had the first-class compartments to ourselves; and we often looked longingly, despite the heat, at the crowded second-class compartments, where many Europeans, nice, intelligent-looking people and interesting families, traveled in sociable numbers. The only companions ever of our first-class solitude were, once, the chief constructor of the railways, who for a sudden short trip had dispensed with his official car; and, again, a young Holland geologist and mining expert returning from a season's survey in Borneo—both traveling at government expense. Only the more extravagant planters, native princes, tourists, and officials with passes or under orders seem to use the first-class cars, although the additional comforts and the extra space are actual necessaries of travel in the tropics. That the second-class carriages were always well filled with Europeans showed that at least one thrifty notion of the Hollanders' home survived transplantation in this matter of railway fares. From the two chance fellow-passengers whom we had the fortune to meet on the train I derived enough, by a day's steady questioning and comment, to atone for the dearth of travelers' talk I had suffered before. Both men were cyclopedias of things Javanese, geologic and botanical, and those were very red-letter days in the guide-bookless land.

There was always interest enough in watching the people by the way; and as the through railway-trains were then novelties of a few days' and weeks' experience in that section of Middle Java, the station platforms were crowded with native sight-seers. Native officials and their trains of attendants, Mohammedan women with gorgeous head-gear and the thinnest pretenses of veils, stolid planters with obsequious, groveling servants, and planters' wives, barefooted, wrapped in scant sarongs, and as often wearing red velvet jackets and other traveling toilets of eccentric combination, the costume of the tropics and a Northern winter at the same time—processions of these entertained us not a little as they went their way to the other compartments of the long train.

After the scorching hours spent running through swamp and jungle, we drew near the mountains; life became more bearable, and we beckoned our Moslem at the next stopping-place.

"Bring the sandwiches; they are not in this basket." He looked blankness, as if a little vaguer and more becalmed in mind than usual. "The sandwiches that you made at the Tjilatjap hotel this morning," I explained slowly. "Where are they?"

"Oh, I eat them—jus' now," said the soft-voiced one, naïvely, his hand unconsciously traveling to the digestive region and comfortably stroking it.

Language was useless at such a crisis, and sadly, silently, I resigned myself to the rest of the ten hours' empty ride. An hour later we reached Tjiawi, near which the finest pineapples of the island are grown; and we bought them on the platform, great fragrant, luscious globes of delight, regardless of the almost prayerful requests made to us on arrival, that we would not touch a pineapple in Java. We did a tourist's whole duty to specialties of strange places for that one day, buying the monster nanas in most generous provision; and we made up for all previous denials and lost pineapple opportunities as we tore off the ripe diamonds of pulp in streaming sections that melted on the tongue; nor did we feel any sinking at heart nor dread of the future for such indulgence. Then, at Tissak Malaya, we bought strings of mangosteens through the car-windows. But after the light, evanescent, six-o'clock breakfast of the country, these noonday feasts of juicy fruits did not satisfy one for long, and soon we hungered again.

At Tjipeundeui, in the shadow of the great volcanic range that walls the west, a local chief, or village head man, was foremost on the station platform, that was crowded with cheerful, chattering groups of natives, hung over with bundles as if come from a fair. With great excitement the chief announced that the Goenoeng Galoengoeng, or "Great Gong Mountain," was in eruption again. Two weeks before it had rumbled, as its name indicates it has a habit of doing, and sent out a shower of stones that ruined a large coffee-plantation, scorching and half burying the budding trees in the hot rocks, pebbles, and sand. It had begun rumbling and shaking again, the village wells had emptied, and the people had fled, remembering too well the eruption of 1822, when one hundred and fifteen villages were destroyed, twenty thousand people were killed, and plantations ruined for twenty miles around by the rain of hot stones and ashes, and the hot water and mud overflowing from the blown-out crater. But such a gentle, happy, cheerful, chattering lot of refugees as they were, saving their best sarongs and finery by wearing them, and tying the rest of their treasures in shapeless bundles, as they went picnicking forth to visit relatives until the volcanic disturbance might subside! They were not a whit more care-worn or anxious than the crowd on the next station platform, where two or three hundred pleasure-seekers were returning from a famous country passer, whose rare meetings attract people from afar. Even the chief of the volcanic village radiated joy and pride all over his wrinkled old brown face as he related the moving events occurring in his bailiwick. Eruptions were evidently his pastime, a diversion quite in his line, since he had only come down to the railway to see his family off to a place of safety, while he would return, play Casabianca on his burning heath, and have it out with the resounding Galoengoeng at his leisure.

We had an hour to wait at Tjibatoe station before the Garoet train left, and the refreshment-room keeper offered tea and biscuits—the inevitable, omnipresent Huntley & Palmer biscuits, that are the mainstay and salvation, the very prop and stay and staff, of tourist life in Netherlands as well as British India, and for whose making the great Reading bakers buy the entire tapioca-crop of Java each year. After a short wait in the room, redolent of gin and schnapps and colonial tobacco, a boy sauntered in the back door with an iron tea-kettle, and the proprietor was about to make the tea with that warm water, when we chorused a protest. He good-naturedly allowed me to gather up tea-pot, tea-kettle, small boy, and all, and go a hundred yards down the road, climb a bamboo ladder laid against a bank, and restore the cooling kettle to its place on the home fire in the airiest, dearest little fancy basket of a home, in which one could imagine grown people playing "keep house." A bright-eyed little woman stirred the fire, gave me a box to sit upon, and herself crouched before the sullen tea-kettle, chattering and crooning like a child at play. "*Bodedit? Bodedit?*" ("Does it boil? Does it boil?") she asked seriously, putting her ear to the spout, or sliding the lid and peering into the still interior; but it finally did boil energetically. We made the tea; and, at risk of every bone, I descended that slanting half-ladder in a gentle rain, and returned to enjoy quite a feast that the kind refreshment-room keeper had conjured up in the meantime.

XXIII

GAROET AND PAPANDAYANG

RAIN blurred the landscape for all of the half-hour run from Tjibatoe down to Garoet, and we lost the panorama of splendid mountains that surround the great green Garoet plain, embowered in the midst of which is the town of Garoet, a favorite hill and pleasure-resort of the island. We did catch glimpses now and then, however, of dark mountain masses looming above and through the clouds, and of flooded rice-fields and ripening crops, with scarecrows and quaint little baskets of outlooks perched high on stilts, where young Davids with slings lay in wait for birds. Boys leading flocks of geese, and boys astride of buffaloes made other pictures afield, and in the drizzling rain of the late afternoon we were whirled through the dripping avenues to the Hotel Hork, home of Siamese royalties and lesser tourists, health- and pleasure-seekers, who visit this volcanic and scenic center of the Preanger regencies.

Our sitting-room porch at this summer hotel, with an endless season, looked on a garden, whose formal flower-beds, bordered with stones and shells, classic vases, and other conventions of their kind, reminded one at once of by-places in Europe; and so also did the bust of Mozart and the copy of Thorwaldsen's "Venus,"—until one noted their protecting palm- and mango-trees. This Garoet hotel is one of the institutions of Java, and the Vrouw van Hork and her excellent Dutch housekeeping are famed from Anjer Head to Banjoewangi. All the colonial types were represented at the long table d'hôte, and every language of Europe was heard. There were always nice neighbors at table, able and anxious to talk English, and the cheery Dutch ladies were kindness and friendliness personified. At no other resort on the island did we receive such a pleasant impression of the simplicity, refinement, and charm of social life in the colony. But, although two thousand feet above sea-level, in a climate of mildly tempered eternal spring, the ladies all wore the sarong and loose dressing-sacque in the morning, as in scorching Batavia or lowland Solo. Even on damp and chilly mornings, when a light wrap was a comfortable addition to our conventional muslin gowns, the Garoet ladies were bare-ankled and as scantily clad as the Batavians; and there were shock and real embarrassment to me in seeing in sarong and sacque the dignified elderly matron who had been my charming dinner neighbor the night before.

There is an interesting passer at Garoet, and besides the lavish display of nature's products, there are curious baskets brought from a farther valley, which visitors compete for eagerly. The town square, or overgrown village green, is faced by the homes of the native regent and the Dutch resident, and by the quaint little messigit, or Mohammedan mosque. The last mufti, or head priest of the prophet, at Garoet was a man of such intelligence and liberality that he had but one wife, and allowed her to go with face uncovered, to learn Dutch, and to meet and freely converse with all his foreign visitors, men as well as women. Travelers brought letters to this mufti and quoted him in their books, but since his death the more regular, illiberal order has ruled at Mohammedan headquarters.

The great excursion from Garoet is to the crater of Papandayang, a mountain whose extended lines (fifteen miles in length by six in breadth) match its syllables; which has been in vigorous eruption within a century; and which still steams and rumbles, and, like the Goenoeng Goentor, or "Thunder Mountain," across the plain, may burst forth again at any moment. At the last eruption of Papandayang, in 1772, there was a great convulsion, a solid mass of the mountain was blown out into the air, streams of lava poured forth, and ashes and cinders covered the earth for seven miles around with a layer five feet thick, destroying forty villages and engulfing three thousand people in one day. The scar of the great crater, or "blow-out hole," near the summit of the mountain, is still visible from the plain, and the plumes and clouds of steam ascending from it remind one of its unpleasant possibilities. We made a start early one rainy morning, and drove twelve miles across the plain, along hard, sandy white roads, continuously bordered with shade-trees. The frequent villages were damp and cheerless, and the little basket houses, that

the people weave as they would a hat, were anything but enviable dwellings then. The sling-shooters' sentry-boxes throughout the fields—perches where men or boys sat to pull sets of strings that reached to scarecrows far away—suggested too much of clammy, rheumatic discomfort to seem as picturesque as usual —strange little Malay companion pieces to the same boxes on stilts that one sees perched in the rice-fields of Hizen and the other southern provinces of Japan.

At Tjisoeroepan, at the foot of the mountain, we changed to clumsy djoelies, or sedan-chairs, each borne by four coolies, whose go-as-you-please gait, not one of them keeping step with any other, was especially trying so soon after coming from the enjoyment of the swift, regular, methodical slap-slap tread of the chair-bearers of South China. Despite their churning motion, the way was enjoyable; and, beginning with a blighted and abandoned coffee-plantation at the base of the mountain, we passed through changing belts of vegetation, as by successive altitudes we passed botanically from the tropic to the temperate zone. The bleached skeletons of the old coffee-trees, half-smothered in undergrowth and vines, interested one more than the beautifully ordered and carefully tended young coffee-trees in newer plantations—sad reminders of those good old days before the war (the Achinese war), the deficit, and the blight. Beyond kina limits there were no more clearings, and then the tree-fern appeared —wan skeletons of trees at first, where much thinning out had left them in range of scorching sunlight; but in the shade of greater trees in the thick of the jungle they stood superb—great, splendid, soft, drooping, swaying, gigantic green fronds, a refined, effeminate, delicate, sensitive sort of palm, the tropic's most tropical, exquisite, wonderful tree. The upper regions of Papandayang are all clothed with real jungle, the forest primeval, with giant creepers writhing and looping serpent-like about the trees, and doing all the extravagant things they are expected to do. Ratans, or climbing palms, enveloped whole trees with their pendant, gracefully decorative leaves; orchids swung in tasseled sprays, starred mossy trunks and branches, and showed in all the green wonderland overhead and around; and in each ravine, where warm streams sprayed the air, a whole hothouse full of blooming, green, and strange loveliness delighted the eye.

We met strings of coolies descending with baskets of sulphur on their backs, the path was yellow with the broken fragments of years' droppings, and infragrant, murky sulphur-streams crossed and ran beside the path, in promise of the stifling caldrons we were fast approaching.

We had a magnificent view back over the Garoet plain, with its checker-board of green and glinting fields, marked with the network of white post-roads and dotted with the clumps of palms that bespoke the hidden villages, and then we passed in through a natural gateway or cutting in the solid mountain-side made by the last eruption. The broad passage or defile led to the *kawa*, or crater, a bowl or depression deep sunk in rocky walls, with pools of liquid sulphur bubbling all over the five-acre floor and sending off clouds of nauseous steam. These pools, vats of purest molten gold, boiled violently all the time, scattering golden drops far and wide from their fretted, honeycombed edges. There was always suggestion of the possibility of their suddenly shooting into the air like geysers, and deluging one with the column of molten gold; or of the soft filigree edges of the pools crumbling and precipitating one untimely into the lakelet of fire and brimstone. Steam jets roared and hissed from all parts of the quaking solfatara, and from the rumblings and strange underground noises one could understand the native legends of chained giants groaning inside of the mountain, and their name for Papandayang, "The Forge." The sulphur coolies stepped warily along the paths between the pools; our shoe-soles were not proof against the steam and scorch of the heaving ground beneath us; and carbonic-acid gas and sulphureted hydrogen were all that one could find to breathe down there on the crater's floor—the undoubted Guevo Upas, or "Valley of Poison."

It is said that one can see the shores both of the Indian Ocean and the Java Sea from the summit of Papandayang, which is seven thousand feet above their level. Although the skies were cloudy and doubtful around the horizon edges, we were willing to take the brilliant noonday sun overhead as augury, and attempt the climb. As there was no path beyond the crater's rest-sheds for the coolies to carry us in djoelies, we started on foot straight up the first steep slope of the crater's ragged wall, through tangles of bushes and the rank bamboo-grass. We drove our servant on ahead, and the poor indolent creature, cheated of his expected lounge after his arduous pony-ride up the mountain and his midday rice-feast, turned plaintive countenance backward, as he picked his reluctant way barefooted through this prickly underbrush.

"What for go here?" he bleated.

"To get to the top of the mountain and see the two oceans."

"Dis mountain no got top," wailed the unconscionable one; but we remembered the waist-deep water he had conjured up to discourage us from Chandi Sewou; nor had we forgotten the Tjilatjap sandwiches with which he had comforted himself such a few days before, and we said, "Go on!"

Then, remembering our perpetual hunt for and expectation of great snakes, he turned mournful countenance and wailed: "*Slanga! slanga!* ["Snakes! snakes!"] always live dis kind grass."

"Very well. That's just what we want to find. Be sure you tell us as soon as you step on one or see it moving."

But, after pushing and tearing our way through bamboo-grass and bushes to the first ridge, we saw only other and farther ridges to be surmounted, with great ravines and stony hollows between. We took such view of the cloudy plains and ranges to northward and southward as we could, seeing everywhere the murky, blue, misty horizon of the rainy season, and nowhere the silver sea-levels, nor the lines of perpetual surf that fringe the Indian Ocean. We saw again the mosaic of rice-fields and dry fields covering the Garoet plain; and looking down upon the foot of an opposite mountain spur, we could study, like a relief-map or model tilted before us, a vast plantation cultivated from tea to highest coffee and kina level.

Nowhere in the slopes below could we see the vale of the deadly upas-tree, that was last supposed to occupy a retired spot on Papandayang's remote heights. The imaginative Dr. Foersch, surgeon of the Dutch East India Company at Samarang in 1773, made the blood of all readers of the last century run cold with his description of himself standing alone, "in solitary horror," on a blasted plain covered with skeletons, with another solitary horror of a deadly upas the only larger object in sight. The Guevo Upas, or "Valley of Poison," was first said to be on the plain southeast of Samarang, but that region was explored in vain; then it was put upon the Dieng plateau, and found not there; and last the valley was said to be on the side of a high mountain far away in the almost unexplored Preanger regencies. Dr. Horsfield, in his search for volcanic data, routed the upas myth from the Papandayang region and exploded it for all time, and the Guevo Upas has gone to that limbo where the maelstrom and other perils of ante-tourist times are laid away. There is a deadly tree in Java, the antiar (*Antiaris toxicaria*), whose sap is as poisonous as serpent venom if it enters a wound, and will produce deep, incurable ulcers if dropped on the skin; and skeletons of animals may have been found beneath and near it. Erasmus Darwin immortalized the deadly upas, or antiar, in his poem, "The Botanic Garden," and this antiar is the only actual and accepted upas-tree of the tropics. It is quite possible that some valley or old crater on the mountain-side, where the carbonic-acid and sulphurous gases from the inner caldron could escape, would be strewn with skeletons of birds and animals, a valley of death to man and beast, and as deadly a place, for the same reasons, as the celebrated grotto at Naples; but no tree could live in those fumes either; and the solitary tree on the "blasted plain" of skeletons, and the Dutch doctor in his "solitary horror," have to be abandoned entire—a last disillusionment in Java.

When we returned from above, our djoelie coolies were squatted under the tiled shed of refuge built for visitors and sulphur-miners, and were as curious a lot of mixed types and races as one could find in an ethnological museum. While the Malays have, as a rule, but scanty beards and no hair on breast or limbs, two of these men were as whiskered and hairy as the wild men of Borneo, or the hirsute ones of Ceylon, the faces narrowed to the countenance of apes by the thick growth of hair, and their breasts shaggy as a spaniel's back. These wild men came from some farther district, but our medium could not or would not comprehend our queries and establish the exact spot of their birthplace by cross-questioning the man-apes themselves; and the missing links sat comfortably the while, submitting their disheveled heads to one and another's friendly search and attentions.

We were reluctant to descend Papandayang at the rapid gait the coolies struck for going down hill, but they whisked us through the different belts of vegetation and down to the serried rows of coffee-trees in seemingly no time at all. The head man of Tjisoeroe-pan had posted the village gamelan, or orchestra, in the little rustic band-stand of the green, and their tinkling, mild, and plaintive melodies reached us through the trees long before we were in sight of them. The musicians played a long program while the djoelies were put away, carts and horses brought round, and the very moderate bill itemized and paid— too modest a bill altogether to need an accompaniment of slow music.

We reached Garoet as the delayed afternoon shower began falling; but the lovely moonlight evening under the shade-trees of Garoet streets was to be remembered, as were the later hours on the porch, with the iron bust of Mozart looking at us from his tropical garden bower. In the middle of the night we heard commotion on our porch, as of bamboo-chairs thrown over and dragged about. "The snake!—at last!" was the first thought and cry; and as the thrashing continued, it was evident that a whole den of pythons must be contorting outside. "A tiger!" and we peered through a crack of the latticed door and saw our Tissak Malaya basket scattered in sections over the garden path, and monkeys capering off with our store of Boro Boedor cocoanut-palm sugar. And this petty larceny of the garden monkeys was our only adventure with wild beasts in the tropics!

XXIV

"SALAMAT!"

THE return from the hill-country to Buitenzorg and Batavia was all too hurried, and the soft Malay "*Salamat*" ("Farewell") found much regretfully left undone. We lingered at the Sans Souci by Salak until the last hour of grace for the necessary steamer preparations at Batavia, as we dreaded the reeking sea-coast with its scorching noondays and stifling nights.

The shady avenues, the wonder-garden, the picturesque passer, and the veranda view of the great blue mountain rising from the valley of palms below were more enchanting than at first. I had come to appreciate and accept the tropics then, to be aware of many fine distinctions unnoted in the first enjoyment of their beauty. I fancied that I could detect greater coolness in the shade of the tamarind than in that of any other tree; the milk of a fresh cocoanut had become the most refreshing and delicious drink; and the palm had established itself in my affections and all associations with the outer world. There had come to be a sense of attachment, almost comradeship, in the constant companion tree, the graceful, restless creature that the natives say will not live beyond the sound of the human voice—dying if the village or habitation it guards is deserted. So nearly human and appealing are these waving cocoas that it is fitting that there should be a census of palms quite as much as of people, and that in the last enumeration it appeared that the people and the palms existed in even numbers —one palm apiece for every one of the millions of inhabitants of the island.

The drives and the scenery about Buitenzorg, the sunset and twilight band-concerts under the great aisles of kanari-trees, had fresh interest, and it was indeed a penance to leave without taking train around to the Preanger side of Mount Gedeh, and driving up to the sanatorium of Sindanglaya, over three thousand feet above sea-level. The cool mountain air at that elevation is cure and tonic for all tropic ills, and with the mercury always 20° lower than at sea-level, Sindanglaya is the one sure refuge for all Malaysia and Cochin China, French officers from Saigon reaching it more quickly than Japan or the highlands of Ceylon. From Sindanglaya one may go to the Gedeh's crater, and to the summit of its twin peak, Pangerango, the highest mountain of the island, where, surrounded by primroses and violets,—the flora of the European temperate zone, islanded there after the period of great cold had retreated northward,—one may look down upon all the Batavia Residency, and out upon the Java Sea, and southward across Preanger hills to the greater Indian Ocean.

There was always some new or strange thing to pique one's interest and implore delay, and the promise of the great talipot-palm of the gardens bursting into its magnificent flower, or the great creeper, the *Rafflesia*, producing one of its gigantic six-foot flowers,—the biggest blossom known to the world,—was an inducement not put away without a pang. There were bird's-nest caves near by on a mountain-side, and over in the highlands toward Bantam a strange colony of "Badouins," more than a thousand refugees from religious persecution, who continue there unhindered the practice of a religion part pagan and part Buddhist, which commands the most severely upright lives. The anthropologist and economist have passed these people by, and one can find little concerning them in English print. Every day held its wonder and surprise, and rumor of more and of greater ones.

Although we were living and walking on the line of one of the great fissures of the earth's crust all that time, and eleven of the forty-five volcanoes of the island are gently active, we did not once feel the tremor of an earthquake. Table d'hôte talk often turned upon the volcanic phenomena one and another guest had experienced, and the eruption of Krakatau—by no means an old story to these colonials—was a topic for which I had an insatiable appetite. They told one thrilling stories of that summer of Krakatau's prolonged activity; of Batavian folk running frequent excursion-steamers to the Strait of Sunda to witness the spectacle of a volcano in eruption; and of that August Sunday of horror when the very end of the world seemed to have come to all that part of Java. A dense pall of smoke covered all of Buitenzorg's sky that day; Salak was lost in the darkness, and it was thought that it or Gedeh was in eruption when crashes and roars beyond those of the most terrific thunderstorms, the bang and boom of the heaviest artillery's bombardment, and the sound of frightful explosions filled the air, shook and rocked the ground, and rattled houses until conversation was impossible. Compass-needles spun around and around, barometers rose and fell, clouds of sulphurous vapors half strangled the people in the gloom of that awful Sabbath night, and no one slept with this dread cannonading and the end of the world seemingly close at hand. The next daylight brought the climax, a series of prolonged and awful roars, and then the very crack and crash of doom, when half of Krakatau's island was torn away with the final explosion. None who endured those days of terror can tell of them without excitement; and those whose plantations were near the Sunda Strait had yet more gruesome times during the days of darkness and of greenish, horrid twilight, when the heavens seemed to be falling about them in the rain of ashes and hot stones. Batavian folk had as terrifying experiences, and each entering ship brought more awful tales of being caught by the waves or the eddies of that sickening sea, with hot stones setting decks and rigging afire, and the weight of hot ashes threatening to sink the vessels in the sea of pumice before they could be shoveled away. Pumice covered the ocean for miles away from Krakatau; and it drifted into Batavia harbor in a surface-layer so deep that planks were laid on it and men walked even a mile to shore, they say.

A Dutch scientific commission investigated and collected reports upon the phenomenal events, and its report, "Krakatau," edited by R. D. M. Verbeek, the eminent geologist and director of mines to the Dutch government, was published at Batavia in 1885, in a quarto volume of 500 pages, in Dutch and French editions, accompanied by charts and an atlas of colored plates that make clear the whole course of the spectacular phenomena.

The Royal Society of Great Britain appointed a "Krakatoa Committee," composed of thirteen of its most eminent geologists, meteorologists, seismists, and specialists in such lines, to collect data concerning this most remarkable eruption of the century, and its report, a quarto volume of 475 pages, edited by G. J. Symons, and published in London in 1888, embodies the result of their inquiries.

M. René Breon's report to the French Minister of Public Instruction was published by his government, and he contributed papers to "La Nature," in the April and May numbers for the year 1885. Mr. H. O. Forbes, the naturalist, was in Batavia in the first weeks of Krakatau's activity, and the record of his excursion to the island and his observations was read to the Royal Geographic Society, and afterward published in vol. vi. of "Proceedings" (1884, pp. 129, 142).

The many official reports and accounts of the Krakatau eruption are best epitomized in Findlay's "Sailing Directory for the Indian Archipelago and China" (p. 78):

In an old Dutch work there is an account of a violent eruption on Krakatau in 1680, since which time it appears to have been quiescent until May 21, 1883, when smoke was observed rising from it, and it quickly became very active. On the 23d a vessel encountered a large accumulation of pumice off Flat Cape, Sumatra; and on the 24th volcanic cinders fell on the island of Timor, twelve hundred miles distant.

For the next eight or nine weeks the eruption continued with great vigor, increasing in activity on August 21st, preparatory to its final great effort. On the evening of the 26th some violent explosions took place, audible at Batavia, eighty miles distant; and between 5 and 7 A. M. on the 27th there was a still more gigantic explosion, followed about 10 A. M. by a detonation so terrific as to be heard even in India, Ceylon, Manilla, and the west coast of Australia, over two thousand miles away. Following on these came a succession of enormous waves, which completely swept the shores of the strait, utterly destroying Anjer, Telok Betong, and numerous villages, the loss of life being officially estimated at over thirty-six thousand souls. The coasts and islands in the vicinity were buried under a layer of mud and ashes.

The effects of this eruption were felt all over the world. Ashes fell at Singapore, 519 miles distant, Bengkalis, 568 miles distant, and the Cocos Islands, 764 miles to the southwestward; and undulations of the sea were recorded at Ceylon, Aden, Mauritius, South Africa, Australia, and in the Pacific. A wave of atmospherical disturbance was also generated, which has been traced three times completely round the world, traveling at the speed of sound. Many months afterward pumice was cast ashore on Zanzibar Island and Madagascar, supposed to have drifted from the Strait of Sunda.

The height of the column of steam and smoke given off by the volcano is estimated at from nine to twelve miles,[1] the consequence being that large quantities of fine dust were discharged into the upper regions of the atmosphere, giving rise to those

---

[1] The Royal Society gives an estimate of seventeen miles as the height of this great column of smoke.

beautiful sunset effects observed all over the world for several months afterward. The amount of solid matter ejected has been computed at over four and a quarter cubic miles.

Such a convulsion has naturally greatly altered the features of the surrounding sea and islands. The northern portion of Krakatau has completely disappeared, and several banks and shoals have been formed between it and Bezee Island, rendering the passage between almost impracticable. It has not otherwise affected the navigation of Sunda Strait, and its activity has now ceased (1889). . . .

Krakatau Island, lying in the middle of Sunda Strait, has been reduced in size from thirteen to six square miles, the site of the northern part of the island now being covered by deep water, no bottom being obtained at 164 fathoms at one spot. The island is now three and a half miles in length, east and west, and two miles wide at its east end. Mount Radaka, its fine conical peak, which still remains, rising boldly up to the height of 2657 feet, may be seen at a considerable distance, and serves as a fairway mark for ships entering the strait from the westward. It is in latitude 6° 9′ S., longitude 105° 27′ E., and its northern side is now a sheer precipice about 2550 feet high. . . . The island was uninhabited, but visited occasionally by fishermen. . . .

Verlaten Island has increased in size from about one and a half to four and a half square miles. Lang Island has altered somewhat in shape, but not much in size. The round islet named Polish Hat has disappeared, but another islet now lies three quarters of a mile west a half-mile from its south point, with deep water between.

Bezee or Tamarind Island, lying ten and a half miles north by east from Krakatau peak, has altered a little in shape, but not in size, and appears to be the northern limit of the volcanic disturbance. . . . Bezee Island formerly produced pepper. . . . The village was on the east side opposite Little Tamarind Island, but the volcanic eruption smothered the island with mud and ashes.

Although we traveled on the island through all the November weeks, we did not experience any of the sensational downpours promised for the beginning of the rainy season, nor the terrific thunder-storms warranted to rend the heavens at the turn of the monsoon, nor any inconvenience or disarrangement of plans through the first instalments of the annual precipitation. The black clouds of the Java Sea did not suddenly envelop our ship in such sheets of rain that the vessel was forced to lay to, the lookout in the bows unable to see ten feet ahead of him, and the double sail-cloth awnings over the decks serving no more purpose than so much gauze. The rain did not descend in a flood or cloud-burst's fury at precisely three o'clock every afternoon, penetrating carriage-curtains and -aprons, filling the carriage-boxes like tanks, and saturating every garment and article. Nor any more did we play billiards by lightning, without lamps, like that British planter who eventually scared away a party of Americans by his account of thunder-storms in Java. This British resident assured the tourists that at his Preanger plantation the thunder-claps shook the house, rocked the furniture, and stopped clocks, and that he had often turned out the reeling lamps for safety's sake, and continued his games of billiards by the lightning's incessant, blinding green glare. And the Americans believed it, and remained away from Java—British humor and American credulity matched to equally surprising extremes.

There were gentle, intermittent drizzles and light showers on several days; many days when the gray skies sulked and seemed about to weep; but the only hard showers were at night. The one vaunted sensational, tropical downpour, with blue-and-green lightning's illumination, made my last Batavian midnight memorable, and put me at last in line with my climatic expectations. Yet that was at the end of November, when the monsoon was supposed to have sent off its irregular fireworks and settled down to the fixed program of a three-o'clock shower every afternoon, in order to precipitate its annual eighty inches of rain.

Even the thermometer disappointed one in this land comprised between the parallels of 5° and 8° south of the equator. Not once in my stay did it register as great a heat as I have once seen it register in Sitka in July—94° Fahrenheit; but as the column of mercury is often small gage or warrant for one's own sensations, he must believe, even if with mental reservations, that Batavia's mean temperature was but 78.69° for twelve years, with a monthly mean range of but two degrees. If one has been out in the sun at that hour, he feels skeptical about Batavia's annual average noonday temperature being but 83°, all of four degrees cooler than Samarang's and Sourabaya's average noon temperature. He may believe that the thermometer very seldom falls below 70° or rises above 90°, but a quality in the air, a weight and appreciable humidity, make Batavia's mean, exhausting, lifeless 83° noondays the climax of one's discomfort.

With the upas-tree, the great snakes, the tigers, the pirates, and the good coffee exposed as myths; the white ants never eating out the contents of a trunk overnight; mildew ignoring the luggage left for over a fortnight at Buitenzorg; and the trunks left at Singapore for more than a month equally innocent of fungus-mold, I felt that the tropics had defrauded me a bit—or else that I had lent too willing an ear to returned travelers' imaginations. Taking my own experience as proof, there might be written a brief chapter about snakes to match that famous one in Horrebow's "History of Iceland." But the disillusionment of disillusionments awaited us on the borders of Bantam, when the last Batavian day brought information that our so-called tiny bantam cock is not from Bantam at all. It was first seen on board a Japanese junk trading at Bantam in the long ago, and the Malays, who are natural and long-descended cockfighters, saw in these little fowls combatants more spirited than any of their own breed, and of more manageable size. The true bantam cocks to the province born are nearly as large as turkeys; long ago Dr. Marsden told of their being as large as Norfolk bustards, and of their standing high enough to peck off the dinner-table, and said that when they sat down on the first joint of the leg they were taller than any common fowls. The introduction of the pretty Japanese fowls revolutionized cock-fighting, and the Dutch imported them through their Nagasaki factory, and introduced them to Europe.

The equator was proved not such a terrible thing as it had been made out to be—a thing that might be spoken of very disrespectfully because of that misplaced awe and veneration; and the tropics not at all as astonishing as they used to be, when illustrated books of travel, museum collections and models, and exposition villages had not made their life and scenery so familiar; when hothouses had not brought even orchids to common acquaintance, and Northern markets to displaying oranges and bananas as commonly and regularly as apples or potatoes.

With the other India—the whole continent of the real, the greater, or British India—before us, we could not delay on the Netherlands isle; and that strange, haunting, indefinite fear, the dread of some unknown, undefinable evil, that shadows and oppresses one so in the tropics, asserted itself more strongly as we approached Batavia. One is not sure whether this vague fear which possesses one under the line is due to the sense of extreme distance, to dread of the many diseases that lie in wait, to fear of the sudden deaths of so many kinds that may snatch one in the lands where the sun swings nearest, or to the peril of volcanic forces that may instantly overwhelm one in some disaster like that of Krakatau. At least, there was always a sensation of oppression, a dread of some impending danger in the midst of one's enjoyment, and an unconscious looking-forward to free breathing and the sensation of safety, when once across the line again, back to the grand route and the world again, safe under the British flag at friendly Singapore, at home again with the English language.

Yet Java, the peerless gem in "that magnificent empire of Insul-Inde which winds about the equator like a garland of emeralds," is the ideal tropical island, the greenest, the most beautiful, and the most exquisitely cultivated spot in the East, the most picturesque and satisfactory bit of the tropics anywhere near the world's great routes of travel. Now that the dark days of Dutch rule are ended and enlightened modes prevail; now that the culture system has developed the island's resources and made it all one exquisite, fruitful garden, and the colonists have begun to take an interest in uncovering and protecting the ancient monuments, the interest and attractions of Java are greater each year. It is alike the scientist's greatest storehouse and the traveler's unequaled tropical pleasure-resort and playground in the East. The antiquities have been merely scratched, explorations in that line are only well begun, leaving to archæologists and anthropologists a field of incalculable richness—more especially to those bent upon arriving at some solution of the great puzzle, some proof of Asiatic and American contact in pre-Columbian times. The puzzling resemblance of the older Javanese ruins to those of Central America has yet to be explained, and the alluring theory of migration from the rich "foodponds" of the waters within the archipelago to other and farther inclosed seas teeming with fishes, until the Malays had followed with the great currents up one shore of the Pacific Ocean and down the other, must be proved. Dutch scientists naturally desire to explore and exploit this treasure-house of Java for themselves; but with a questioning world and many eager inquirers bent on solving all the mysteries and problems of race origin and migrations, the prize must be won by the swiftest.

If Baedeker or Murray would only go to Java and kindly light the tourist's way; if the Dutch government would relax the useless vexations of the toelatings-kaart system, and the colonists welcome the visitor in more kindly spirit, Java would rank, as it deserves to, as a close second to Japan, an oasis in travel, an island of beauty and delight to the increasing number of round-the-world travelers, who each year are discouraged from visiting the country by less heedful ones who have ventured there.

Whether, as pessimists foretell, a Mohammedan rebellion shall desolate the isle; whether it remains in Dutch leading-strings, arrives at even the limited independence of a British colony, or succumbs to Germany's colonial ambitions, as the French so freely prophesy, Java is certain soon to loom larger in the world's view, and for a time at least to occupy the stage.

INDEX

Achin, 4, 10.
Antiar. See Upas.
Arabs, 37, 38, 227, 265.
Ashantee. 10, 72.
Asoka, 194.
Ayudya, 269.

Badouins, 326.
Baloeboer-Baloeboer-Limbangan, 154.
Bananas, 8, 80.
Bandong, 150.
Bantam, 42, 333.
Banteng, 133.
Batavia, 21, 25-48.
Batavian Society, Museum of, 34, 35, 36.
Baths, 60, 131.
Battek, 42, 45, 46.
Betel-nut, 42.
Bilimbi, 84.
Birds' nests, 304.
Birds, tropic, 13, 130.
Block-printing, 261.
Boro, Boedor, 167-169, 182-202.
Botanical Garden, 66-70.
Brambanam, 218.
Breadfruit, 85.
Breon, M. René, 328.
Bromo, Mount, 265, 299.
Brumund, Herr, 169, 197.
Buddhism, 168, 169, 187, 190, 193, 194.
Buddhist art, 36, 167, 190, 223, 224.
Buffalo, water-, 55.
Buitenzorg, 49, 62-76, 79, 324.
Burglary, 271.

Cacao, 58, 129.
Carambola, 84.
Central America, 186, 232, 238, 263.
Chandi Sewou, 228-234.
Chicago Exposition, 143, 144, 145.

Chinese, 22, 37, 38, 39, 40, 80, 261, 262, 290.
Christianity, 55, 56.
Cinchona-culture, 70, 104, 150.
Climate, 21, 49, 127, 331, 332.
Coffee, 65, 115, 116.
Coffee-culture, 95, 103, 104, 142, 317.
Coinage, 20.
Courts of law, 271.
Culture system, 94-125.

Daendels, Marshal, 22, 95, 97, 270, 275, 276.
Dancing-girls, 188, 288.
De Charnay, M. Désiré, 186, 232, 238, 263, 264.
Delsarte, 293.
Depok, 55.
Dhyani, 193.
Dieng plateau, 237, 238.
Dishabille, 26, 66.
Djokjakarta, 170, 213, 269-282.
Dodok, 132, 156, 163, 246, 252, 297.
Duku, 83.
Durian, 85, 86.

Education, 56, 57.
Egypt, 263.

Fergusson's "History of Indian and Eastern Architecture," 169, 189, 220, 264.
Ferns, tree-, 317.
Findlay's "Sailing Directory," 328-330.
Forbes, H. O., 328.
Frangipani, 68, 92, 93.
Fruits, 80-91.

Gamelan, 143, 287, 290, 297, 322.
Garoet, 312, 313.

INDEX

Gautama Buddha, Prince Siddhartha, 187.
Gecko, 59, 212.
Gedeh, 325.
Government, colonial, 31, 32, 119, 120.
Gulden, 20.

Heyden, General Van der, 11.
Hotel life, 25, 26, 29, 58, 59, 61, 313.

Indigo-culture, 104.

Jamboa, 84.

Kalaidon, 151, 152, 153.
Kali, Goddess. See LORO JONGGRAN.
Kanari-trees, 67, 158, 302, 304.
Kawi language, 72, 283, 284, 293.
Khublai Khan, 227.
Kina. See CINCHONA.
Krakatau, 11, 326–330.
Kris, 35, 154, 242, 257, 258, 259, 272, 289.

Land laws, 119.
Laundering, 60.
Lawu, Mount, 263.
Leemans, Dr., 197.
Leles, plain of, 152, 153.
Literature, native, 283, 284.
Lizards, 59, 212, 248, 305.
Lombok, 278.
Loro Jonggran, 220, 223.

Macartney, Lord, 21, 289.
Mahabharata, 283, 284.
Majapahit, 241, 265, 269.
Malacca, Straits of, 1, 3, 8.
Malays, 2, 3, 41, 42, 121.
Mangosteen, 30, 87, 88.
Marco Polo, 227.
Mataram, 269, 278.
"Max Havelaar," 110.
McKinley Bill, 77.
"Menac," 298, 299.
Mendoet, 209, 210.
Merapi, 180, 263.
Merbaboe, 180, 263.
Metzger, Emile, 273.
Missions, 55.
Mohammedans, 38.
Money, J. W. B., 113, 114.
Monkeys, 224, 282, 323.
Monsoon, 18.
Mortality, 21.
Music, 143, 287, 290.

Nanko, 85.
No dance, 293.
Noesa Kambangan, 303.
North, Marianne, 126, 186.

Opium, 107.

Pajajaran, 241, 269.
Pajong, 174, 209, 246, 253, 254, 274, 296.
Pakoe Alam, Prince, 278, 290, 294–300.
Palaces, 36, 67, 246, 249.
Palms, 62, 72, 91, 205.
Pangerango, 325.
Panji, 258, 290.
Papandayang, 314, 319.
Papaya, 86, 87.
Parakan Salak, 128, 136.
Paranaks, 39, 261, 290.
Passer, 42, 79, 161, 176, 206, 254, 272, 313.
Passports. See TOELATINGS-KAART.
Pawnshops, 257, 273.
Perk, Herr, 228.
Pineapple, 87, 308.
Polo, Marco, 227.
Pomelo, 87.
Population, 17, 21, 22, 176.

Raden Saleh, 47, 71.
Raffles, Lady, 69, 75.
Raffles, Sir Stamford, 1, 3, 96, 97, 168, 169, 227, 264, 269, 283.
Railway, 5, 50, 51, 52, 164, 307.
Ramayan, 283.
Rambutan, 83.
Rice-fields, 52, 53, 147, 312.
Riz tavel, 30.
Royal Society of Great Britain, 328.

Sadoe, 19.
Salak (fruit), 84.
Salak, Mount, 18, 62, 127, 128.
Salt monopoly, 105.
Sarong, 26, 45, 46, 66, 257, 260, 281, 289, 312.
Siddhartha, Prince, 187.
Sinagar, 128-146.
Sindanglaya, 325.
Singapore, 1.
Singa Sari, 237.
Slavery, 101.
Snakes, 165, 166, 320.
Social life, 30, 33, 66, 129, 289, 294, 295, 313.
Soembing, 180.
Soerabaya, 265.
Soerakarta. See SOLO.
Solo, 240–264.
Staunton, 21, 289.
Steamships, 7.
Stirrup, 254.
Sugar-culture, 98, 115, 205.
Suku, 263, 264.
Sultan of Djokja, 274.
Sumatra, 9–11.
Susuhnan, 241–246, 269, 270.

Tailors, 79, 162.
Tandjon Priok, 18, 19.

Tapioca, 310.
Tea-culture, 102, 103, 137, 138, 141.
Tengger, 265.
Terra ingrata, 163, 164.
"Thousand Temples." See CHANDI SEWOU.
Tissak Malaya, 156–162.
Tjilatjap, 301, 302.
Toekoe Oemar, 11.
Toelatings-kaart, 23, 170, 211, 215.
Topeng, 278.
Tosari, 265.

Upas, 319, 321.

Verbeck, R. D. M., 328.
Volcanoes, 18, 67, 150, 180, 265, 309, 314, 318.
Vorstenlanden, 240.

Wallace, Alfred Russel, 12, 23, 114, 126, 169.
"Wandering Jew," 47.
Water Kastel, 257, 277.
Wayang-wayang, 143, 287, 288.
Wilsen, Herr, 198.

Ylang-ylang, 92.
Yucatan, 238, 239, 264.

www.ingramcontent.com/pod-product-compliance
Lightning Source LLC
Chambersburg PA
CBHW031855220426
43663CB00006B/631